HISTORY IN THE MAKING
Series Editor: J. A. P. Jones

5 The Twentieth Century

HISTORY IN THE MAKING

John Hamer

Head of History,
Collyer's Sixth Form College, Horsham

5 The Twentieth Century

Macmillan Education

First published 1980
Reprinted 1981 (twice)

Published by
MACMILLAN EDUCATION LIMITED
Houndmills Basingstoke Hampshire RG21 2XS
and London
Associated companies in Delhi   Dublin
Hong Kong   Johannesburg   Lagos   Melbourne
New York   Singapore and Tokyo

Printed in Hong Kong

British Library Cataloguing in Publication Data
History in the making.
   Vol. 5: The twentieth century
   1. World history
   I. Hamer, John
   909   D21
ISBN 0-333-22358-6

Changes in the teaching of history over the last decade have raised many problems to which there are no easy solutions. The classification of objectives, the presentation of material in varied and appropriate language, the use and abuse of evidence and the reconsideration of assessment techniques are four of the more important. Many teachers are now encouraging their pupils individually or in groups to participate in the processes and skills of the professional historian. Moreover such developments are being discussed increasingly in the context of mixed ability classes and the need to provide suitable teaching approaches for them.

History in the Making is a new course for secondary schools intended for pupils of average ability. It is a contribution to the current debate, and provides one possible way forward. It accepts many of the proven virtues of traditional courses: the fascination of the good tale; the drama of human life, individual and collective; the need to provide a visual stimulus to the written word.

But it has built on to these some of the key features of the 'new history' so that teachers can explore, within the framework of a textbook, many of the 'new' approaches and techniques.

To this end each chapter in this volume has four major components.

1   **The text**   This provides the basic framework of the chapters, and although the approach is essentially factual, it is intended to arouse and sustain the interest of the reader of average ability.

2   **The illustrations**   These have been carefully selected to stand beside the written pieces of evidence in the chapter, and to provide (so far as is possible) an authentic visual image of the period/topic. Photographs, artwork and maps are all used to clarify and support the text, and to develop the pupil's powers of observation.

3   **Using the evidence**   This is a detailed study of the evidence on one particular aspect of the chapter. Did the walls of Jericho really come tumbling down? Was the death of William Rufus in the New Forest really an accident? What was the background to the torpedoing of the *Lusitania*? These are the sort of questions which are asked, to give the pupil the opportunity to consider not only the problems facing the historian, but also those facing the characters of history. Different forms of documentary evidence are considered, as well as archaeological, architectural, statistical, and other kinds of source material; the intention is to give the pupil a genuine, if modest, insight into the making of history.

4   **Questions and further work**   These are intended to test and develop the pupil's reading of the chapter, and in particular the *Using the evidence* section. Particular attention is paid to the development of historical skills, through the examination and interpretation of evidence. The differences between primary and secondary sources, for example, are explored, and concepts such as bias in evidence and its limitations. By applying the skills which they have developed, pupils may then be able to formulate at a suitable level and in appropriate

language, ideas and hypotheses of their own.

History in the Making is a complete course in five volumes, to meet the needs of pupils between the ages of 11 and 16 (in other words up to and including the first public examination). However, each volume stands by itself and may be used independently of the others; given the variety of syllabuses in use in schools today this flexibility is likely to be welcomed by many teachers. *The Ancient World* and *The Medieval World* are intended primarily for 11–13 year old pupils, *The Early Modern World, 1450–1700* for 12–14 year old pupils, *Britain, Europe and Beyond, 1700–1900* for pre-CSE pupils and *The Twentieth Century* for CSE examination candidates.

It is our hope that pupils will be encouraged, within the main topics and themes of British, European and World History, to experience for themselves the stimulus and challenge, the pleasure and frustration, the vitality and humanity that form an essential part of History in the Making.

J. A. P. Jones

Contents

List of Maps

Empires beyond the seas

On 22 January 1901, after the longest reign in British history, Queen Victoria died. Her grieving family, members of most of the royal houses of Europe, stood at the frail old lady's bedside. Wilhelm II, Emperor of Germany, had held his grandmother's arm for the last hours of her life.

King and emperor

Victoria had been the ruler of the United Kingdom of Great Britain and Ireland, and (since 1877) Empress of India. These titles now passed to her son, Edward VII. Parliament added another title: Edward was also ruler 'of the British Dominions beyond the Seas'. The empire over which he reigned was the largest and richest in the world. It covered a fifth of the earth's land surface and included 400 million people, a quarter of the world's population.

Not all parts of this vast empire, however, were governed in the same way. Some had greater freedom to manage their own affairs than others.

At the time of Victoria's death there were two dominions – Canada and Australia. During the next ten years they were joined by New Zealand and South Africa. In their parliaments and government offices were the descendants of the early white settlers. Their laws, their customs, and their sports, were very like those of people in Britain. An Englishman visiting an Australian farm at the end of the nineteenth century found not the near-savages he expected, but 'a high-bred English family – English in everything except that they were Australian-born'.

King Emperor Edward VII

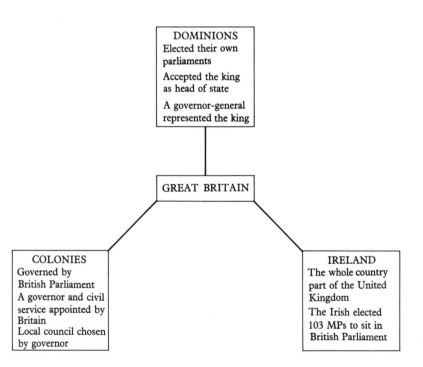

DOMINIONS
Elected their own parliaments
Accepted the king as head of state
A governor-general represented the king

GREAT BRITAIN

COLONIES
Governed by British Parliament
A governor and civil service appointed by Britain
Local council chosen by governor

IRELAND
The whole country part of the United Kingdom
The Irish elected 103 MPs to sit in British Parliament

The British Empire, 1900

The British in India: a picnic at Narayanpore

Outside the dominions, the countries which formed the British Empire had far less independence. The 300 million people of India were ruled by a viceroy appointed by the king, and five thousand British officials. After spending some thirty years in India, most of these officials would return to England. They did not settle there as Britons had done in Australia.

There were those who did not believe that Indians would ever be capable of governing the country themselves.

Unless Indians can govern India wisely and well, in accordance with modern national ideas, they have no more right to India than Hottentots have to the Cape, or the black fellows to Australia. In my opinion, Hindoos would never govern Hindostan half, quarter, nay, one tithe [tenth] as well as Englishmen.

Many Indians disagreed. When the Prince of Wales, the future King George V, visited India in 1905, he asked an Indian leader, 'Would the peoples of India be happier if you ran the country?' 'No, sir,' was the reply, 'I do not say they would be happier, but they would have more self-respect.' Changes were made, but the rule of the king-emperor lasted until the reign of Edward's grandson.

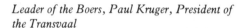

The hero of Mafeking, Baden-Powell, seen here in 1929

Leader of the Boers, Paul Kruger, President of the Transvaal

Britons and Boers

Victoria had died in the middle of a war. Since 1899 British soldiers had been fighting in the Transvaal in southern Africa. This was the country of the Boers, Dutch farmers whose ancestors had arrived in Africa two hundred years previously. The discovery of gold in the Transvaal had threatened their way of life, and most of them heartily disliked the foreigners who came to mine for the wealth under the soil. Like their president, Paul Kruger, they wished to rid the country of these *'uitlanders'*, outsiders. As many of these *uitlanders* came from the British parts of South Africa, they appealed to the British government for support against the Boers. British troops were moved to the borders of the Transvaal. When Britain refused to remove them, Kruger declared war.

The British expected an easy victory, but the Boers were tough soldiers and expert riflemen. They attacked the three towns of Lady-smith, Mafeking and Kimberley, and trapped the British forces there. The longest of the sieges, at Mafeking, lasted for 217 days. When it was finally relieved in May 1900, there was wild rejoicing in the streets of London. The British commander there, Baden-Powell, who later started the Boy Scouts, became a national hero.

But the war in the Transvaal was far from over. It took a further two years, more than 300 000 soldiers, and very brutal tactics to defeat the Boers. The Transvaal was added to the British Empire. Other countries regarded Britain as a vicious bully.

Home from South Africa, a company of the City Imperial Volunteers parade through London in 1900

Portsmouth welcomes the return of the relief force from Ladysmith. During the siege naval guns mounted on wheels had been used to bombard the Boers

■	British
(dotted)	French
(diagonal hatch)	German (many islands in the Pacific were German possessions)
(fine dotted)	Italian
(wavy)	Belgian
(horizontal lines)	Portuguese

Major European colonies in 1914

Colonial rivalry

In a letter to a friend, the American ambassador to Britain wrote, 'I guess they really believe that the earth belongs to them.' But there was competition. Colonies were thought to increase a country's wealth and power, and European rule had spread to many parts of the world.

During the thirty years before 1914, almost the whole of Africa was colonised. Resist as they might, the Africans had little hope of success against the more powerful and better-armed Europeans. Although the colonial powers occasionally quarrelled over the spoils, they never actually fought each other for them. In 1898 Britain and France came close to war over the Sudan. In 1906 and again in 1911, Germany protested about French influence in Morocco. But in the end, such incidents were settled peacefully.

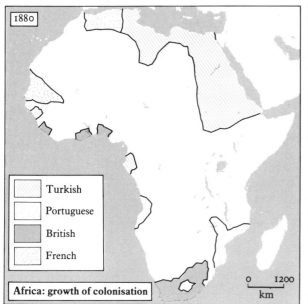

1880

Turkish
Portuguese
British
French

Africa: growth of colonisation

0 ___ 1200
km

1914

Morocco
Tunisia
Rio de Oro
Algeria
Libya
Gambia
French West Africa
Egypt
Eritrea
Portuguese Guinea
Anglo-Egyptian Sudan
Somaliland
Sierra Leone
Nigeria
French Equatorial Africa
Liberia
Gold Coast
Cameroon
Ethiopia
Togoland
Spanish Guinea
Belgian Congo
British East Africa
German East Africa
Angola
South West Africa
Rhodesia
Mozambique
Bechuanaland
Madagascar

Belgian

Union of South Africa

Naval race

The world's largest empire was protected by the world's biggest navy, and Britain was proud of her navy. British policy was 'that our fleet should be equal to the combination of the two strongest navies in Europe'.

At the beginning of the twentieth century this naval supremacy was challenged. 'Our future,' declared Wilhelm II in 1898, 'lies upon the ocean.' Germany began to build more battleships. Anxious not to lose her lead, so too did Britain. Under the direction of the First Sea Lord, Admiral Sir John Fisher, attempts were also made to make the Royal Navy even stronger. He developed a new, improved type of battleship. The first of them was launched in 1906 – HMS *Dreadnought*.

Colonial rivalry in Africa: eight years later Britain and France clashed at Fashoda in the Sudan, but war between the two countries was avoided

First of a new class of battleships, HMS Dreadnought *in 1906*

A twelve-inch (30·5 cm) gun could fire a shell more than thirteen kilometres. At this range a dreadnought was superior to two older battleships. Germany began to build dreadnoughts.

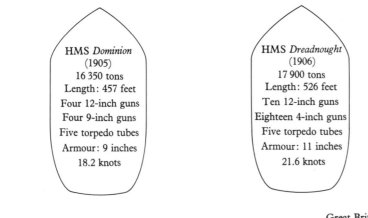

A 1905 battleship and HMS Dreadnought

HMS *Dominion*
(1905)
16 350 tons
Length: 457 feet
Four 12-inch guns
Four 9-inch guns
Five torpedo tubes
Armour: 9 inches
18.2 knots

HMS *Dreadnought*
(1906)
17 900 tons
Length: 526 feet
Ten 12-inch guns
Eighteen 4-inch guns
Five torpedo tubes
Armour: 11 inches
21.6 knots

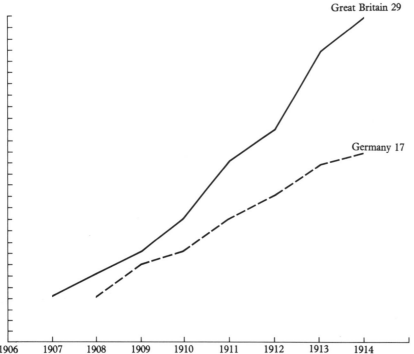

The naval race 1906–14

Great Britain 29

Germany 17

1906 1907 1908 1909 1910 1911 1912 1913 1914

1 When did Germany start to build dreadnoughts?
2 Why did many people in Britain want an increase in the country's shipbuilding programme in 1909?
3 In which year did Britain build the most dreadnoughts?

Before the First World War, countries measured the strength of their navies by the number of battleships they possessed. But, although few people believed it possible before 1914, a very different kind of vessel was to play a greater part in the war at sea. It was Germany's sub-marines, not her battleships, which came closest to defeating Britain.

Using the evidence: the Boer War

Look again at the account of the Boer War given in this chapter. How do
we know that this is what really took place?

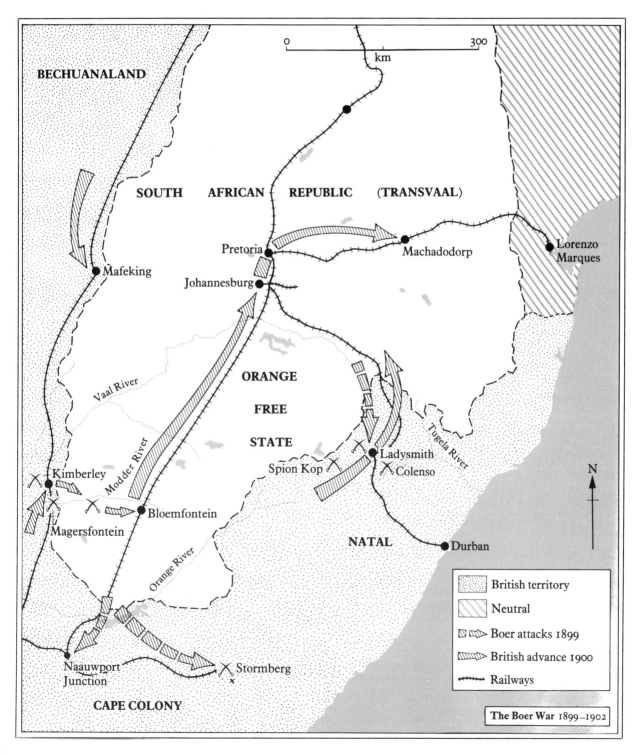

BECHUANALAND

SOUTH AFRICAN REPUBLIC (TRANSVAAL)

Pretoria

Machadodorp

Lorenzo Marques

Mafeking

Johannesburg

Vaal River

ORANGE

FREE

STATE

Modder River

Spion Kop

Ladysmith

Colenso

Tugela River

Kimberley

Bloemfontein

Magersfontein

NATAL

Durban

Orange River

Naauwport Junction

Stormberg

CAPE COLONY

N

British territory

Neutral

Boer attacks 1899

British advance 1900

Railways

The Boer War 1899–1902

In order to describe past events we have to rely upon information which is available to us now – to use the evidence. These are examples of some of the evidence which the historian writing about the Boer War may use:

(1) The condition of Your Majesty's subjects in this state has become well-nigh intolerable. ... They are still deprived of all political rights, they are denied any voice in the government of the country, they are taxed far above the requirements of the country. ... The education of *uitlander* children is made subject to impossible conditions. The police afford no adequate protection to the lives and property of the inhabitants of Johannesburg; they are rather a source of danger to the peace and safety of the *uitlander* population.

(May 1899)

(2) ... (b) That the troops on the borders of this republic shall be instantly withdrawn. (c) That all reinforcements of troops which have arrived in South Africa since 1 June 1899, shall be removed from South Africa within a reasonable time. ... (d) That Her Majesty's troops now on the high seas shall not be landed in any part of South Africa.

(Note from the Transvaal government to the British government, 9 October 1899)

(3) Extract from the *Daily Mail*, 19 May 1900, announcing the relief of Mafeking: ... the historic home of the Lord Mayor was surrounded by a crowd of no fewer than 20 000 madmen, all yelling: 'Mafeking is relieved!' or singing 'God Save the Queen' in all the notes possible to music.

Women absolutely wept for joy and men threw their arms about each other's necks – strangers' necks for the most part; but that made no difference, for Mafeking was relieved. ...

1 Which three statements in the account of the Boer War on pages 12–13 are supported by each of these items of evidence?

One of the bloodiest battles of the war was fought at Spion Kop ('Look-out hill') in January 1900.

(4) At 9 p.m. we started to march to the top of Spion Kop. ... There was a mist on the hill, and it was difficult to get the exact crestline for a good field of fire, and the boulders made it difficult to dig, but we made a rough trench and breastwork ... the mist rose about 8 a.m., when the rifle fire on both sides became heavy, and the Boers opened fire from three guns and a Maxim-Nordenfelt. The shrapnel fire was very accurate, sweeping the whole plateau. I sent out more men to the flanks as the Boers were working round, and the replacing of casualties gradually absorbed all the men of the force. The firing became hotter on both sides. The Boers closed in on the right and centre. Some men at right end of trench got up and put up their hands; three or four Boers came out and signalled their comrades to advance. I was the only officer in the trench on the left, and I got up and shouted to the leader of the Boers that I was the commandant, and that there was no surrender.

A. W. Thorneycroft, *Spion Kop Despatches* (Parliamentary Papers, 1902), quoted in *The Historians' History of the World*, Vol. XXII, *The Times*, 1908

(5) An account of Spion Kop written by a historian using the sort of evidence given in document 4: At 8.30 p.m. on 23rd January the column of attack, under the command of Major-General E. R. P. Woodgate and guided by

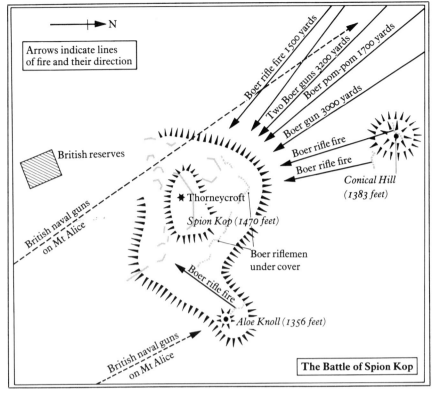

Map of the battle of Spion Kop –
simplified from one in the official
British history

Lieut-Colonel A. W. Thorneycroft, advanced through the drizzle. . . . From
the south-west British gunners began to bombard the northern slope. The
objective was taken. . . .

At about 9 a.m. the mist lifted and gave way to bright sunshine. An arc of
accurate fire from artillery and rifles was directed on the 2000 or so men packed
on Spion Kop. The British, who had been convinced they were the conquerors, were surprised, trapped, and without cover. From their hastily built,
shallow, and badly positioned trenches, which were rapidly becoming clogged
with dead and wounded, the British fiercely fought to hold their position. . . .

At one stage the men of one company, having lost most of their officers, were
holding up white handkerchiefs, and the Boers were advancing to take the
surrender. Thorneycroft in a fury strode over with a pistol and roared to the
Boer commander: 'Take your men to hell, there's no surrender here.'

Purnell's History of the Twentieth Century

2 Study the evidence on the battle of Spion Kop carefully.
  (a) How accurate are the following statements in Document 5:
      (i) at 8.30 p.m. the column of attack advanced;
      (ii) from the south-west British gunners began to bombard the
      northern slope;
      (iii) at about 9 a.m. the mist lifted?
  (b) What reasons are given in Document 4 for the British trenches
      being 'hastily built, shallow, and badly positioned'?
  (c) Compare the two versions given here of the attempt to surrender.
      How does the account in Document 5 differ from the evidence of
      Document 4, and why do you think this might be?

2 News from the Balkans

On 28 June 1914 a nineteen-year-old student, Gavrilo Princip, shot the Archduke Franz Ferdinand in the neck, and his wife, the Duchess Sophie, in the stomach. Within six minutes both were dead.

During the previous twenty years five European rulers and one American president had been assassinated. Yet the shooting of Franz Ferdinand is particularly remembered: six weeks later the greater part of Europe was involved in a war which was eventually to spread to include countries as far apart as Japan and the USA.

The Balkans

The assassination took place in Sarajevo, the capital of Bosnia, which is now part of Yugoslavia. This area of Europe, the Balkans, had once been part of the Ottoman (or Turkish) Empire. Since the seventeenth century, Turkey's power there had steadily declined. Some Balkan countries had gained their independence, others had become part of different empires. Bosnia, though in name still part of the Turkish Empire, had in practice been governed by Austria-Hungary since 1878,

An arrest at Sarajevo. It used to be thought that this showed police arresting Gavrilo Princip, but almost certainly one of his fellow-conspirators is shown

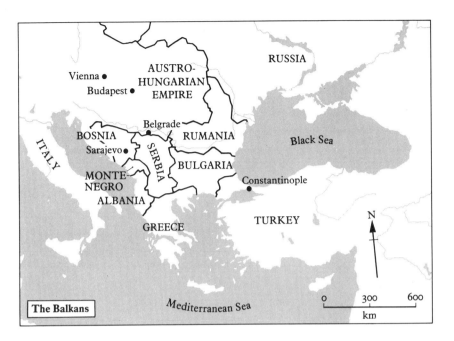

The Balkans

before being taken over completely by Austria-Hungary in 1908.

Among Bosnia's neighbours, one in particular – Serbia – opposed this enlargement of the Austro-Hungarian Empire. Scattered in the various countries of the Balkans were people of many different nationalities – Greeks, Bulgars, Magyars and Serbs. As the boundaries dividing one country from another had been drawn in earlier centuries, there were those who found themselves living outside the country to which they felt they rightly belonged. Like the young Gavrilo Princip, a Serb living in Bosnia, many were nationalists. They believed that all people of the same nationality should be part of the same country; that Bosnia should be joined to Serbia, not to Austria-Hungary. Within Serbia itself organisations sprang up whose aim was to free all Serbs from Austrian rule. To bring this about, they were prepared to use any means, however violent. Princip had connections with one of these societies, the one usually known as the 'Black Hand'. Whether he and his fellow conspirators were actually members of the Black Hand is uncertain. But it is known that they had acquired their lethal collection of bombs, pistols and suicide packets of potassium cyanide (which failed to work) in Serbia.

Heir to the Hapsburg Empire

The Dual Monarchy of Austria-Hungary had been formed in 1867. It was really two states. There were two parliaments and two governments ruling from Vienna and Budapest. The two states shared three ministries and one emperor – Franz Josef I. Conscientious, dignified and powerful, Franz Josef was the head of the Hapsburg family, which in the sixteenth century had ruled over most of Europe. At the time of the

Sarajevo murder he had reigned for sixty-six years. The victim, Franz Ferdinand, was Franz Josef's nephew and heir.

Already, in 1908, Austria-Hungary and Serbia had nearly gone to war over Bosnia. War had been avoided, though the dispute over the Bosnian Serbs was not the only cause of their quarrel. From the map on page 21 you will see that Serbia suffered from one grave disadvantage if she was to safeguard her independence and develop her trade abroad – she had no outlet to the sea. Austria-Hungary, anxious to keep Serbia weak, was determined not to let her expand westwards.

Old Spider and Young Turk

Austria-Hungary was not alone in having ambitions in the Balkans. What made it a particularly explosive area was that two other empires – those of Turkey and Russia – had interests there. In 1878 it was not only in Bosnia that Turkish rule had been replaced. Turkey had lost control of nearly all her European possessions. Tyrannical and inefficient, the government of Sultan Abdul Hamid II had been powerless to prevent the loss. The highly superstitious sultan trusted nobody. Hidden away for most of the time in his palace, Abdul Hamid employed an army of spies, so suspicious was he of those around him. To many observers his behaviour verged on the insane. The Secretary of the British Embassy in Constantinople wrote:

The whole system is rotten to the core. The sultan wandering from room to room during the night; snatching an hour or two on this and that divan; calling up his sheikhs, astrologers and attendants at all hours to try and get some solace and consolation from some new terror which seizes him; this is the sad picture of the terrible life he leads. The ex-Sultan Murad, soused in raki, plentifully supplied by his affectionate brother, sits slobbering and dazed, while his palace is the haunt of all that is despicable and depraved.

After tottering for thirty years the government of Abdul Hamid finally fell in 1908. A successful revolt in the army, led by the 'Young Turk' organisation, brought a new government to power. A year later the 'old spider' was sent into exile. Although a new sultan took his place, real power lay not with him but with the leader of the Young Turks, Enver Bey.

The Young Turks proved to be no more successful in hanging on to the shreds of empire than Abdul Hamid had been. In 1912 Turkey was faced by an alliance of four countries in the Balkan League. Their enthusiasm for finally dismantling Turkey's European empire had, for once, overcome their hatred for each other. Hopelessly outnumbered and outclassed, the Turks were defeated. They lost all but a small strip of territory around Constantinople. Some of it they recovered almost immediately in the Second Balkan War of 1913 when, encouraged by Austria-Hungary, the victors fought over the spoils. But by 1914 the once-great Turkish Empire stretched only as far west as Adrianople.

Turkey was not the only country to emerge disappointed from these Balkan wars. The Serbs had made considerable gains to the south, but their country was still landlocked. Austria-Hungary had used her influence to deny them the route to the sea they so badly wanted. To Franz Josef and his government the growing strength of Serbia was an increasing threat to their empire in the Balkans. It was a danger which would have to be stopped before too long.

An ice-free port

The third empire eager to stake a claim in the Balkans was Russia. Stretching across Asia to the Pacific and southwards to the borders of India, Russia was by far the largest of the three. But she needed a harbour which was open to ships all the year round. The ports on the Baltic and Vladivostok on the Pacific were icebound for part of the year. There were the Black Sea ports, but ships going to and from there had to pass through the narrow Dardanelles Straits. If countries hostile to Russia dominated the Balkans, this vital link might be cut. Its safety could only be assured if Russian influence there was strong.

In 1898 Russia had acquired Port Arthur on the Pacific, which was permanently free of ice. However, this success was short-lived. After a brief but disastrous war, Russia was forced to hand Port Arthur over to Japan in 1905. Again she looked towards the Balkans and an outlet to the Mediterranean.

The alliance system

The three empires (the Austro-Hungarian, the Turkish and the Russian) had powerful friends. Since 1879 Austria-Hungary had been joined with Germany in the Dual Alliance. As the Turkish Empire had

Japanese troops attack: a scene from the war between Russia and Japan (1904–5)

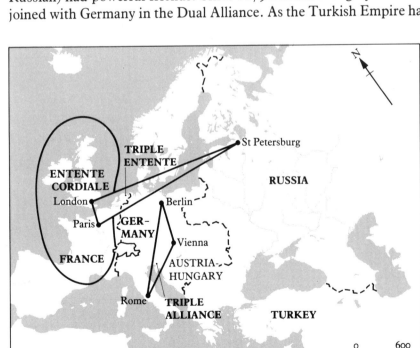

Europe 1914: empires and alliances

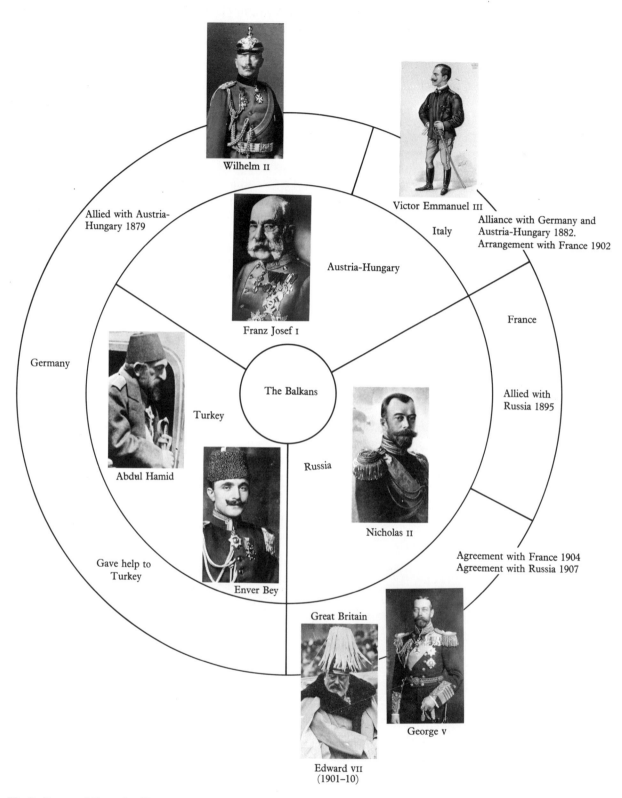

Wilhelm II

Victor Emmanuel III

Allied with Austria-
Hungary 1879

Italy

Alliance with Germany and
Austria-Hungary 1882.
Arrangement with France 1902

Austria-Hungary

Franz Josef I

France

Germany

The Balkans

Turkey

Allied with
Russia 1895

Abdul Hamid

Russia

Nicholas II

Gave help to
Turkey

Enver Bey

Agreement with France 1904
Agreement with Russia 1907

Great Britain

George V

Edward VII
(1901–10)

The Balkans and Europe's alliances

declined she had sought help; Germany had been happy to oblige. By 1914, Russia had agreements with both France and Britain.

Wilhelm II

The newest of the European empires was Germany. It had come into being in 1871 after the defeat of France in the Franco-Prussian War. As a result France had lost Alsace and Lorraine to Germany. These were valuable provinces, rich in iron and coal deposits. It was a loss which France had not forgotten.

Third in the line of German emperors was Kaiser Wilhelm II. (Like Tsar, the title Kaiser comes from the Latin for emperor – Caesar.) His two most prominent physical features, emphasised by unfriendly cartoonists, were his left arm which had been withered since birth, and his upturned moustache. The empire over which he ruled had by 1900 become a leading military and industrial power. Germany produced more coal, more iron and more steel than any of her continental rivals. Nor was her supremacy limited to these older industries. Similarly in the newer products of the twentieth century – electrical goods, chemicals, motor cars – Germany was rapidly establishing a lead.

Although not the largest in Europe, the German army was certainly the most efficient. From the professional general staff to the conscript required to do two to three years' military service, it was a well-organised, highly-trained, and totally disciplined force. In one of his more bloodthirsty speeches, Wilhelm II told German troops about to leave for China to crush an uprising:

Give no quarter! Take no prisoners! Anybody who falls into your hands must

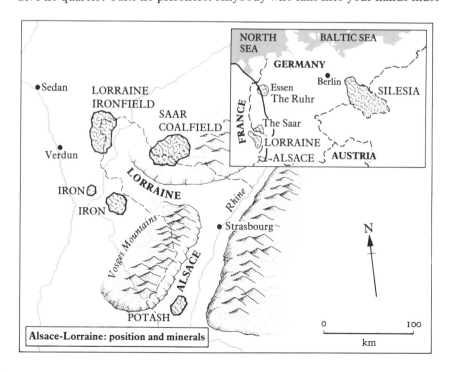

Alsace-Lorraine: position and minerals

be destroyed. Just as a thousand years ago Attila's Huns made a reputation for ruthless violence that still resounds through the ages, so let the name of Germans, through your actions in China, acquire a similar reputation that will last for a thousand years, so that never again will a Chinaman dare to look even askance at a German.

That was in 1900. In 1914 the name 'Hun' was to be heard again.

To equip this army, Germany possessed the world's biggest arms factory. It was owned by the Krupp family. From their factories in the Ruhr came the artillery needed by modern armies. Perhaps the best-remembered member of the family was to be the great-grand-daughter of the founder: a huge 420 mm howitzer used by the German army in the First World War was christened 'Big Bertha' by British troops.

Founder of the world's biggest arms factory, Alfred Krupp with his wife and son in 1869

Right The Kaiser and his generals, Hindenburg, Wilhelm II and Ludendorff. Note the Kaiser's pose. Can you suggest why he might be standing in this position?

Ultimatum

In the afternoon of 28 June 1914 a telegram from Mr Jones, the British vice-consul at Sarajevo, reached the Foreign Office:

According to the news received here heir-apparent and consort assassinated this morning by means of an explosive nature.

How would the Great Powers react to yet another crisis in the Balkans? In 1912 and again in 1913 their armies had not been involved. Could they be kept out of it this time, or would Austria-Hungary regard this as an opportunity for a final showdown with Serbia?

For a time little appeared to happen. But secretly, in palaces, embassies and government offices, urgent discussions took place and vital decisions were taken. Austria-Hungary sought the support of her German ally before moving against Serbia. Once that was given, events moved more swiftly. On 23 July, Austria-Hungary presented her demands to the Serbian government. Serbia was to stop all activity against Austria. All Serbian officials to whom Austria objected were to be dismissed. Austrians were to be allowed into Serbia to investigate the assassination. Altogether there were ten demands in the ultimatum. Serbia was given forty-eight hours to agree, or it was war.

Austria-Hungary expected the Serbian government to refuse these terms. The Serbs agreed to all of them – except one. They would not allow Austrian judges into their country. It was not enough. On 28 July, Austria-Hungary declared war on Serbia. Russia now prepared to go to the aid of her friend – Serbia.

The following day, Germany tried to persuade Russia to halt her call-up of troops. But once millions of soldiers have started to move, it is difficult to stop them, particularly when neither side trusts the other. The mobilisation continued. Germany declared war on Russia on 1 August, and on France two days later.

It began as the most popular war in history: cheering recruits in Berlin, 1914

'Not our fault'

The worst had happened. The armies of the Great Powers were on the march. Would Britain too be swept into the conflict? Unlike the alliances between the other Powers, Britain's agreements with France and Russia did not bind her to go to war in their support, but one event made it certain that Britain would declare war.

For years German military planners had wrestled with the problem of fighting a war on two fronts – against France in the west, and Russia in the east. Their answer was the Schlieffen Plan, named after the general who devised it. It was based on the belief that the Russian army, although larger than the French, would be slower to move. Schlieffen's plan was to defeat France quickly, by aiming a massive knock-out blow at the point where French defences were weakest – through Belgium.

Off to the war: a young German soldier leaves home in 1914

The spread of war

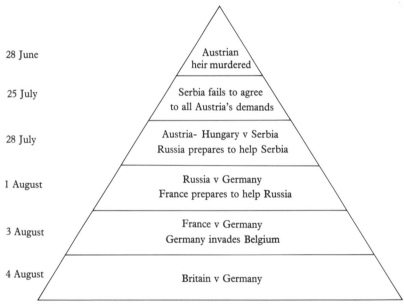

28 June	Austrian heir murdered
25 July	Serbia fails to agree to all Austria's demands
28 July	Austria- Hungary v Serbia Russia prepares to help Serbia
1 August	Russia v Germany France prepares to help Russia
3 August	France v Germany Germany invades Belgium
4 August	Britain v Germany

With France defeated, Germany could then turn the full weight of her army on Russia.

But Belgium was a neutral country, and her neutrality had been guaranteed by both Germany and Britain. When the Germans invaded Belgium, Britain declared war. It would in any case have been difficult for Britain to remain a spectator. British and French naval planning had, since 1912, been too closely linked for this. But it was Germany's refusal to withdraw from Belgium which was given as Britain's reason for going to war on 4 August.

King George V wrote in his diary:

4 August Warm, showers & windy. At work all day.... I held a Council at 10.45 to declare war with Germany; it is a terrible catastrophe but it is not our fault.... When they heard that war had been declared the excitement [of the crowds outside the palace] increased & it was a never-to-be-forgotten sight when May & I with David went on to the balcony, the cheering was terrific. Please God it may soon be over & that He will protect dear Bertie's life.

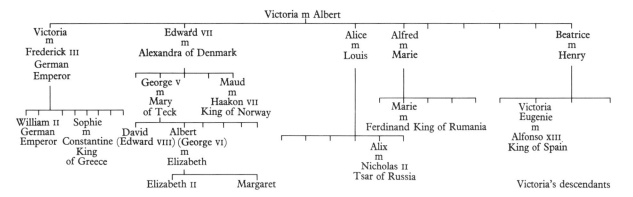

Queen Victoria's descendants

There is no easy explanation of why Europe went to war in 1914. The Great Powers did not fight because they had different religious or political beliefs. The kings of Germany and Britain were cousins; another cousin was married to the tsar of Russia (see the diagram on page 29). But they feared each other and felt threatened. France feared Germany and remembered the war they had fought forty-three years earlier. Germany was afraid of Russian might. Austria-Hungary was afraid of losing her empire in the Balkans. Britain felt her naval power was being threatened by Germany. Each was afraid that their enemies might strike the first blow.

The Schlieffen Plan in action: German troops march through Belgium

The powers of Europe were joined by a series of alliances and agreements; they possessed the armies and weapons to wage war; their overseas empires meant that a war which began with an assassination in the Balkans would spread beyond Europe. When the war came there were cheering crowds in all the capitals; it began as the most popular war in history. King George V was not alone in feeling that it was 'not our fault'. Both sides believed they were in the right and in churches throughout the continent they appealed to God for support.

1879	Dual Alliance of Austria-Hungary and Germany (expanded to Triple Alliance in 1882, when Italy joined)
1894	Franco-Russian Alliance
1899-1902	Boer War
1902	Alliance between Britain and Japan
1904	Entente Cordiale between Britain and France
1904-5	War between Russia and Japan
1906	First Moroccan crisis
	HMS *Dreadnought* launched
1907	Agreement between Britain and Russia
1908	Rising of Young Turks
	Bosnia part of Austro-Hungarian Empire
1911	Second Moroccan crisis
1912	Anglo-French naval agreement
1912-13	First and Second Balkan Wars
1914	Start of First World War (The Great War)

Using the evidence: (1) What happened at Sarajevo?

How do we know?

The historian asks of any event, (i) what happened and (ii) why?

Often neither question is easy to answer, and historians arrive at different conclusions. This can be true of quite recent events where a lot of evidence is available.

Historians obtain their information in a number of different ways. Some of the evidence used in chapter 1, for example, was from a newspaper report of the time. But newspapers, although valuable, are only one source of information.

This chapter began with the assassination of the Archduke Franz Ferdinand. How do we find out what actually happened at Sarajevo on 28 June 1914?

Accounts by those directly involved

(1) When the second car arrived, I recognised the heir-apparent. But as I saw

that a lady was sitting next to him I reflected for a moment whether I should shoot or not. At the same moment I was filled with a peculiar feeling and I aimed at the heir-apparent from the pavement – which was made easier because the car was proceeding slower at that moment. Where I aimed I do not know. But I know that I aimed at the heir-apparent. I believe that I fired twice, perhaps more, because I was so excited. Whether I hit the victims or not, I cannot tell, because instantly people started to hit me.

Gavrilo Princip to the investigating judge,
forty-five minutes after the shooting

Eye-witness accounts

(2) I stood about ten steps from the assassin. I had instructions not to look at the car, but to watch the crowd. Standing like this and doing my duty, I heard a revolver shot. I turned my head to the left; there was nothing. I looked to the right; a second shot was echoing. I plunged through the crowd, overtaking everybody else, and charged at the assassin, grabbing him by the arm; then somebody ambushed me and landed a fist in my stomach.

A detective at the trial

Official records

(3) *The charge against Princip*: I open against you the preliminary judicial investigation of the crime of murder which you committed today through shooting treacherously from the closest distance with a Browning pistol at the Heir-Apparent and his wife, the Duchess of Hohenberg, with the intention to kill them, and hitting them both, which caused their death a short time afterward.

Photographs

(4) *Archduke Franz Ferdinand and his wife walking down the steps of the Town Hall at Sarajevo*

(5) The hat, tunic, gloves and Bauchband worn by Franz Ferdinand on the day of his assassination

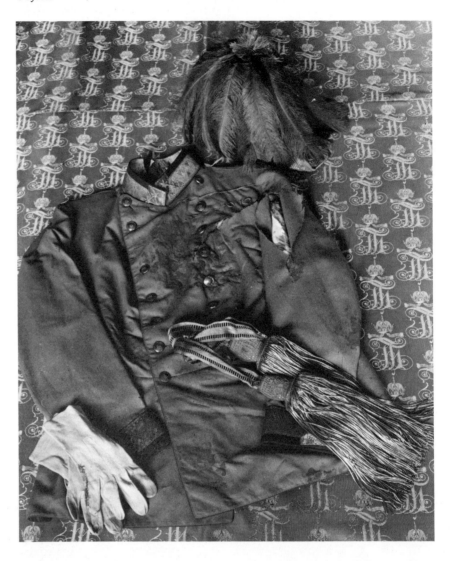

These are all examples of *primary sources*. That is, evidence from the time the event took place, which help the historian to build up a picture of what happened.

1 What examples of (i) written primary sources, (ii) other kinds of primary sources, are there in the chapter you have just read?

If you wrote about the Sarajevo assassination, you would probably use *secondary sources* for your information. That is, you would read accounts written by historians who were not there, usually written quite a long time after the event. This is part of one such account:

(6) As the procession moved along the Appel Quay there were a few shouts of 'Zivio!' (Long may he live!) from a thin crowd that stood under the shade of the houses and trees. It was very hot. The river side of the street was almost empty.

In a nearby street, a huge, poorly-fastened black-and-yellow flag above the ironmonger's Racher and Babic, located opposite the Catholic cathedral, shook, wobbled and finally fell among the spectators.

Vladimir Dedijer, *The Road to Sarajevo*

2 What is there in Document 6 to suggest that the writer is using some primary sources of evidence for his information?

Questions and further work

Differences in the accounts given by historians may arise because the primary sources are confused or misleading.

1 (a) Look again at the story told to the judge by Princip.
On what points is he quite certain?
On what points is he uncertain?
Suggest reasons why he is unsure on these points.
(b) In what ways do the eye-witness account and the official report clear up some of the doubts in Princip's story?

Sometimes photographs can be used in a way which is misleading. Look at the photographs on pages 32 to 34, and their captions. Compare them with what is said in Document 9, (a) to (c), and answer the questions that follow.

(7) *The archduke and his wife about to drive away from the Town Hall*

(8) 'Last picture of Franz Ferdinand and his wife – taken shortly before his assassination'

(9a) [Franz Ferdinand] was dressed in the ceremonial uniform of an Austrian cavalry general, with a blue tunic, a high collar with three stars, and a hat adorned with pale-green feathers. He wore black trousers with red stripes down the sides and around his waist a Bauchband, a gold-braided ribbon with tassels.

Vladimir Dedijer, *The Road to Sarajevo*

(b) ... at a quarter to eleven the archduke left the town hall. He was again in the third car. Lieutenant-Colonel Harrach stood on its running board, on the side of the car nearest to the river.

Vladimir Dedijer, *The Road to Sarajevo*

(c) Franz Ferdinand cried out, 'Sopherl! Sopherl! Don't die! Stay alive for the children!' His plumed hat had fallen off, and now as his aide tried to prop him upright he slumped over his wife's body murmuring only one last phrase of well-bred politeness, 'It is nothing'.

Dorothy G. McGuigan, *The Habsburgs*

2 (a) These descriptions match only two of the photographs and not the third. Which are the two photographs?
In what ways do these descriptions support the view that only two of the photographs are genuine?
(b) What piece of non-written evidence is there which might also support this view?

On the same day, a bomb was thrown at the archduke's car, but he escaped unhurt. These are three secondary accounts of that event:

(10a) ... one conspirator, a 19-year-old printer, ... threw a bomb at Franz Ferdinand, who managed to deflect it by raising his hand.

Jere Clemens King, *The First World War*

(b) The driver ... seeing a black object flying towards him, accelerated, and the bomb fell on the folded roof. The archduke threw up his left arm to protect the duchess, and the missile bounced off into the street.

Vladimir Dedijer, *The Road to Sarajevo*

(c) The bomb hit the hood and ricocheted off into the street where it wounded several bystanders and an aide of the Bosnian governor riding in the car behind.

Dorothy G. McGuigan, *The Habsburgs*

3 (a) There are two versions here of what happened to the bomb. What are they?
(b) Refer to the question 1, and suggest reasons for this difference.
(c) Which of these three descriptions do you think gives the most likely account of what happened and why?

Using the evidence: (2) Why the Great War?

The historian deals with complicated events. The reasons why they happened are complicated also. The simplest way to look at an event is to use three headings:

(i) What was the immediate cause?
(ii) What were the conditions which made it possible?
(iii) Why did the people involved act as they did (i.e. what were their motives)?

This is an account of an imaginary road accident:
Mr Simmonds was driving home from work in a hurry. He was late, and there was a TV programme he wanted to watch. It had been raining and the roads were very wet. The street lighting was poor. As he entered a sharp right-hand bend his car skidded and crashed into a wall. Mr Simmonds was badly injured. When they examined his car the police found that the two front tyres were bald.

4 Write a report on the accident to show:
(a) the immediate cause;
(b) the conditions which made it possible;
(c) the reasons why Mr Simmonds drove as he did.

5 From what you have read in the last two chapters on the causes of the war which started in 1914, decide:
(a) what was the immediate cause;
(b) what were the conditions that made it possible;
(c) what were the motives of the Great Powers?

3 Tactics, trenches and tanks

Where shall we go?

At 4 p.m. on 5 August the British prime minister called a Council of War. It was a large meeting. All the leading politicians, generals and admirals attended. They had to consider two questions – where should the British army be sent; and how many men should go? Some suggested Belgium, others France. There was even a suggestion that the army should invade the north coast of Germany itself. After a long and confused discussion, the decision was made. They would follow a plan drawn up in 1911. The British Expeditionary Force would join the left wing of the French armies at Maubeuge in northern France. It would consist of one cavalry and six infantry divisions – the whole of the regular army. The next day it was decided to reduce this slightly. One hundred thousand British soldiers crossed the Channel. The German navy did not try to stop them, and they were in position by 20 August.

'Over by Christmas'

In its early stages the First World War was a war of movement. Huge armies marched, or were transported, about Europe. Both sides were

A war of movement: British cavalry retreating from Mons

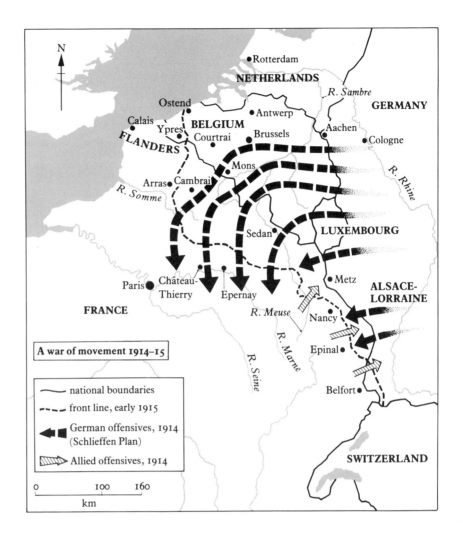

N

NETHERLANDS

• Rotterdam

• Antwerp

R. Sambre

GERMANY

Ostend

Calais •

Ypres •

FLANDERS

BELGIUM

Courtrai

Brussels

Aachen

• Cologne

R. Rhine

Mons

Arras • Cambrai

R. Somme

Sedan •

LUXEMBOURG

Château-
Thierry

Paris •

Epernay

FRANCE

R. Meuse

Nancy •

• Metz

ALSACE-
LORRAINE

Epinal •

R. Marne

R. Seine

Belfort •

A war of movement 1914–15

—— national boundaries

- - - front line, early 1915

◀ German offensives, 1914
(Schlieffen Plan)

▷ Allied offensives, 1914

SWITZERLAND

0   100   160

km

certain that it would all be over by Christmas at the latest. In some cases, soldiers stowed away in troop trains, they were so keen not to miss the fight.

Within a few days of their arrival, the British met the Germans at Mons. A million men had invaded Belgium and were now advancing towards Paris. The BEF could only delay the Germans at Mons, before being forced to retreat. It was not until the Germans were almost in sight of Paris that their onrush was stopped. They were turned back at the Battle of the Marne by French troops rushed from the capital in taxis.

The Germans retreated as far as the River Aisne. There they began to dig trenches. The British and French dug in opposite the Germans. Each side tried to get round the other; neither could. At one end they reached the sea, at the other the mountains of Switzerland. The Germans occupied most of Belgium, but their attempts to capture the Channel ports were defeated at Ypres. By December the war of movement was over in the west and trench warfare had begun.

Deadlock

For the next four years the armies on the Western Front moved no more than a few kilometres either way. The trenches were dug deeper. They were strengthened with sandbags, wood, concrete and steel. They were protected in front by several kilometres of barbed-wire, and supported behind by lines of reserve and communication trenches. Above all, they were defended by machine-guns.

It was nearly impossible to attack such defences successfully. This had already been shown during the Boer War and in the war between Russia and Japan. But this was war on a much more massive scale than those. How were the armies to break through? No commander on either side found the answer, but their attempts cost the lives of millions of men.

The solution tried most often had two stages. First there would be a huge artillery bombardment, with the intention of destroying the enemy's dugouts, barbed-wire and machine gun posts. At the battle of the Somme in 1916, for example, the British bombardment lasted for eight days: on a twenty-four-kilometre front, 52 000 tonnes of ammunition were fired from 1750 guns. Then, in great waves, the infantry would cross no-man's-land between the lines of trenches, to attack the enemy.

This method seldom had much success. It took a long time to collect the guns and men which were needed for such an attack. It could not be

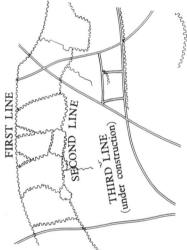

Typical arrangement of trenches: these face westwards

Going over the top: British troops at the Battle of the Somme, 1916

done secretly. The enemy had plenty of warning. They knew that when the guns stopped, the infantry would be coming. Many of the trenches were too deep for the men in them to be killed by shellfire. The shells destroyed some of the barbed-wire, but they could also turn no-man's-land into a swamp. Soldiers carrying rifles and packs were forced to move slowly. Some were drowned in water-filled potholes. They were easy targets for the machine-gunners. On the first day of the battle of the Somme, the British Army lost 60 000 men killed or wounded. It was the greatest loss in a single day in the history of war.

Much has been written by the men who took part, about the horror of this war. One of them described it in a radio programme long afterwards:

Now came disillusionment for us who had joined up in a fine spirit of adventure. The frenzied butchery of this war, indefensible even on a military basis, was eventually to kill at least ten million young men. After being dressed in uniform, fed and drilled, cheered and cried over, these ten million were then filled with hot lead, ripped apart by shell splinters, blown to bits, suffocated in mud, or allowed to die of diseases after rotting too long in trenches that they shared with syphilitic rats and typhus-infested lice. Death, having come into his empire, demanded the best, and got it.

Stalemate at sea

Much the same state of deadlock existed in the war at sea. Winston

Churchill, the First Lord of the Admiralty, had dreamt of a glorious British naval victory to end the war, but no such victory occurred. Both sides laid mines. A few small-scale battles were fought. The great dreadnoughts spent most of the war in harbour – an unused threat. As long as the British fleet remained intact, Britain need not fear invasion; troop ships could cross the Channel; German ships could not enter or leave port safely. The Commander-in-Chief of the British Grand Fleet, Admiral Jellicoe, felt that by losing his ships he could lose the war in an afternoon.

There was only one major naval battle – the battle of Jutland in the North Sea in 1916. The British lost more ships than the Germans, but the German Fleet retired, and did not leave Kiel harbour again.

The war at sea: HMS Indefatigable steams into action at the Battle of Jutland

New weapons: (above right) a gas sentry rings the alarm; (right) the tank

New weapons: aircraft of the Great War

New weapons

New means were used to try to break the deadlock. In February 1915 the Germans experimented with flame-throwers. In April poison gas was used for the first time. Despite the dangers to friend as well as foe, it continued to be used by both sides. The new British invention, the tank, made its first appearance at the Somme. The tanks stuck in the mud. A year later, however, on hard ground at Cambrai in 1917, tanks were much more successful.

Powered flight was in its very early stages at the beginning of the war. At first aeroplanes were used mainly for reconnaissance and directing artillery fire. Occasionally pilots shot at each other with pistols, or dropped small bombs by hand. Larger bombs were carried by hydrogen-filled airships, but the airships were liable to explode if hit by bullets. As the war progressed, aeroplanes became bigger, stronger and faster. New tactics, including formation-flying, were developed. Bomb-sights were invented. By 1916 fighter planes carried machine-guns which were synchronised to fire through the propeller. As the war ended, four-engined bombers were being prepared to raid Berlin.

At sea, the most important development was the submarine. In 1901 the first five British submarines had entered the navy. But it was the Germans who used them to greatest effect. In one month of 1917 they sank nearly one million tonnes of merchant shipping. This was a serious threat to Britain's food supplies. The problem was largely overcome by ships sailing in convoys, where they could be more easily protected.

A German submarine surrenders at the end of the war

The Eastern Front

In an effort to break the deadlock, Winston Churchill put forward a plan for attacking Turkey in 1915. Turkey had entered the war on the

The Eastern Front – a German artillery observation post at the Battle of Tannenberg, August 1914. The German army drove the invading Russians out of Germany

side of Germany and Austria-Hungary in October 1914.

The fighting in eastern Europe had not become as bogged-down as that in the west. At the beginning of the war, Germany expected the Russian armies to be slower to move than the French. To their surprise, the Russians successfully attacked parts of Germany and Austria. German troops had to be sent to stop the Russians in the east. This was one of the reasons for the breakdown of the Schlieffen Plan. Churchill's scheme was to help Russia by defeating Turkey.

British, French and Anzac (Australian and New Zealand) troops were landed on the Gallipoli peninsula. They got no farther than the beaches. There they remained in trenches throughout the summer. The plan failed. In November the soldiers were withdrawn, but by that time Churchill had already been forced to resign.

'If only peace would come!'

At the end of 1916, a German soldier wrote home: 'Hans is dead. Fritz is dead. Wilhelm is dead. There are many others. I am now quite alone in the company. . . . This is almost unendurable. If only peace would come!'

In 1917 peace seemed as far away as ever. Britain and France gained one ally, and lost another. So many American ships were sunk by German submarines that the United States of America declared war in April. In November, after the Communist revolution (see chapter 6) Russia made peace with Germany.

Now Germany had to fight on only one front. Before America could enter the war in strength, the Germans made a last mighty effort. It very nearly succeeded. They advanced deep into territory held by the British and French, before being driven back. Large numbers of German troops surrendered. German sailors mutinied when ordered to put to sea. In Germany people were starving. Wilhelm II abdicated. The new government agreed terms with the Allies.

On 11 November 1918 the message was sent to the men in the trenches:

Hostilities will cease at 11.00 hrs today Nov 11. Troops will stand fast on line reached at that hour. . . . Defensive precautions will be maintained. There will be no intercourse of any description with the enemy until receipt of instructions from Army HQ.

For them the war was over: captured German troops

Total war

Before 1939, the 1914–18 war was called the Great War. Athough it was fought mainly in Europe, every continent was involved. Never before had populations been called upon to make such a total effort. Millions of people were involved. Millions of soldiers and civilians were killed or maimed. By 1918 casualty figures were no longer given to the newspapers.

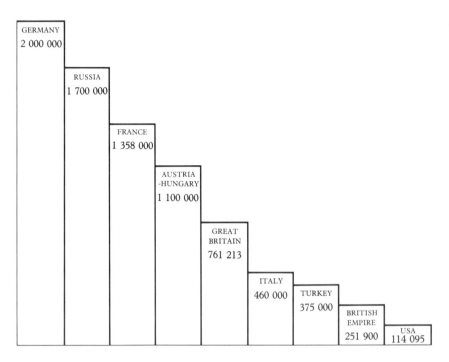

War losses 1914–18 (only military losses are shown)

GERMANY
2 000 000

RUSSIA
1 700 000

FRANCE
1 358 000

AUSTRIA
-HUNGARY
1 100 000

GREAT
BRITAIN
761 213

ITALY
460 000

TURKEY
375 000

BRITISH
EMPIRE
251 900

USA
114 095

War memorial in Brussels

The numbers of those killed were so high that they are difficult to grasp. Every town, village and school had its war dead. Their memorials can still be seen. Families throughout the world received telegrams similar to this:

> Deeply regret to inform you that Capt E. R. Cooke Irish Fusiliers was killed in action 26th April Lord Kitchener expresses his sympathy.
>
> Secretary War Office

1914	British Expeditionary Force sent to France
	Retreat from Mons
	Paris saved by the battle of Marne
	Beginning of trench warfare
1915	Gallipoli campaign
1916	Battle of the Somme
	Battle of Jutland
1917	Entry of the USA into the war
	Russian withdrawal from the war
1918	Final German offensive
	End of the Great War

Using the evidence: the sinking of the Lusitania

How do we know?

This exercise is designed to look for the truth behind this headline, by asking both 'what?' and 'why?' You are asked to make a number of decisions. You can work through these individually, in pairs or in small groups, and at the end of the exercise, compare your decisions with those reached by other members of the class. Two helpful references are: *Lusitania* by Colin Simpson (Penguin) and *Lusitania* by Barry Turner in *History of the Twentieth Century*, Purnell.

The SS *Lusitania*

On 1 May 1915, the British liner SS *Lusitania*, one of the largest and fastest ships afloat, left New York bound for Liverpool. On the afternoon of 7 May she was torpedoed by a German submarine off the south coast of Ireland. The ship sank within eighteen minutes; 1201 people lost their lives. Of these, 128 were Americans. As a result, the USA nearly entered the war against Germany.

These are the bare facts of the tragedy; but a lot of questions still remain unanswered.

1   On 4 February, Germany had announced that submarines would be used against all enemy merchant shipping in the war zone. The war

Daily Express, 8 May 1915

Daily Express

NO. 4,706. LONDON, SATURDAY, MAY 8, 1915. ONE HALFPENNY.

The World's Greatest and Foulest Crime.

NO WARNING GIVEN.

GREAT LINER GOES DOWN IN EIGHT MINUTES.

GRAVE MESSAGES.

BETWEEN 500 AND 600 SURVIVORS LANDED AT QUEENSTOWN.

MANY HOSPITAL CASES.

The Secretary of the Admiralty announced at one o'clock this morning that the following message had been received from the admiral at Queenstown:—

Survivors from the Lusitania ... being landed. Those wounded ... being sent to naval and military hospitals.
...o names yet received.

...rtly afterwards the Secretary ... Admiralty issued the following ... message from the admiral at ...stown:—

...etween 500 and 600 survivors ...m Lusitania now landed.
...any hospital cases. Several ...e died.
...lso some have been landed ...sale. Number not yet received.

... soon as the news of the sinking ... the Lusitania became known ... London the Cockspur-street ... of the Cunard Company were ...ged by anxious inquirers.

...tish staff officers in uniform ... a number of Americans were ... the first callers. The case ... middle-aged American woman ...ated on obtaining confirma... the sinking was typical of ... distressing incidents which ... during the evening.

...irst details of the outrage ...ntained in the following ... written in blue pencil, ... was posted up inside the ... 7 p.m.:—

...d Head of Kinsale wires:—
...out twenty boats Lusitania ... vicinity where ship sank. ...t sixteen more boats are ...ing for spot to render assist... Weather beautifully fine.

...ORK OF RESCUE.

... announcements made at ...s were as follows:—

...sitania was sunk without ...ing. She sank in eight min...

...ves of passengers have been ...l. A boatload of survivors ...ing towed into Kinsale by a ...k steamer.

...veral passengers have been ... by rescuing steamers. ... of them are making for ...ale, others steering a course ... Queenstown.

...e following message from ... Admiralty:—

...lley Head, 4.25 p.m.—Seve... boats, apparently survivors, ...-east nine miles; Greek ...ner proceeding to assist.

...tor fishing boat carrying ... boats; probably number pas... ...rs about fifty. Tug Storm... also taking passengers and ... from motor fishing boats. ...ing boats probably proceed... ...o Queenstown. Majority of ... vessels now apparently ...ing Queenstown.

...ptain Turner, of the Aqui... was in command of the Lusi... said an official of the ... Company to a "Daily Ex... representative. "The cap... who is, I believe, a Lancashire ... was relieving Captain Dow, ...usitania's regular comman... who was taking a rest for a ... of voyages.

THE BRITISH FLAG.

"The Lusitania was flying the British flag, and carried a number of Americans in addition to British and other passengers.

"The large number of lifeboats in the Lusitania had a capacity of from fifty to eighty passengers each, and with the rafts and collapsible boats there was more than sufficient accommodation for every soul on board."

In addition to her general cargo the liner probably had bullion on board.

Several inquiries were made whether the sailing of the Cunard liner Ascania from Liverpool on Sunday would be cancelled, but the company announced that nothing had yet been decided.

The American Ambassador sent representatives to the offices, and asked that all the messages received should be telephoned to him.

Arrangements were made to keep the offices open all night, and chairs were placed in the vestibule for inquirers. As the hours passed the crowd of anxious friends of passengers largely increased, and there were many expressions of indignation and anger, particularly among Americans.

ALTERED VIEWS.

"I am a New York citizen," said one American Association representative, "and have so far agreed with the neutral attitude taken up by my country. This affair, however, has changed my views, and, if I mistake not, has altered the minds of thousands of my fellow countrymen."

One of the most pathetic sights was that of an elderly woman and man with grey hair, who sat quietly and composedly in a corner. They were a clergyman and his wife, waiting for news of their son who was returning in the Lusitania after a lecture tour in America.

An American stated that he was anxious for news of his wife, who went to America in the Adriatic four weeks ago.

"I cabled to her to come back by the Lusitania," he said, "as that was the only boat that could get away from the German submarines."

One or two women went tremblingly to the counter and broke into tears, but most of the anxious people stood talking quietly, and tried to buoy each other up with remarks about the possibility of a liner remaining afloat until the passengers were taken into the boats.

When a message indicating the possibility of lives being lost was posted up a woman who had been keenly interested in the announcements uttered painful screams and went into hysterics. She was carried out of the building struggling piteously.

The offices are not large, and the crowd made them almost unbearably warm. Inquirers made fans of their newspapers and jugs of water were brought by the officials.

Outside several thousands of people came to read the messages in the outer passage, and the police had to regulate the flow. Among the late callers were Sir Samuel Evans and Sir Henry Norman, M.P.

LUSITANIA TORPEDOED & SUNK IN EIGHT MINUTES.

German piracy reached its climax yesterday when the great Cunard liner Lusitania, with 1,978 souls on board, was sunk without warning by a submarine twenty-three miles west of Queenstown.

Up to a late hour last night only the scantiest details of the outrage had been received in London. Between 500 and 600 survivors, many of whom were injured and were taken to hospital, were landed last night at Queenstown. Some others have been landed at Kinsale. As the liner sank eight minutes after she was torpedoed there may have been considerable loss of life. Many prominent persons had booked passages in the Lusitania, including Mr. Charles Frohman, Mr. Alfred Vanderbilt, Mr. D. A. Thomas, Sir Hugh Lane, Lady Mackworth, and Lady Allan, wife of Sir Hugh Allan, of Montreal.

While the incident may impress the imagination by reason of the size of the liner, it will in no degree impair the courage of the nation, and will not have the slightest effect on the course of the war. It is simply an act of piracy and nothing more.

The Lusitania left New York on Saturday last with passengers and mails for Liverpool. Just before she sailed the German Embassy, on instructions from Berlin, published in the New York newspapers a warning to travellers that they embarked in British liners at their own risk. Anonymous warnings were also sent to persons who had booked berths, but little attention was paid to these communications, and the number of passengers created a record for the time of the year. There were on board:—First Class Passengers, 290; Second Class Passengers, 662; Third Class Passengers, 361; Crew, 665. Total, 1,978.

The first indication that the Germans might attempt to carry their threat into effect was afforded on Thursday afternoon by the presence of an enemy submarine in Dunmanus Bay, next to Bantry Bay, on the south-west coast of County Cork and eighty miles west of Queenstown. The submarine came close to the shore, and, having manœuvred on the surface for some time, dived and was not seen again. Rumours were current in the City yesterday afternoon that the Lusitania had been attacked, and at 5.30 the Admiralty announced that she had been torpedoed and sunk off the Head of Kinsale, south of County Cork. Soon after the news became known in London the offices of the Cunard Company in Cockspur-street were besieged by friends of passengers, including many Americans, and expressions of indignation were heard on every hand. In New York the news caused intense excitement, and the stock market collapsed, all stocks falling from 5 to 10 points.

During the day it became known that two other large Liverpool steamers had been sunk in St. George's Channel on Thursday by German submarines. They were the Candidate, of 5,856 tons, bound for Jamaica, and the Centurion, of 5,945 tons, bound for Durban.

CAPTAIN TURNER,
The Lusitania's Commander

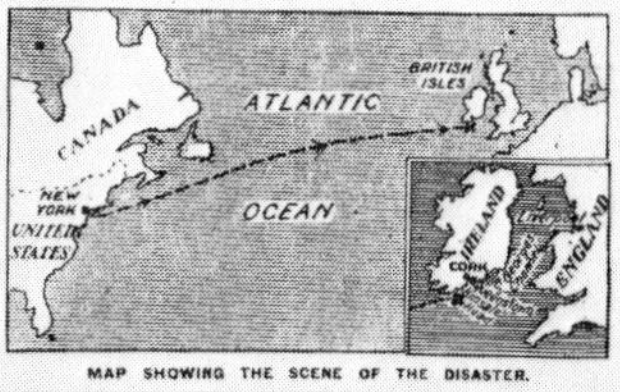

MAP SHOWING THE SCENE OF THE DISASTER.

"COME AT ONCE."

LINER'S LAST MESSAGE FOR HELP.

Only the scantiest details reached London from Queenstown up to a late hour. There were brief announcements of the sinking issued by the Admiralty, Lloyd's, and the Cunard Company, and little else.

The Queenstown correspondent of the Central News states:—

"The Lusitania was torpedoed off Galley Head on the other side of Kinsale at 2.25 p.m., and within eight minutes the liner sank. A fleet of steamers was immediately despatched from this port to rescue passengers.

"When the disaster occurred the weather was beautifully fine, with a hot sun and a gentle southerly breeze. Among the rescuing boats sent out was a fleet of ten trawlers, and one had the Queenstown lifeboat in tow.

"Several rescuing steamers have been sighted laden with Lusitania passengers making towards Kinsale and Queenstown."

The Press Association's correspondent states:—

"It appears that the Lusitania was noticed to be in difficulties from the signal station at the Old Head of Kinsale, at 2.12 p.m. At 2.33 she had completely disappeared.

"A wireless message was received here from the vessel at 2.15, stating:

"Come at once. Big list."

"Immediately Vice-Admiral Sir Charles Coke despatched all the available tugs and steam trawlers to the scene of the disaster. It would take most of them about two hours to reach the spot where the vessel went down."

FOR MURDER!

IRON CROSSES FOR THE MEN WHO PLANNED THE DISASTER.

Wireless news from Berlin, tapped by the Marconi Company yesterday, contained the following significant item:—

A telegram from the German Admiralty to Boy-Ed in Washington states that the Iron Cross of the Second Class has been awarded to Boy-Ed and Moeller.

Captain Boy-Ed is the German naval attaché in Washington, who was suspected of plotting the issue of false passports to German reservists in order that they might return to Germany.

"Moeller" is Max Moeller, the superintendent at New York of the North-German Lloyd, who declared on Monday last:—

"As for the Lusitania, we will get her surely."

THE LUSITANIA.

EXCITEMENT IN NEW YORK.

COLLAPSE OF THE STOCK MARKET.

NEW YORK, Friday, May 7.

The news of the sinking of the Lusitania has created intense excitement here.

As soon as the intelligence became known the market collapsed, all stocks falling from five to ten points.

The state of demoralisation into which the New York Stock Exchange was thrown by the news may be imagined from the fact that some stocks fell more than fifteen points, recovering to ten in the last half hour.

Bethlehem Steel fell seventeen and a half, subsequently recovering to twelve.

Public indignation is overwhelming.—Central News.

OFFICIAL ATTITUDE.

"Express" Correspondent.

NEW YORK, Friday, May 7.

The State Department announces that the sinking of the Lusitania falls in the same category as that of the ship Falaba, and both will be handled along the same lines so far as America's interests are concerned.

THE PASSENGERS.

FAMOUS PEOPLE WHO WERE ON BOARD.

Among those who had booked passages by the Lusitania were:—

Mr. Alfred Vanderbilt, son of the late Mr. Cornelius Vanderbilt, and his principal heir. Director of the International Horse Show Association of London, where he has made his home for many years, having withdrawn from active participation in the Vanderbilt interests in America.

Dr. F. S. Pearson, American financial magnate and well-known engineer.

Mr. Herbert Stone, son of Mr. Melville Stone, general manager of the Associated Press of America.

Sir Hugh Lane, great traveller and collector of works of art; director of the National Gallery, Ireland; has presented a collection of modern art to the City of Dublin, and formed the collection for the Johannesburg Municipal Gallery, offered £10,000 to the Red Cross funds for the right to name two sitters for Sargent portraits.

(Continued on Page FIVE.)

WAS THERE A CONVOY?

QUESTIONS RAISED BY THE GREAT DISASTER.

SPEED AND ROUTES.

STOPPING TO PICK UP A PILOT.

The "Daily Express" naval correspondent writes:—

Many questions are raised by the sinking of the Lusitania which have not figured in the sinking of other merchantmen.

Every one will be curious to learn whether there was a warship convoy for the liner, in view of the published threats against her;

Whether, and, if so, why, she followed her usual course after the unmistakable warnings; and

Whether from any cause her speed was reduced.

On the correct answers to these questions rests the whole solution of the mystery which at present enshrouds the loss of this ship.

The question of the course of the ship is of redoubled importance in view, first, of the threats made in New York before she sailed that she would be sunk, and the fact that at least two German submarines of modern type are known to have been haunting the waters south of Ireland since last Saturday.

RUNNING RISKS.

It is conceivable that there were imperative reasons why she should call at Queenstown, though one finds it difficult to believe that anything could have compelled her to run untold risks with so many passengers on board. It is true that the practical closing of the North Channel between the Irish and Scottish coasts by the British minefield made a passage round the north of Ireland direct to Liverpool one of considerable peril. Fishguard also was open to objection, in view of the activity of enemy submarines both off the Scillies and off Waterford.

Plymouth, however, seems to be indicated as a possibly safer destination than Queenstown, and it will be interesting to learn what explanation is offered for the failure to divert the Lusitania to the Channel port.

The question of the convoy by warship is a naval problem, and on the answer to it a great deal depends.

It is almost unbelievable that the Lusitania was allowed to navigate these waters under the circumstances without an attendant flotilla of fast warships. If there was no convoy the nation will have every right to demand to know the reason.

In the meantime we must assume that proper precautions were taken, and consequently we are faced with the fact that even a fast convoy is not an infallible protection against underwater attack.

SCREEN OF DESTROYERS.

Hitherto we have found in the course of the naval operations that a screen of destroyers served very well ... disaster from large vessels, e... they were compelled to steam ... the commander of the submari... sank the Lusitania outwitted ... ships of the convoy, we shall ... more to revise our opinion of th... water peril.

In the same way, the answ... question about the Lusitania's ... of the first importance to all m... She was nominally able to do t... knots. So far as is at prese... there was no fog at the time sh... proaching the Old Head of Kin... ...as she, then, torpedoed while moving fast through the water?

An affirmative answer to this will shake the growing belief that speed is the most adequate defence against submarines. But that affirmative will only be serious in its effect if the attack was made at long range. Provided the submarine could fire the torpedo at a very short distance from her target, let us say, for example, 150 yards, the chances of success were, of course, enormous. A torpedo travelling at forty knots, against a liner travelling at twenty, at that range could hardly miss.

In connection with the question of the influence of speed on the loss of the Lusitania, it may be well to bear in mind that vessels entering the Cork Harbour district are required to take a pilot.

The Old Head of Kinsale, where the disaster occurred, is a pilotage station, and it is possible that the Lusitania had stopped to pick up a pilot at the time she was torpedoed. Under those circumstances she would offer as easy a mark as did the Hogue and the Cressy when they went to the help of the sinking Aboukir and lay-to for the work of rescue.

PREVIOUS DISASTERS.

The following table shows the total loss of life in the worst shipping disasters of this century:—

Titanic sunk after striking an iceberg on April 11, 1912	1,503
Empress of Ireland sunk by collision with the collier Storstad in the St. Lawrence, May 29, 1914	1,014
General Slocum burnt at New York, June 1904	1,000
Norge wrecked on Rockall Reef, June 1904	637

The worst disaster caused by a warlike act at sea was the sinking of the West African steamer Falaba on March 27 last, when 111 lives were lost.

zone was the sea area around Great Britain and Ireland. Neutral ships were advised to avoid it. This was in response to the British blockade of German ports. A notice from the German Embassy warning travellers of the dangers, had appeared in American newspapers the morning the *Lusitania* was due to sail. In some papers this appeared next to a list of departure dates.

2   But Cunard received very few cancellations. There were, however, some facts which the passengers did not know, and which might have altered their decisions. This additional information is given below.

INFORMATION SHEET A

2a *The cargo*

(i) The boxes of cartridges were addressed to the Royal Arsenal at Woolwich. Each box contained 1000 rounds of .303 ammunition.

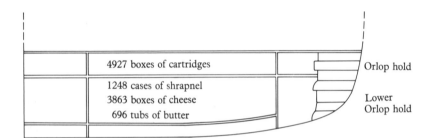

Part of the Lusitania's *hold*

(ii) On the loading-bill there were 1248 cases of shrapnel (small pieces of metal). On the shipping note of the company which supplied them, they were described as '1248 cases of 3-inch Shrapnel shells filled'.
(iii) The cheese and butter were addressed to a box number in Liverpool. The box number was that of the Superintendent of the Naval Experimental Establishment at Shoeburyness.

TAKE UP THE SWORD OF JUSTICE

A British recruiting poster: 'Avenge the Lusitania'

2b *The passengers*

On the evening of 30 April, sixty-seven men, two women and a baby boarded the *Lusitania*. The two couples were Mr and Mrs R. Matthews, and Mr and Mrs Palmer.

Male body identified as Lt (Temporary)/Capt. R. Matthews of the 6th Winnipeg Rifles by certificates and papers found in his pockets. (Report on a body washed up on the Irish coast, 8 May)

2c *The ship*

(i) Under strict secrecy the *Lusitania* entered dry-dock at Liverpool on 12 May 1913. . . . The shelter deck was adapted to take four six-inch guns on either side, making a total complement of twelve guns or a broadside of six guns each firing a shell containing high explosive . . . they (the Cunard liners) could mount a heavier broadside than the *Bacchante* or E-class cruisers then charged with the defence of the Channel. . . .By 8 August [1914] the *Aquitania* had her guns installed and the *Lusitania* was moved into the Canada dry-dock on Merseyside to be similarly equipped.

Colin Simpson, *Lusitania*

(ii) It was only to be expected that the enemy would attempt to justify his heinous [hateful] work by proclaiming that the vessel was armed. . . . This was proved to be totally unfounded. . . . Another German lie exposed!

From an account of the sinking of the *Lusitania* published in October 1915 by the Cunard Company, owners of the ship.

1 Consider carefully the information given and then look at the statements below. Write out those with which you would agree.

(i) The *Lusitania* was carrying a large amount of ammunition and other explosives;

(ii) Only a small part of the cargo was ammunition, and this did not endanger the ship;

(iii) The *Lusitania* was a troop-ship;

(iv) There were no troops on board;

(v) A few of the passengers were soldiers, but most were ordinary travellers;

(vi) The *Lusitania* carried some guns to defend herself, which made the ship safer to travel in;

(vii) The *Lusitania* was not armed;

(viii) The *Lusitania* could be used to attack enemy ships.

Winston Churchill, First Lord of the Admiralty

3 On the morning of Wednesday 5 May, there was a meeting in the Plot Room of the British Admiralty. Those present were:

Winston Churchill – First Lord of the Admiralty. He was deeply involved in the Gallipoli campaign, and was about to leave for Paris. He was anxious not to miss his train.

Admiral Lord Fisher – First Sea Lord. He was now seventy-four years old. He had quarrelled violently with Churchill over Gallipoli and resigned on 15 May.

Vice-Admiral Henry Oliver – Chief of Naval War Staff.

Captain Reginald Hall – Director of Naval Intelligence.

Commander Joseph Kenworthy – Worked in Naval Intelligence. He had written to Churchill about the political results of an ocean liner being sunk with American passengers on board.

INFORMATION SHEET B

Notes (*refer to the map on page 50*)

Notes (*refer to the map on page 50*)

(i) U30 was well to the west of Ireland, heading north.

(ii) U20 had been sighted at 9 a.m. a few miles north-west of Fastnet.

(iii) *Lusitania* was approaching the south coast of Ireland. If U20 remained stationary, the two would meet at dawn on 6 May.

(iv) HMS *Juno* had orders to meet the *Lusitania* south-west of Fastnet.

Admiral Lord Fisher, First Sea Lord

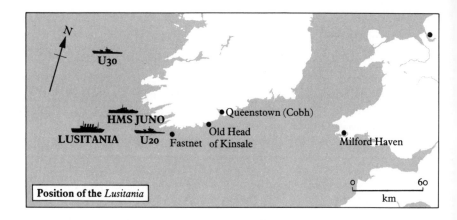

Position of the *Lusitania*

Juno was an old cruiser of a type that was known to be very liable to sink if hit by a torpedo.

(v) There was a destroyer flotilla stationed at Milford Haven.

4 The situation which they saw on the plot is shown above. They had to decide what action to take.

2 Five possible courses of action are listed below. Choose which of these you consider to be the best plan, which the next best and so on. If you think (a) is the best, number it as 1; if you think (b) is the next, number it as 2, and so on until you can list all five in the order you have decided on.
(a) Leave *Lusitania* and *Juno* on their present courses;
(b) Provide an escort of destroyers;
(c) Divert *Lusitania* round the west coast of Ireland and leave *Juno*;
(d) Divert *Juno* and leave *Lusitania*;
(e) Divert both *Lusitania* and *Juno*.

5 The decision that was made was (d). *Juno* was to return to Queenstown, travelling at night, and avoiding Fastnet by eighty kilometres. *Lusitania* was not informed.

3 Compare this decision with the one you made in question 2. In your view was the decision made a good one or not?

6 No one knows who made it, or why, but Churchill and Fisher controlled naval policy, and they must share the responsibility. It is difficult to determine what their motives were. Below are three possibilities, with some reasons for and against each one.

a The Lusitania *was considered to be safe*
For: The *Lusitania* would not reach the point where the U20 had been sighted for nearly twenty-four hours, by which time the submarine might well have moved. In any case the *Lusitania* was faster than a submarine.
Against: The U20 was bound to stay in the area through which ships would have to pass on the way to Liverpool. In the past even ships carrying mules had been diverted when submarines were known to be about.

b The danger was not realised

For: Both Churchill and Fisher had many other things on their minds. They were at loggerheads with each other. Churchill was anxious to leave for Paris. Fisher was too old to do his job properly.

Against: Fisher in particular was very experienced, and similar situations had occurred before. In any case, there were three other people at the meeting who would have pointed out the danger to them.

c The Lusitania *was deliberately sent into a dangerous area*

For: Churchill wanted the USA to enter the war. If American lives were lost there was a good chance that this would happen.

Against: Politicians would not gamble with civilians' lives in this way. There was no certainty that the USA would declare war; especially as the Americans on the *Lusitania* were aware of the risk they were taking.

4 Consider these possible motives carefully. Decide which one you think is the most likely, which the next most likely and which the least likely.

(a) The *Lusitania* was considered to be safe;

(b) The danger was not realised;

(c) The *Lusitania* was deliberately sent into a dangerous area.

4 The civilians' war

Horatio Bottomley at work: a recruiting speech in Trafalgar Square, 1915

'What did YOU do in the Great War?'

In the issue of 12 September 1914, the editor of the magazine *John Bull* told his readers:

'The mills of God grind slowly, but they grind exceeding small!' Aye, friend, and the slower they grind the smaller they crush. And that is why Kaiser William the Second – the Butcher of Berlin – will assuredly be crushed, utterly and for everlasting.

The editor and owner of *John Bull* was Horatio Bottomley who set up in business to recruit men for the armed forces. Bottomley became very popular and his business was highly profitable. His standard charge for a recruiting speech was £50, or £100 for the more stirring version. Bankrupt at the beginning of the war, he made a small fortune during it, before being imprisoned for fraud and dying in poverty in 1933.

Once the hope of a quick victory disappeared in the trenches of the Western Front, the most urgent need was for men. Unlike the other countries of Europe, Britain relied entirely for the first eighteen months of the war on volunteer recruits. Government posters, music-hall songs and speakers like Bottomley, urged men to do their duty for king and country, family and friends. Members of the Women of England's Active Service League pledged themselves to persuade their sons and boyfriends to join up, and to have nothing to do with those who refused. In some parts of the country, white feathers were handed out to men who were thought to be shirking. In the face of this combined appeal to their patriotism and assault on their manhood, thousands rushed to the recruiting offices. The army had the greatest difficulty in coping with such numbers.

Lord Kitchener, the Secretary for War, and one of the few men who did not believe it would all be over by Christmas, asked initially for 100 000 men. Not far short of twice that number volunteered in the first week of September. By the end of the month 750 000 had enlisted. When compulsory military service was introduced in March 1916, the number had reached 2½ million.

Business as usual

In northern France and Belgium civilians were immediately caught up in the fighting. But this was not so for most Britons and Germans. At first, life for the majority of the civilian population continued much as usual. In 1915 the east-coast towns of Bridlington, West Hartlepool, Scarborough and Whitby were shelled by German cruisers, and the first bombing raid on London by Zeppelins took place in April. But although such raids caused widespread alarm, few civilians were killed. The only refugees Britons saw were 100 000 Belgians, who, after the first enthusiasm had worn off, were heartily disliked. Despite rumours

Victims of the war: Belgian refugees in Holland

of one million Russian troops seen marching south from Aberdeen, the only soldiers people saw were men in training or on leave, or the wounded arriving in hospital trains at Waterloo and Victoria. War, as it had been in the past, was waged away from home.

'The trenches are in Tonypandy'

It became increasingly obvious, however, that the demands made by war on such a scale could only be met by governments controlling all of a country's population, industry and resources. The armies and navies had to be provided with weapons and ammunition, clothed and transported. Replacements had to be found to fill the jobs left vacant by soldiers. Everybody had to have enough to eat. Civilians, as well as soldiers, had to get used to hardship and taking orders, as government control spread into all areas of life. It was, as one British politician called it, 'war socialism'.

In Germany, the industrialist, Walter Rathenau, was appointed to run German industry. Companies were told what to produce. Workers were told where to work, and were not allowed to leave.

Because many of her richest industrial areas were occupied by Germany, France was in a particularly difficult position. She was forced to borrow heavily from her allies. All governments ran up mounting debts by raising loans from their own populations and from outside, mainly from the USA. By the end of the war these had reached staggering totals.

In Britain, the Defence of the Realm Act (known, not always affectionately, as Dora) was passed at the outbreak of war. It gave the government considerable powers which were repeatedly strengthened. The government took over the running of the railways; rents and prices were controlled; the mines were nationalised; news was censored. Government action even went so far as to order the watering down of beer and the putting forward of clocks by one hour in the summer. When the army complained of a lack of shells in May 1915, the first of a number of new ministries was formed – the Ministry of Munitions. Although the minister, Lloyd George, did not have as much power as Rathenau, he encouraged employers and trade unions with a mixture of threats and promises. New factories were built; more workers were brought in. When the great Women's War Pageant marched through the streets of London demanding the right to work, Lloyd George responded. Hundreds of thousands of women were employed for twelve hours a day, seven days a week, making munitions. The output of shells and weapons increased enormously. The changes and restrictions were not always accepted. In some industries there were strikes, although fewer than before the war. General Smuts, a former Boer leader and later a member of the War Cabinet, told striking miners in South Wales, 'You know that the front is not only in France, but that the front is just as much here as anywhere else. The trenches are in Tonypandy'. The men went back to work the next day.

Above Women filling machine-gun belts

Below Knitting 'comforts' for the troops, Punch 1914

THE HI

Changing attitudes

At the beginning of the war, women in Britain, unlike France or Germany, were given little opportunity to do more than make bandages and 'comforts' for the troops. By 1918 this had changed. Women came to play a greater part in the war effort in Britain than elsewhere. It was not only on the factory floor that they replaced men. In offices female typists took the place of male clerks. Women worked on buses in London and drove underground trains in Paris. There were women in the police and in the armed forces. Their very appearance changed. The fashionably small waist disappeared as the restricting corset was abandoned. Shorter hair and skirts became the fashion. Land Girls were known to wear trousers even when off duty.

The employment of women in jobs previously thought suitable only for men brought about changes in their behaviour and in the relationship between the sexes; the changes lasted after the war, even though many of the jobs did not. Their work during the war helped women in Britain to gain the right to vote (but only if they were over thirty).

This breaking down of the barriers between men and women, or between soldiers and civilians, was not the only social effect of the war. Often for the first time, people from one part of society came into close contact with people from a very different part. Rich met poor, the aristocracy met the working class.

AIR OF MITTENS.

A Land Girl

Humping coke

The muddiest, dirtiest commonest soldier from the slums or the factories or the fields was a hero before whom great ladies were eager to kneel in devotion and love, to cut away his bloodstained clothes, to dress his wounds. . . . In the trenches or in the ruins under shellfire young officers wrote home about their men:'They're too splendid for words! . . . I am proud to command such a topping crowd. . . . They make me feel ashamed of things I used to think about the working man. There is nothing too good for them!'

Sir Philip Gibbs, *Ten Years After*

Such feelings did not generally last long after the guns had stopped.

What most of the men wanted was to get far away from the trenches as quickly as possible. People at home believed that the war was glorious and heroic. The soldiers at the front knew better. From what they read in the newspapers, heard in speeches, or saw in posters and advertisements, civilians in Britain viewed the Germans as evil monsters who must be conquered, whatever the cost. Civilians in Germany felt the same about Britons.

In *All Quiet on the Western Front*, a German novelist, Erich Maria Remarque, told the story of a young soldier home on leave.

After I have been startled a couple of times in the street by the screaming of the tramcars, which resembles the shriek of a shell coming straight for one, somebody taps me on the shoulder. It is my German-master, and he fastens on me with the usual question: 'Well, how are things out there? Terrible, terrible, eh? Yes, it is dreadful, but we must carry on. . . .'

He drags me along to a table with a lot of others. They welcome me, a headmaster shakes hands with me and says: 'So you come from the front? What is the spirit like out there? Excellent, eh? Excellent?'

I explain that no one would be sorry to be back home.

He laughs uproariously. 'I can well believe it! But first you have to give the Froggies a good hiding. . . .'

A British soldier who took part in the battle of the Somme remembered that 'When a chap was going on leave his pals used to say to him , now, don't forget, tell 'em what the truth is, you know, in England, no fighting on for ever.'

1917

For civilians throughout Europe, 1917 was the worst year of the war so far. The U-boat campaign against Britain, which had lessened after 1915, began again even more fiercely. By April there was only enough wheat left for another six weeks. Although this desperate situation was saved by the introduction of the convoy system, fear of food shortages remained. *The Times* reported on 18 February 1918 that 'In all parts of London on Saturday long queues of people gathered to buy meat, butter and margarine.' Some of the queues were four thousand strong, with people arriving in the early hours of the morning. A week later rationing was introduced and the queues disappeared.

Shortages, queues and rationing had long been part of everyday life in France and Germany. From the beginning, Britain had used her naval strength to stop goods entering Germany, either directly or through

'Collect locks of women's hair! Our industry needs it for driving belts for machinery'

neutral ports. This blockade was so successful that Germans were forced to rely ever more heavily on *ersatz* (substitute) food and materials. The coffee they drank was a mixture of barley, rye, chicory and figs. There was a lively trade in potato-peelings. Cars had tyres consisting of strips of metal mounted on springs. Human hair went to make belts for driving machinery. Everything had a use, nothing was wasted. But how long would people continue to put up with these conditions?

In Russia the lack of food had become so serious that there were bread riots. The most violent took place in Petrograd. Soldiers, sickened by the slaughter of their comrades, which they blamed on inefficient government and bad generals, joined in. Russia entered a period of revolution and civil war (the full story of which is told in chapter 6) and withdrew from the war against Germany altogether.

'Stab in the back'?

Within a year there was revolution in Germany. With their ally, Austria-Hungary, on the point of surrendering and with the prospect of Germany's defeat growing, many of the half-starved people of Kiel joined the mutinous sailors. There were demonstrations and street fights. By 3 November, Kiel was in the hands of a revolutionary council. Six days later, as the Kaiser crossed the frontier into Holland, the rebellion reached Berlin. The new republican government, fully occupied with preventing further uprisings, agreed to the terms dictated to them. Although her armies had not been defeated in battle, Germany had lost the war.

Out of these events, came the view that the German army 'was stabbed in the back'. 'In spite of the superiority of the enemy in men and materials,' Field Marshal Hindenburg said later, 'we could have brought the struggle to a favourable conclusion if determined and

The Kaiser defeated, 1918

A soup kitchen in Berlin, 1916

unanimous co-operation had existed between the army and those at home'. But could Germany, alone and facing an enemy growing in strength, really have avoided defeat? Even Hindenburg's chief of staff General Ludendorff, had insisted at the end of September that the war was lost. Although he changed his mind later, his doubts helped to bring about the collapse at home.

In the victorious countries, the news of the armistice was greeted with wild enthusiasm. When the the celebrations ended, and in the middle of an influenza epidemic which killed more people than had died in the war, the politicians began planning the final peace.

Using the evidence: propaganda

(1a) According to what *The Times* has heard from Cologne, via Paris, the unfortunate Belgian priests who refused to ring the church bells when Antwerp was taken have been sentenced to hard labour.　　　　*Corriere della Sera*

(b) According to the *Kölnische Zeitung*, the clergy of Antwerp were compelled to ring the church bells when the fortress was taken.　　　　*Le Matin*

(c) According to information which has reached the *Corriere della Sera* from Cologne, via London, it is confirmed that the barbaric conquerors of Antwerp punished the unfortunate Belgian priests for their heroic refusal to ring the church bells by hanging them as living clappers to the bells with their heads down.　　　　*Le Matin*

(d) When the fall of Antwerp became known, the church bells were rung (i.e. at Cologne and elsewhere in Germany).　　　　*Kölnische Zeitung*

(2a) Herr Carl Rosner, the correspondent of the Berlin *Lokalanzeiger* on the Western Front, who lately gave such glowing accounts of the devastation of France, published last Tuesday the first definite German admission concerning the way in which the Germans use dead bodies. In a description of the battlefield north of Reims he writes:

'We pass through Evernigcourt. There is a dull smell in the air, as if lime were being burnt. We are passing the great Corpse Exploitation Establishment (*Kadaververwertungsanstalt*) of this Army Group. The fat that is won here is turned into lubricating oils, and everything else is ground down in the bones-mill into a powder which is used for mixing with pigs' food and as manure.'

Herr Rosner conveys this information with no comment but the remark that 'nothing can be permitted to go to waste'.　　　　*The Times*, 16 April 1917

(b) A 'Corpse-conversion' Factory
   A peep behind the German lines

Out of their own mouths, the military masters of Germany stand convicted of an act of unspeakable savagery which has shocked the whole civilised world, including probably, now that the truth has come out, many of the German people themselves. Attila's Huns were guilty of atrocious crimes, but they never desecrated the bodies of dead soldiers – their own flesh, as well as the fallen of the enemy – by improvising a factory for the conversion of human corpses into fat and oils, and fodder for pigs. . . .

How was the discovery made? Quite simply. Herr Karl Rosner, the Special Correspondent of the Berlin *Lokalanzeiger* on the Western Front, made the announcement in his published dispatch of 10 April.

Department of Information pamphlet

(3) *A telegram from the American ambassador to Britain*

September 11, 3 a.m. Confidential to the President
No.645
Accounts of atrocities are so inevitably a part of every war that for some

time I did not believe the unbelievable reports that were sent from Europe, and there are many that I find incredible even now. But American and other neutral observers who have seen these things in France and especially in Belgium now convince me that the Germans have perpetrated some of the most barbarous deeds in history. Apparently credible persons relate such things without end.... Can any one longer disbelieve the completely barbarous behaviour of the Prussians?

PAGE

(4) Translated from the *Frankfürter Zeitung*:

ANGLO-FRENCH OFFENSIVE
ENEMY'S HEAVY LOSSES AND MINIMAL GAINS
15 Enemy Planes Shot Down
Advance on Eastern Front

Correspondent: W. B. Amtlich   *General Headquarters, 2 July*

Western Front

After a whole week of the heaviest artillery and gas bombardment, there began today on a wide front of some forty kilometres the big Anglo-French mass offensive which has been in the process of preparation – with limitless resources – for several months.

On the Somme, from the river Ancre at Gommecourt to the area around La Boiselle the enemy gained no advantage of any consequence, but sustained heavy losses. However, on both the French and British fronts their leading troops finally penetrated our front line at a few points. It was thought better, therefore, to withdraw our divisions from the front trenches, which had been totally destroyed by the heavy fire, to the reserve line between the first and second positions.

As is normal in these circumstances, some equipment – permanent front-line fixtures which had been made useless – was lost.

How do we know?

In considering documents, pictures, or other kinds of evidence, you should ask yourself what the writer's or artist's intentions were.

Possible intentions might be:
(i) to persuade people to act in a particular way
(ii) to persuade people to think in a particular way
(iii) to arouse people's feelings
(iv) to present more than one point of view
(v) to present events in what he considers to be their most favourable light.

Questions and further work

1(a) Look carefully at the evidence on pages 58–61. In each case decide the purpose for which it was produced. (The writer or artist may have had more than one intention.)

(b) Are there any other intentions which are not included in the list above?

July 3, 1916 THE DAILY MIRROR Page 3

ADVANCE OF ALLIES IN THE WEST STILL CONTINUES

Capture of Fricourt by British with Substantial Progress—French Take Curlu.

HAUL OF PRISONERS NOW AMOUNTS TO 8,500

Germans Admit Front Line Trenches Were Taken—"Immovable Material Lost"—"Allies' Heavy Losses."

(BRITISH OFFICIAL.)

GENERAL HEADQUARTERS, Sunday, 5.5 p.m.

Substantial progress has been made in the vicinity of Fricourt, which was captured by our troops by 2 p.m. to-day.

Up to noon to-day some 800 more prisoners have been taken in the operations between the Ancre and the Somme, bringing the total up to 3,500, including those captured on other parts of the front last night.

(FRENCH OFFICIAL.)

PARIS, Sunday.—The following communiqué was issued this afternoon:—

To the north of the Somme fighting was furious during the night. The Germans launched violent counter-attacks against our new positions on the outskirts of Heudicourt

Our curtain fire and our rifle fire inflicted serious losses on the enemy, who had to fall back in disorder, leaving 200 prisoners in our hands, of whom six were officers.

Pursuing our advantage on the right bank of the river, we gained possession after a sharp fight of the village of Curlu, which we occupied completely.

South of the Somme we have maintained all the positions captured by us yesterday, and have made some progress in the course of the night between Herbecourt and Assewillers.

According to further information to hand, the total figure of unwounded German prisoners captured by the French troops yesterday exceeds 5,000.

Between the Oise and the Aisne we captured a German patrol which tried to approach our lines near Bailly.—Reuter.

"PENETRATED OUR FIRST LINE TRENCHES."

(GERMAN OFFICIAL.)

The German official communiqué issued yesterday, says the Wireless Press, is as follows:—

The great English-French offensive "mass attack," which has been extensively prepared for during many months past, began yesterday over a front of twenty-five miles, after strong artillery and gas preparation lasting six days.

On both sides of the Somme, and likewise the Ancre Brook, from Gommecourt as far as the region of La Boiselle, the enemy obtained no advantages worthy of mention. He sustained, however, very heavy losses.

On the other hand, he was successful in penetrating at several points the first-line trenches of our division in the region abutting both banks of the Somme, and was able to advance.

This division had to be withdrawn from their heavily-shelled first-line trenches into the position arranged for, checking an advance from the first to the second lines.

The material in the first line, which was immovable and had been rendered useless as is customary in such cases, was lost.

In connection with these extensive operations there were many artillery actions and numerous minor attacks on the adjoining front, and also west and south-east of Tahure. They were everywhere unsuccessful.

FRENCH HOLD FAST TO THIAUMONT FORT.

German Attempts at Recapture Easily Repelled.

(FRENCH OFFICIAL.)

PARIS, Sunday.—The following communiqué was issued this afternoon:—

Champagne Front.—In Champagne we made a number of reconnaissances along the enemy front, several of which penetrated the German trenches, and swept them clear with hand grenades. We brought back fifteen prisoners.

Verdun Front.—On the left bank of the Meuse a German attack delivered yesterday evening against our positions north-west of the Avocourt Wood, after succeeding in penetrating the advanced elements of our trenches, was completely thrown back by our counter-attack.

On the slopes of the Mort Homme we effected a successful coup de main. In the course of the fighting which took place in the enemy trench some fifty Germans were killed and some twenty were made prisoners and brought back to our lines. Two machine guns were also left in our hands.

On the right bank several enemy attempts against the Thiaumont Work, in which we are established, were easily repelled.

In this sector a strong German party, having come into contact with some first-line elements, was dispersed with heavy losses.

We made sixteen prisoners, of whom two are officers. On the front west and south of Vaux there has been great artillery activity on both sides.—Reuter.

(GERMAN OFFICIAL.)

The following German communiqué was issued yesterday, says the Wireless Press:—

East of the Meuse the enemy with the aid of strong reinforcements repeated his attacks many times, both yesterday and this morning, on the Froide Terre Hill and especially against the fortified work of Thiaumont, but was compelled by our curtain fire to retire.

The enemy's aerial service displayed great activity.

Our squadrons gave battle at various points and inflicted upon him heavy losses.

For instance, in the region of the front attacked and that of the Meuse fifteen enemy aeroplanes were shot down, eight English and three French falling within our lines.

BRITISH MONITORS FIRE ACROSS DUNES?

Dutch Report of Heavy Gunfire from Warships Off Coast.

AMSTERDAM, Sunday.—The *Telegraaf* reports from the frontier that unusually violent artillery action was heard from the Yser front, beginning about two o'clock yesterday afternoon, and shortly afterwards heavy gunfire from warships off the coast was also heard.

It is believed British monitors were firing on the Germans across the dunes to render impossible any advance by the German infantry.—Central News.

'ENGLISH GOING FORWARD'

Writing on the British part in the great offensive in the *Berliner Tageblatt*, Major Moraht says:—

The British offensive has begun, and the English are going forward very systematically and cautiously.

Map showing Thiaumont Work.

"A VERY SATISFACTORY FIRST DAY."

Further Developments Can Be Awaited with Confidence.

ALLIES' LOSSES SLIGHT.

PARIS, Sunday.—A semi-official statement issued last night says:—

The chief fact of July 1 on the western front was the beginning of the Franco-British offensive.

By a very extended bombardment, the enemy was kept in ignorance as to the possible field of attack, and consequently had to divide his reserve effectives and to disperse his artillery.

The attack began at half-past seven in the morning and was preceded for half an hour by an artillery preparation the violence of which has never yet been equalled.

At nine o'clock the advanced defences of the German lines had fallen into our power.

The enemy's retreat made us masters of the villages of Montauban and Mametz, in the English zone, Becquincourt, Bussu and Fay, in the French zone.

According to the first information, our losses are few, as the result of the efficacy of our preparatory work, while the Germans', on the other hand, are heavy.

The number of prisoners taken is also important. The French have 3,500 and the British at the first reckoning have over 2,000.

The first day of the offensive is, therefore, very satisfactory.

The success is not a thunderbolt, as has happened earlier in similar operations, but it is important above all because it is rich in promises.

From to-day the first results of the new tactics permit one to await developments with confidence.—Reuter.

THE GREAT SQUEEZE.

BRITISH—North of Somme: We break into German forward defences on front of sixteen miles. Serre, Montauban, La Boiselle taken; Fricourt surrounded; German labyrinth of trenches on seven-mile front to depth of 1,000 yards captured. Prisoners: 2,000.

FRENCH—South of Somme: Dompieres, Becquincourt, Bussu, Fay and Curlu taken. Prisoners: 5,000.

ITALIAN—Italians still rolling back the Austrians to the Trentino.

RUSSIAN—Russians still moving ahead in Galicia and Bukowina. Total haul of prisoners: 217,000.

WOUNDED HEROES HOME.

Four hundred wounded soldiers were on board the steamer Salta, which arrived at North Wall, Dublin, yesterday.

The men had been engaged quite recently at the front, and with the exception of eight, who belonged to Ireland, they were all members of English and Scottish regiments.

A special train conveyed 132 of their number for treatment to Belfast.

DESPERATE BLOWS AT RUSSIANS REPULSED.

Retreating Germans Fired On by Own Artillery.

BALTIC SEA SCRAP.

(RUSSIAN OFFICIAL.)

PETROGRAD, Saturday (received yesterday).—The communiqué issued to-day says:—

Western Front.—In the region between the Stokhod and the Styr the enemy is maintaining violent artillery fire.

Desperate fighting has begun in the village of Zatourtsy, where, in spite of a bombardment by the enemy of extreme violence, our troops have already repulsed nine successive attacks with heavy losses for the enemy.

In our sector of this region the Germans who were falling back were fired upon by their own batteries and forced to return to the attack.

The whole ground in this district is covered with enemy corpses.

Yesterday afternoon the enemy artillery produced gusts of fire in the region of Koptchie, Ghelenovka and Zabary, south-west of Sokul.

An energetic infantry attack then followed, but was repulsed.

MASSED ASSAULT STOPPED.

South-east of Kisseline our fire stopped an offensive by massed formations of the enemy in the village of Semerinka, and in the same region near the village of Zubilno there was a warm engagement.

South of the village of Zaturtsy, near the village of Koscheff, we stopped an Austrian offensive by a counter-offensive.

We repulsed hostile attempts to cross the river Schara south-west of Lipsk, south of Baranovitchi.

Our left wing continues to throw the enemy back on the front south of the Dniester and has occupied several points north of Kolomea.

South-west of that town our troops, after hot fighting, repulsed the enemy towards the heights near the village of Brezevo.

We have already taken part of these heights.

North-west of Kimpolung the enemy, who endeavoured to take the offensive, was thrown back to the west.

217,000 PRISONERS NOW.

In this region our troops are pressing closely upon the enemy and have taken some strongly organised mountain positions.

The total number of prisoners taken by General Letchitsky during June 28 and 29 is 305 officers and 14,574 men. Four guns and thirty machine guns were also taken.

The grand total of prisoners taken from June 4 to June 30 is 217,000, officers included.

In the Baltic yesterday a detachment of several of our cruisers and torpedo-boats, searching for enemy forces between the Island of Gothland and the Swedish coast, discovered no big naval unit.

At daybreak our cruisers were attacked by a flotilla of enemy torpedo-boats, who were easily repulsed by the fire of our guns.

Attacks by enemy submarines were also unsuccessful.

Our detachment regained its base without loss and without having been damaged.—Reuter.

BIG GERMAN CLAIMS.

(GERMAN OFFICIAL.)

The German official communiqué yesterday, says the Wireless Press, was as follows:—

General von Linsingen's Army.—The attack is going forward. The number of prisoners has increased by seven officers and 1,410 men.

At various points enemy counter-attacks were easily repulsed.

Count von Bothmer's Army.—German and Austro-Hungarian troops stormed the Hill of Vorobijowka (south-west of Tarnopol), which had recently been occupied by the Russians, and took from the enemy seven officers, 892 men, seven machine guns and two mine throwers.

WHERE'S WHERE OF 'PUSH'

The following are places mentioned in the communiqués:—

The Gommecourt salient is a little more than a mile north of Hebuterne.

The River Ancre is an important tributary of the Somme, which it flows into at Etampes.

Albert is situated on the Ancre, and three miles to the east lies Fricourt, a place of considerable military value.

A mile to the east of Fricourt is Mametz, which is now occupied by British troops.

Montauban is three miles almost due east of Fricourt. Close by lies the main road running due north to Bapaume.

Contalmaison is a mile and three-quarters north of Fricourt.

La Boiselle lies immediately north of Contalmaison.

Serre is a mile and a quarter south of Hebuterne.

Hamel lies midway between Serre and the Ancre.

Curlu is four miles south-east of Mametz and the Faviere Wood.

A typical London street scene after the arrival of Saturday's great news.

2 The newspaper extracts in Document 1 (a) to (d) are from a book by Robert Graves about his experiences during the First World War, called *Goodbye to All That*.

(a) In the book they were given in chronological order. Here they have been given out of sequence. Re-arrange them in the order in which you think they appeared.

(b) In what year do you think the extracts originally appeared?

(c) Which of the newspapers supported the Allied side, and which the German?

(d) Compare the first and last extracts in your re-arranged list. How do they differ?

3 Each side accused the other of committing numerous atrocities. Look at the evidence on pages 58–61, and list the various accusations which are made against the Germans.

4 What reason does the American ambassador in Document 3 give for believing the atrocity stories? Do you agree with his conclusion?

5 Document 2 gives one of the most famous propaganda stories of the war. Not until 1925 was it admitted in the House of Commons that the story was a lie put about for propaganda purposes.

(a) The Germans did probably use corpses for various purposes, but is there any indication in Herr Rosner's account that these were human corpses?

(b) What might they have been?

(c) How does the Department of Information pamphlet try to make its story believable?

(d) Why do you think many people did believe it?

6 Compare the two newspaper accounts of the first day of the Battle of the Somme (see Document 4 and the newspaper on page 61).

(a) In what ways do they differ?

(b) How does each one attempt to present the battle in the most favourable light?

(c) Write an account of the first day's fighting, trying to be as unbiased as possible.

(d) Why is it very likely that there will be differences between a contemporary newpaper report and a later historical account of the events?

7 Which of the posters reproduced here do you think is likely to have had the greatest impact on people during the war?

5 The world made at Versailles

The peacemakers

The victors began their meetings to decide the terms of the peace in Paris in January 1919. There were no representatives from Germany or Austria-Hungary, nor from Russia. When the discussions seemed to be getting nowhere, the leaders of Britain, France, the USA and Italy set themselves up as the Council of Four. In fact only the Big Three (Woodrow Wilson, the American president, Lloyd George and Clemenceau, the prime ministers of Britain and France) really mattered. Orlando, the prime minister of Italy, had little influence.

The Council of Four: left to right – Orlando, Lloyd George, Clemenceau and Wilson

The Inter-Allied Conference in session at Versailles

The Council of Four held most of their meetings in a room in the house of the French president. They were surrounded by interpreters, secretaries and advisers. The meetings were not very orderly. Clemenceau, the chairman, seldom spoke, and when he did the effort was liable to bring on a violent attack of coughing.

Both Lloyd George and Orlando had to return home several times. Wilson, the first American president to leave the country whilst in office, went back to America for a month. Clemenceau was seriously ill for a time, after being shot in the chest in an assassination attempt.

The Treaty of Versailles: signatures of some of the delegates

Right German delegates leave their hotel at Versailles

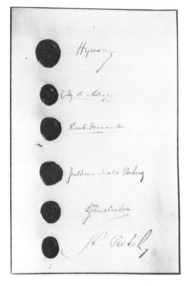

The peace

Despite these interruptions, the treaty was eventually drawn up and presented to the Germans in May. They were angry and horrified at the terms. No discussion was allowed, but they could make objections in

A children's party in the East End of London to celebrate the end of the Great War

writing. Some slight changes were made, and two months later, in the face of the Allied threat to re-start the war, Germany was forced to agree. On Saturday, 28 June, two civilian representatives of the German government were escorted into the Hall of Mirrors in the Palace of Versailles, just outside Paris. They were both very pale and walked with their eyes fixed firmly to the ceiling. 'We are here', Clemenceau told them, 'to sign a treaty of peace.' The two Germans signed first, followed by the delegates of the other countries. Outside the crowd cheered, the guns fired a salute and the fountains spurted. The war with Germany was finally over.

Although it was the most important, Versailles was only one of the peace treaties made between the countries who had fought in the war. They were named after the various palaces in and around Paris where they were signed. But, in looking at the main results, it is easier to consider them together.

The peace treaties of 1919

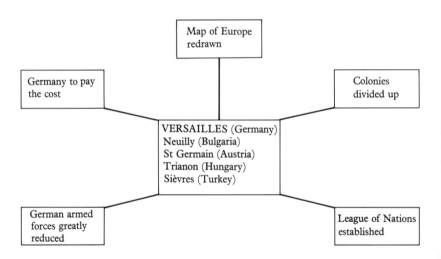

Europe re-drawn

The politicians had spent many months poring over maps. An American delegate remembered that, 'One of the most picturesque scenes of the conference took place in Mr Wilson's drawing-room in Paris, with the president on all fours in front of a large map on the parquet floor . . . with Orlando crawling like a bear to get a better view.' The Empire of Austria-Hungary was to be broken up. Frontiers had to be decided on. New independent countries like Yugoslavia and Czechoslovakia were created. Poland, which had last existed as an independent country in 1772, re-appeared. This is what the statesmen were doing as they crawled around the floor. When they had finished, the map of Europe, as you can see opposite, looked very different.

The nationality problem

Many people, and not only Germans, were very critical of the results. But the task had been a very difficult one. As you saw earlier, the

Austro-Hungarian Empire had contained people of many nationalities, with different languages and religions. The peacemakers had tried to follow the principle that these various nationalities should form their own separate countries. If you apply this principle to the map of a fictitious area of Europe on the right, it will help you to understand the difficulties that could arise.

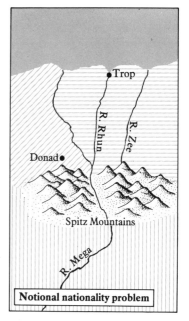

Notional nationality problem

(1) People of three nationalities live in the differently shaded areas.
(2) The main industry of the city of Donad is the manufacturing of cutlery.
(3) The ore and coal needed for this comes from south of the Spitz mountains.
(4) Most of the cutlery is shipped from the port of Trop.
(5) To the east of the River Rhun is a fertile plain from which Donad gets most of its food.

(a) What would happen to the city of Donad if the principle of 'national self-determination' outlined above were followed?
(b) How could the frontier be drawn so that all these problems were avoided?
(c) How many different nationalities would now live in the country of which Donad was a part?

It was because of difficulties like these that over three million Germans found themselves living in Czechoslovakia, and that the 'Polish Corridor' which gave Poland a route to the sea, divided East Prussia from the rest of Germany. These areas, and the frontier between Germany and France, were to be the trouble-spots of the future.

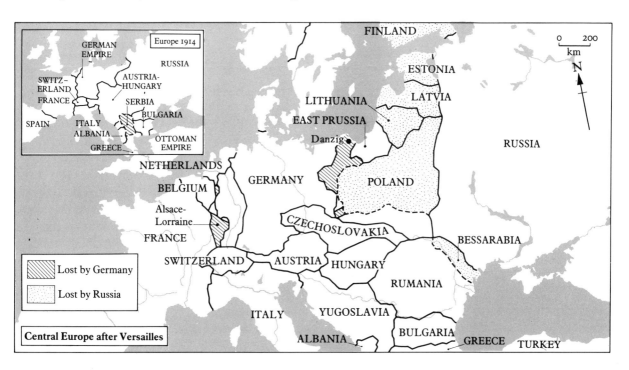

Central Europe after Versailles

Lost by Germany

Lost by Russia

The distribution of colonies

Germany renounces in favour of the Principal Allied and Associated Powers all her rights and titles over her oversea possessions

(Article 119, Treaty of Versailles)

The colonies taken from Germany were distributed amongst the victorious countries. They were to govern them on behalf of the new League of Nations, and agreed to accept certain conditions. These mandates as they were called, were of three types. Those countries labelled A in the maps below were to become independent in the near future. Those marked B were to remain colonies for a much longer period, whilst colonies of type C were considered to be too underdeveloped for independence, and were given to those countries who had conquered them from Germany. None of the people who lived in these parts of the world had any say in what was to happen to them.

As a result, the empires of Britain and France increased considerably.

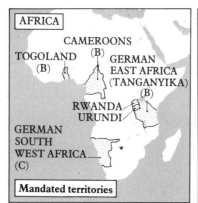

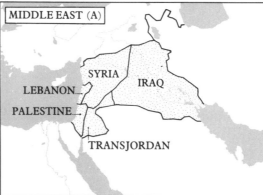

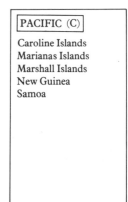

So too did that of Japan, who had played little part in the actual fighting. This distribution of colonies seemed most unfair, not only to Germany, but also to Italy. Italy had lost half a million men in the war, yet gained very little.

International peace and security

The High Contracting Parties,
In order to promote international co-operation and to achieve
international peace and security. . . .
Agree to this Covenant of the League of Nations

(Part I, Treaty of Versailles)

In a speech he made almost a year before the war ended, President Wilson put forward his Fourteen Points for world peace. In the last of these he called for the setting up of a 'general association of nations'. Wilson was not alone in wanting this, but he was its most powerful and passionate supporter. By his efforts in Paris he was the politician most responsible for the establishment of the League of Nations. The Covenant, or rules, of the League, formed part of each of the peace treaties.

President Woodrow Wilson of the USA: his Fourteen Points formed the basis of the peace treaties, but he could not persuade his fellow countrymen to join the League of Nations

The Swiss government offered to have the headquarters of the League in Geneva. Their offer was gratefully accepted, and the first assembly opened there on 14 December 1920, attended by the delegates of the eighteen member countries.

Of those countries who were absent, the most surprising was the USA. President Wilson had persuaded Europe to accept the League of

The first session of the Council of the League of Nations, 1920

Nations, but he could not persuade America. After three weeks touring the country, appealing to the people, he was struck down by a severe illness from which he was soon to die. The United States Senate threw out the Treaty of Versailles, and with it, American membership of the League.

Germany and Russia were also missing from that first meeting in Geneva. Germany was admitted in 1926; Russia in 1934. But it was the permanent absence of the USA, rapidly becoming the world's richest and most powerful country, which seriously weakened the League.

Ten years later there had been some successes. Membership had increased (altogether fifty-nine countries joined); disputes, such as the one between Greece and Bulgaria in 1925, had been settled. A Court of International Justice, and the International Labour Organisation to improve working conditions, had been set up. A considerable amount of help had been given to backward countries. But the next ten years were to show how weak the League really was.

With no armed force at its command, the only way the League could bring pressure to bear was by means of sanctions, which meant that it could ask members to stop trading with any country which would not carry out the League's wishes. When Japan, Italy and Germany decided to expand in the 1930s, however, sanctions did not stop them. The great hope that the League of Nations could prevent wars and protect the weak was dead within fifteen years.

Germany pays the price

One of the things which helped to kill it, was the price that Germany was forced to pay for losing the war. Under the terms dictated at Versailles, Germany had to demolish her military forces, and was forbidden ever to build them up again.

Navy

Article 181:

... the German naval forces in commission must not exceed:
  6 battleships of the *Deutschland* or *Lothringen* type,
  6 light cruisers,
12 destroyers,
12 torpedo boats, ...
No submarines are to be included.

Army

Article 160:

By a date which must not be later than 31 March 1920, the German Army must not comprise more than seven divisions of infantry and three divisions of cavalry. After that date the total number of effectives in the Army ... must not exceed one hundred thousand men. ...

Air force

Article 198:

The armed forces of Germany must not include any military or naval air forces.

Far more damaging, however, was Article 232 of the treaty, which required Germany to 'make compensation for all damage done to the civilian population of the Allied and Associated Powers and to their property. ...' In the language used at the time, Germany was to make 'reparation'.

The end of the Imperial German Navy: surrendered German destroyers sinking after being scuttled in Scapa Flow

How much was Germany to pay? The French in particular, were anxious that the bill should be a heavy one. After much discussion it was finally presented in 1921. The figure arrived at was a colossal £6500 million, to be paid in instalments, partly in money, partly in goods. Not surprisingly, Germany found it impossible to keep up the payments, and in 1923 French troops occupied her main industrial area, the Ruhr. The workers there went on strike and sabotaged the machines. German industry declined rapidly and with it the currency. By the end of 1923 the mark was all but worthless. One million marks (which was a small

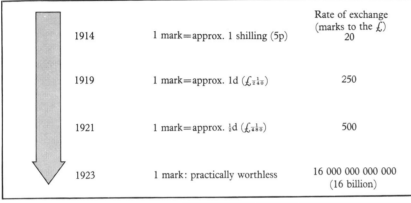

The decline of the mark

		Rate of exchange (marks to the £)
1914	1 mark=approx. 1 shilling (5p)	20
1919	1 mark=approx. 1d ($\pounds\frac{1}{240}$)	250
1921	1 mark=approx. $\frac{1}{2}$d ($\pounds\frac{1}{480}$)	500
1923	1 mark: practically worthless	16 000 000 000 000 (16 billion)

Bags full of worthless paper money just withdrawn from a bank in Berlin, 1923

Demobilised German soldiers

fortune worth some £50 000 in 1914) was now not enough to post a letter or buy a newspaper. It was cheaper to paper walls with money rather than buy wallpaper.

In the confusion, there was fear and unrest throughout Germany. In the south, an ex-soldier, Adolf Hitler, led a revolt against the government. It failed, and he was sent to prison for five years. By the time he was released, after serving less than a year of his sentence, the turmoil had died down. The French had withdrawn from the Ruhr. The economy had been saved with American help. In these more prosperous times, Hitler found little support.

1918 President Wilson's Fourteen Points for world peace
1919 Versailles Peace Conference
1920 First meeting of the League of Nations
1923 French occupation of the Ruhr
      Collapse of the German currency

Using the evidence: was Germany guilty?

(1) The Allied and Associated Governments affirm and Germany accepts the responsibility of Germany and her allies for causing all the loss and damage to which the Allied and Associated Governments and their nationals have been subjected as a consequence of the war imposed upon them by the aggression of Germany and her allies.

Article 231, Treaty of Versailles

(2) It was a peace of vengeance. It reeked with injustice. It was incapable of fulfilment. It sowed a thousand seeds from which new wars might spring. It was as though the Devil, in a jester's cap-and-bells, had sat beside Clemenceau in his black gloves, and whispered madness into the ear of Wilson, and leered across the table at Lloyd George, and put his mockery into every clause. In that Hall of Mirrors at Versailles the ideals for which millions of men had fought and died – liberty, fair play, a war to end war, justice – were mocked and outraged, not by men of evil, but by good men, not by foul design, but with loyalty to national interests. Something blinded them. . . .

But it was on the economic side of the treaty and in its interpretation that the statesmen of the Allies seemed to be stricken with insanity, which infected many of their peoples until recent months. Germany, they insisted, had to pay all the costs of the war, for the damage she had inflicted and the ruin she had caused. Theoretically, that was just as if one took the view that every German peasant, every German mother in a cheap tenement, every German worker on starvation wages, every little sempstress, or university student, ten or twelve years old when the war began, shares the responsibility of those war lords and militarists who challenged the world in 1914. . . .

It might have been just . . . if it is justice that the individuals in a nation and their children and children's children are responsible for the guilt of their governments. But, justice or injustice apart, the absurdity, the wild impossibility, of extracting all that vast tribute from the defeated enemy . . . ought to have been manifest to the most ignorant schoolboy of thirteen or fourteen years of age.

Sir Philip Gibbs, *Ten Years After*

(3) I say until we are satisfied – and we cannot be satisfied until we have proved it – that in the German there is a changed heart and a changed mind, no single scapegoat can bear their sins. They have made their bed and they must lie upon it.

The Life and Letters of Austen Chamberlain

(4) TO THE BELGIAN PEOPLE
It is to my very great regret that German troops find themselves obliged to infringe the Belgian frontier. They act under pressure of unavoidable necessity, Belgium's neutrality having been violated by French officers who, in disguise, have crossed Belgian territory by car to enter Germany. . . .

German proclamation, August 1914

(5) In January 1919, the peace conference set up a body called The Commission on the Responsibility of the Authors of the War and on Enforcement of Penalties. These are extracts from their report:

(a) . . . the Commission, after having examined a number of official documents relating to the origin of the World War, and to the violations of neutrality and of frontiers . . . has determined that the responsibility for it lies wholly upon the powers which declared war in pursuance of a policy of aggression. . . . This responsibility rests first on Germany and Austria, secondly on Turkey and Bulgaria. The responsibility is made all the graver by reason of the violation by Germany and Austria of the neutrality of Belgium and Luxembourg, which they themselves had guaranteed. It is increased, with regard to both France and Serbia, by the violation of their frontiers before the declaration of war.

(b) Many months before the crisis of 1914 the German emperor had ceased to pose as the champion of peace. Naturally believing in the overwhelming superiority of his army, he openly showed his enmity towards France.

(c) . . . the ultimatum to Serbia had been jointly decided upon by the governments of Berlin and Vienna . . . no illusions were cherished, either at Berlin or Vienna, as to the consequences which this threatening measure would involve. It was perfectly well known that war would be the result.

(6) Both during and after the peace conference, many German politicians gave a different interpretation of events. These are some of the conclusions of one of them:

(a) Germany's preparations for war were on a considerably smaller scale than those made by France. . . . From 1913 onwards, even her actual numerical peace strength was less, in respect of white troops, quite apart from the steadily increasing strength of the French coloured troops.

(b) The possibility that the Austro-Serbian war . . . might lead to further complications, was well weighed, but the risk was thought very small, in view of the special provocation. After the publication of the Serbian reply, Germany no longer thought war advisable, even against Serbia. . . .

(c) By her (France's) false statements regarding Germany's preparations for war . . . by magnifying insignificant incidents on the frontier into invasions of French territory . . . An impression was produced in London that 'the opponents of the Entente were the aggressors'.

Count Max Montgelas, *The Case for the Central Powers*

(7) **Dr Bell:** We must take a stand on the guilt question. One might explain that the march through Belgium was motivated by erroneous assumptions. (1) This was an emergency, in which ordinary rules did not apply, and (2) Belgium had a secret agreement with the Entente. We have since realised our mistake. We are, therefore, responsible for repayment of damages.

Noske: I still think that in extreme emergencies one fends for oneself as best one can. I cannot even recognise German guilt in Belgium. Nor in U-boat warfare, either – it was a counter-measure to starvation blockade. I agree that payments should be spread over a long period.

Count Rantzau: We can justify submarine warfare by the hunger blockade. Other guilt questions will be taken up under point 10. . . .

Landsberg: . . . The question of guilt and reparations cannot be separated. The march into Belgium resulted from an emergency, but was not self-defence. Emergency conditions do not relieve us from the responsibility for damages, so we should consent to making restitution. The payments should be small. . . .

Erzberger: Let us maintain, according to the Note of November 5, that reparations be limited to damage in occupied areas. No other demands should be recognised. . . .

Meeting of the Reich Ministry, 21 March 1919

How do we know?

At the end of chapter 4 we looked at examples where a biased point of view is deliberately presented, as propaganda. But, when people feel strongly about events, they may interpret them very differently. This is especially true of such a shattering event as the Great War. Even after it was over, feelings against Germany ran so high that quite simple acts could be given a sinister meaning.

Compare these two accounts of the behaviour of Count Brockdorff-Rantzau, head of the German delegation at Versailles:

Count Brockdorff-Rantzau

(8) With Clemenceau still standing, the pale, black-clad Count Brockdorff-Rantzau, head of the German delegation, began reading his reply – *seated*.

An almost perceptible gasp swept the room, for the failure of the German to rise was taken as a studied discourtesy. Some felt that he was too nervous and shaken to stand. Others felt that he wanted to snub his 'conquerors'. The truth is that he planned to sit, not wishing to stand like a culprit before a judge to receive sentence.

T. A. Bailey, *Woodrow Wilson and the Lost Peace*

(9) His first speech at the Conference was made sitting down. Lloyd George was 'completely chilled by this one exhibition of inexcusable boorishness', but learnt later that 'the poor man was so nervous that he was physically incapable of standing up'. In his speech Brockdorff-Rantzau said: 'We are required to admit that we alone are war-guilty; such an admission on my lips would be a lie'.

M. Gilbert, *Britain and Germany Between the Wars*

Questions and further work

1 (a) List the various interpretations of Brockdorff-Rantzau's behaviour given in Documents 8 and 9.
(b) Which do each of the two writers consider to be the correct interpretation?
(c) What do you consider was the most likely explanation of Brockdorff-Rantzau's failure to stand?

2 When Count Brockdorff-Rantzau said, 'We are required to admit that we alone are war-guilty', to which part of the Treaty of Versailles was he referring?

3 The invasion of Belgium was one of the charges of aggression brought against Germany to prove her guilt. Both at the time, and later, attempts were made to justify this invasion. Who put forward each of the following reasons?

(i) French troops had entered Belgium in order to attack Germany;

(ii) Germany mistakenly believed that Belgium had a secret agreement with France and Britain;

(iii) The attack on Belgium was necessary because a state of emergency existed.

What do you feel was the most likely reason for the German march on Belgium?

4 The case for and against German war guilt has been strongly argued. From the evidence presented to you, defend Germany against each of the charges in this list.

(i) Both Germany and Austria knew that the ultimatum to Serbia would lead to war;

(ii) Germany had been preparing for war before 1914;

(iii) German troops crossed into France before war was declared;

(iv) The U-boat campaign was not in accordance with the rules of warfare.

On balance, do you agree or disagree with the verdict of the peacemakers?

5 Not everybody, even amongst the victors, agreed with the terms of the Treaty of Versailles.

Read carefully the extract from Sir Philip Gibbs (Document 2). Which of these points does he agree with?

(a) The peacemakers were evil men;

(b) The peacemakers were more concerned with the interests of their own countries than with justice for Germany;

(c) Germany should not pay for any of the cost of the war;

(d) Germany should not pay for all the cost of the war;

(e) Not all the German people should be held to be equally responsible;

(f) The Allies demanded an impossible price from Germany.

6 Compare Documents 2 and 3. Make out a case to show that:

(a) Only the Kaiser and the German government, not the German people as a whole, were guilty of aggression;

(b) It was fair that all the German nation should suffer the consequences.

Which do you feel is the stronger case?

Russia: Revolutions and civil war

Simbirsk, now known as Ulyanovsk, is a small city on the River Volga in central Russia. There in 1870, in a wooden house which is still standing, Vladimir Ilyich Ulyanov was born. His father was an inspector of schools who was later made a member of the lesser nobility for his services to the province. His mother was the daughter of a doctor whose family had originally come from Germany. Vladimir was their second son. A photograph taken when he was four years old, shows him as rather a chubby child with curly, sandy-coloured hair and a high forehead. As a schoolboy he was exceptionally clever, but inclined to make fun of his teachers – a habit which did not make him very popular.

Tsarist rule

The Ulyanov family were unusual in nineteenth-century Russia. Ninety per cent of the population of 130 million were peasants. Until they were freed in 1861, more than half the peasants had been serfs, little better than slaves. But their freedom cost them dear. In return for the land they received, they had to make annual payments to the government for the next forty-nine years. The burden of this debt was made worse by the difficulties of using primitive tools to cultivate plots of land, which were often too small or infertile. In many areas land was farmed in common, but seldom efficiently. For the 'dark masses' of Russia, three-quarters of whom could neither read nor write, the days were spent in an exhausting struggle against the weather, poverty and starvation. Squalor, violence and drunken brutality were part of everyday life.

Unlike the countries of Western Europe, Russia had scarcely started to develop her industry by 1870. It was not until the last quarter of the nineteenth century that Russia, often with foreign help, began to build the factories, mine the coal and construct the railways which would turn her into an industrialised country. By 1900, although it was to be another four years before it was possible to travel the 10 500 kilometres from St Petersburg to Vladivostok by rail, there were 1½ million indus-

Vladimir Ilyich Ulyanov aged 17

A public eating-house in a Russian town at the end of the nineteenth century

trial workers. Their numbers were to nearly double before the outbreak of war.

Conditions in the mines and factories were nearly as wretched as on the land. Hours were long, wages were low. The labour force in a great number of the factories was a thousand or more strong. For many of the men, home was a large, barrack-like building which they shared with hundreds of their fellow workers. Discontent and plans for bringing about change could spread more quickly there than amongst the widely-scattered peasants.

Russia was the world's largest country, but less than half the population were Russians. There were Poles, Rumanians, Finns, Ukrainians

A life of squalor: Russian workers at the turn of the century

A beggar in Nizhni Novgorod, 1912

and Tartars. They spoke many languages, belonged to different religions and dreamt of independence.

At the head of this vast empire, ruling in splendour from the capital, St Petersburg, was the tsar. His power was absolute. He alone appointed and dismissed ministers and army officers. He dictated policy and passed laws. The first of the Fundamental Laws of the Empire stated that 'To the Emperor of All the Russias belongs the supreme autocratic and unlimited power. Not only fear, but conscience commanded by God himself, is the basis of obedience to this power.' The tsars believed that they were answerable only to God for their actions. To protect themselves against those who disagreed, they relied on an army of $1\frac{1}{2}$ million men and the powerful Okhrana, the Secret Police.

Nevertheless, the lives of the tsars and their ministers were con-
stantly threatened by those who felt that, under the circumstances, the
bullet or the bomb were the only means of change. Ministers of the
Interior were particularly popular targets. Alexander II, who had freed
the serfs, was blown up in 1881. His successor died peacefully, despite
various attempts to assassinate him.

The revolutionary

Vladimir's elder brother, Alexander, took part in one such plot. He was
arrested and hanged in the fortress of Schlusselberg in St Petersburg.
Vladimir was then seventeen, and his brother's death had a deep effect
on him.

It was about this time that he first read the books of Karl Marx. They were to influence the rest of his life. Marx, who had died in 1883, believed that there would be revolution in all the industrial countries. The downtrodden workers would one day rise up and overthrow their masters, the capitalists, who owned the industries and governed the country. Once this had happened, wealth and power would be shared by all the people. Marx expected this to happen first in Britain and Germany where there was more industry, and where factory workers were more numerous. But in Russia too, more and more men were leaving the land for the steelworks and textile mills in the towns. It was here, Vladimir argued, not amongst the peasants, that the revolution should begin. He joined revolutionary groups working in St Petersburg.

His name was now on the files of the Okhrana. In 1898 he was caught trying to smuggle propaganda into the country in the false bottom of a trunk, and sent to Siberia. It was to this thinly-populated area, with its harsh climate, that all those who opposed the government were liable to be sent. Here, thousands of kilometres from the capital, their ideas were less likely to spread.

The revolutionary: Vladimir Ilyich Ulyanov in 1895

The two years Vladimir spent in exile in Siberia were not unpleasant. He married a serious-minded young girl he had met earlier, Nadezhda Krupskaya. Together they skated, cultivated their garden and wrote secretly to friends in Europe. Their exile over, the Ulyanovs left Russia. For the next seventeen years, apart from a brief return in 1905, they moved from house to house in one European city after another. They travelled under various names. The man who was born Vladimir Ilyich Ulyanov used well over a hundred names in his lifetime. But the one by which he is best known is Lenin.

The Bolsheviks

The years abroad were spent writing pamphlets, making speeches and editing a newspaper, all with the aim of spreading Marx's ideas. News from Russia reached Lenin in letters from revolutionaries still living there. To avoid the prying eyes of Okhrana agents, these letters contained secret messages which only became visible when the paper was heated over a stove.

There were many revolutionaries in exile in Europe, like Lenin, scheming and plotting for the day when they would return and overthrow the tsar. But they disagreed violently with each other about how it should be done. In 1903 the Russian Social Democratic Party met in Brussels. When they were forced to break off their discussions, the meeting moved to England. Where exactly in London they held their meeting is not known. In some hall or warehouse, like the one used in Brussels, Lenin argued with the other members. Ignoring food and sleep, he shouted and threatened for days on end. To many his rantings were those of a madman. When sheer exhaustion brought the arguments to an end, the Party was split into two groups. On the one side were those who wanted the Party to work with the other revolutionary groups to gain the support of all the workers. On the other were those, like Lenin, who wanted to form a small party of highly disciplined and trained professional revolutionaries. As he had managed at one point to gain the support of just over half the members for his views, Lenin called this group by the Russian word for majority – Bolsheviks. Those who had opposed him were Mensheviks – the minority.

Bloody Sunday

Two years later, after a disastrous war with Japan, there was revolution in Russia, but Lenin arrived too late to play any part. On 22 January 1905, 200 000 workers led by a priest, Father Gapon, marched in procession to the tsar's Winter Palace in the middle of St Petersburg. They carried a petition appealing to him to improve working conditions and to give them the right to vote. 'For us,' it said, 'that terrible moment has come when death is better than the continuance of the most unbearable torments.' As they approached the Palace, the waiting troops opened fire. Hundreds of the unarmed marchers were shot down. Hundreds more were killed as the panic-stricken crowd stampeded. In his description of the scene, Father Gapon wrote: 'Bodies lay prostrate around me. I cried to them, "Stand up!" But they lay still, their arms stretched out lifelessly, and the scarlet stain of blood upon the snow. Horror crept into my heart.' This was Bloody Sunday.

It was followed by strikes, demonstrations and riots. The crew of the great battleship *Potemkin* mutinied and threw their officers overboard. Whole provinces were no longer under the government's control.

Faced with the total collapse of his government, Tsar Nicholas II was persuaded to agree to the election of a parliament, or Duma. It was to be formed to advise the tsar and his ministers. They remained free to accept or ignore its advice. Four elections later, the weakness of the

Bloody Sunday, 22 January 1905

Duma was glaringly obvious. The power of Nicholas II remained absolute.

The soviets

More significant for the future than the formation of the Duma, were the elections in 1905 in St Petersburg and other cities, of soviets, or workers' councils. These sent representatives to a central soviet. For a short time, the soviet controlled some areas of the country more effectively than the government. Not until the end of the year was it crushed, and the members sentenced to exile in Siberia. Among them was the young co-chairman, Leon Trotsky, who had opposed Lenin in London. Somehow, he managed to escape, and fled once more to western Europe. By 1917 he had joined the Bolsheviks.

The last of the tsars

Although little appeared to have been achieved by the 1905 revolution, there were some changes during the next ten years. Until he was killed in 1911, the new and very able prime minister, Stolypin, introduced reforms which improved life for the peasants. Industry continued to grow. The people were allowed rather more freedom. To Lenin, back in Switzerland, the overthrow of the tsar seemed as far away as ever.

This peaceful progress was shattered by the war with Germany. The huge Russian army, badly led and poorly-equipped, suffered enormous losses. As the Germans over-ran large areas of the country, the transport system broke down. Factories had to shut down owing to the shortage of fuel and materials. Food became very scarce. No one in the government or army seemed to know how to stop the hunger at home, or the slaughter at the front. Tsar Nicholas and his wife came to be dominated by a sinister peasant with hypnotic powers called Rasputin. He was, they believed, the only man who could save their son from the deadly blood-disease from which he suffered. On Rasputin's advice, one incompetent minister after another was appointed and dismissed.

Rasputin was murdered by a group of nobles in 1916. According to some accounts, he survived massive doses of poison and several bullets, before being thrown in a river, where he drowned. But his death could not save the tsar's government. In March 1917 there were more mass strikes and food riots in Petrograd (the old name, St Petersburg, had been changed in 1914, as it was considered too German-sounding). Soldiers who were sent to restore order, shot their officers and joined the rioters instead. The Duma met hurriedly and set up a provisional government. With few people prepared to obey his commands any longer, and no powerful supporters, Nicholas II abdicated. Quietly, and almost without a struggle, the rule of the tsars ended.

Lenin returns

There were now, in effect, two governments in Russia. As in 1905, workers and soldiers set up their own soviets. They controlled the army, the factories and the railways. The Petrograd soviet was at least as powerful as the provisional government. Together they ruled the country.

For the second time there had been a revolution in Russia, with Lenin only a spectator. He was desperate to get back; but how? From the beginning, Lenin had argued that the war with Germany was a capitalist war in which socialists should play no part. To the Germans it now seemed that he might be used to bring Russia out of the war. It was arranged that he should travel in a special train from Switzerland, across Germany, to Russia. Thirty Bolsheviks travelled with him. They arrived in Petrograd on 16 April.

During the next six months, Lenin worked fiercely to carry out the plans he had made during his years in exile. There must be no co-operation with the Mensheviks in the provisional government. The war had to be stopped. 'Bread, Peace and Freedom' was to be the Bolshevik slogan. On his arrival, the Bolsheviks had been a small minority. In November they overthrew the provisional government and began creating the Communist state.

They succeeded because government leaders insisted on continuing the war. But Kerensky, first as Minister of War and later as Prime Minister, was no more successful than Nicholas II had been. Thousands of soldiers deserted. In the general war-weariness, the Bolsheviks came to dominate the soviets. Although he was forced to go into hiding again in July, Lenin continued to mastermind the final revolution. On the night of 6–7 November, Red Guards, under the direction of Lenin's Military Revolutionary Committee, occupied Petrograd and seized the Winter Palace. As his fellow ministers were being arrested, Kerensky fled for safety abroad. Lenin was now the most powerful man in Russia.

Left Lenin two years before his death. His wife Krupskaya is sitting next to him, together with his sister, his nephew and the daughter of a worker

Reds v Whites

In the three years which followed the November Revolution, Lenin's ability to hang on to power was severely tested. The Bolsheviks had gained only a quarter of the votes in the election for the new assembly which met at the beginning of 1918. Lenin's answer was to bring its meetings to an end on the second day with a display of armed force, and form a minority government. In March this government signed away a large proportion of Russia's land, population and wealth to Germany at Brest-Litovsk. Two months later they were fighting for survival in a civil war.

This was a time of appalling misery in Russia. Countless millions were killed, or died from starvation and disease. Britain, France, Japan and the USA sent troops to support the anti-Bolshevik forces, and continued to give them aid after the Great War ended. But the Whites, as these forces were called, were not united in their aims. They fought each other almost as often as they fought the Bolsheviks. The Red Army of 60 000 men, brilliantly led by Trotsky, slowly defeated them. By 1921, the whole of Russia was under their control. Lenin proclaimed the birth of the Union of Soviet Socialist Republics.

The father of his country

Peace had been gained – but at a high price. Freedom was strictly limited by the terror of the Cheka, the secret police force which Lenin had formed to root out and destroy opponents. Bread scarcely existed. It was vital that the farms, the factories and the mines increase their output. Lenin announced a change of policy. Peasants would be allowed to sell some of the food they grew for profit; no longer would all of it go to the government. This New Economic Policy was seen as a step

Top Countless millions died: funeral procession of men killed in the civil war, Petrograd, 1921

Above Lenin with Red Army commanders in Moscow, May 1918

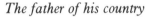

Timechart	
1870	Birth of Lenin
1903	Beginning of the Bolshevik Party
1905	Bloody Sunday
	Beginning of the Duma
1917	7–15 March: March revolution
	Abdication of Tsar Nicholas II
	Formation of provisional government
	16 April: Arrival of Lenin in Petrograd
	7 November: Bolshevik revolution
1918	Treaty of Brest-Litovsk
	Beginning of civil war
1921	End of civil war
	New Economic Policy
1924	Death of Lenin

backwards to capitalism, to private rather than state ownership, but it worked. Production figures in both agriculture and industry gradually rose.

Lenin lived for only three years after the end of the civil war. He suffered from three strokes which left him dumb and scarcely able to write. When he died on 21 January 1924, his body was embalmed and placed in a tomb in Red Square in Moscow. Whilst pilgrims flocked to see the father of modern Russia, his successors struggled for control of the state which he had created.

Note Until 1918, Russia used the old Julian calendar. This was thirteen days behind the Gregorian calendar used elsewhere. Thus, in the old style, the Bolshevik revolution in 1917 is the October, not the November, Revolution. The dates here are given in the new style.

Using the evidence: death at Ekaterinburg

How do we know?

On 15 March 1917, Tsar Nicholas II abdicated. Under the protection of the provisional government, he joined his family at Tsarkoe Selo, their country house twenty-six kilometres from St Petersburg. In August they were moved to Tobolsk in Siberia, where it was thought they would be safer. It was whilst they were in Tobolsk, that news reached them of the successful Bolshevik revolution. Now in the hands of the soviets, the tsar and his family were moved yet again in the spring of 1918 – this time to Ekaterinburg, 480 kilometres away in the Ural mountains. There they were kept under close guard in Ipatiev House. Two months after their arrival, on the night of 16 July, the guards murdered the former tsar and his wife, their four children, two servants, the family doctor and a pet dog. Those who were still alive after the hail of bullets, were finished off with bayonets.

Apart from variations in detail, this is the widely accepted story of the fate of the last tsar and his family. But is it the correct one? Ever since, there have been rumours that some members of the family escaped from

Children of the tsar, a photograph taken after the Revolution: left to right – Olga, Alexei, Anastasia and Tatiana. There was also a fourth daughter, Maria

that bloodbath in the basement of Ipatiev House. Even that there were no killings at all; that the whole family were smuggled out of Russia to live in secret exile.

Perhaps the full truth of what happened at Ekaterinburg will never be known; evidence which might finally settle the mystery may never be discovered.

This exercise is designed to examine some of the evidence that is available, to look for gaps in it, and to question motives.

The fate of the Romanovs

The announcement

(1) Saturday, July 20 1918
The President of the Central Executive Committee, Sverdlov, at a meeting of the Presidium of the Committee of 18 July, announced that he had received information by direct wire from the District Soviet of the Ural of the execution of the ex-tsar, Romanov.

During the last days, the capital of the 'Red' Ural, Ekaterinburg, was seriously threatened by the danger of an advance of Czechoslovak gangs, and at the same time a new counter-revolutionary plot was discovered, which had the object of snatching out of the hands of the Soviet government the crowned hangman. In view of all these circumstances the Presidium of the District Soviet of the Ural decided to execute, by shooting, Nikolai Romanov, which decision was duly carried into effect on 16 July.

The wife and son of Nikolai Romanov have been sent off to a secure place. The documents respecting the discovered plot have been forwarded to Moscow. . . .

Petrograd Telegraph Agency

(2) Tell Sverdlov entire family suffered same fate as head officially family perished in evacuation

Telegram sent 17 July 1918

1(a) Which members of the tsar's family are not mentioned in the first telegram?
(b) How do the telegrams differ concerning the fate of the imperial family?

The investigation

The best-known investigation of the events at Ekaterinburg was carried out by Judge Nicholas Sokolov, a White Russian. He began his investigation in February 1919, and his findings were published in 1924.

After examining Ipatiev House and analysing some pieces of wood from the basement room, Sokolov reported:

(3) It is demonstrated that between 17 and 22 July 1918, when Ipatiev renewed the interrupted possession of his house, a murder occurred in it.

This did not occur on the upper floor, where the imperial family lived; there is not even a hint that violence was employed there against anyone.

The bloody carnage took place in one of the rooms of the lower, basement, floor.

The selection alone of this room speaks for itself: the murder was strictly premeditated. . . .

The murder was perpetrated with revolvers and bayonets.

More than thirty shots were fired, because it cannot be assumed that all the blows were transpiercing and that no bullets remained in the bodies of the victims.

Several people were murdered, because it cannot be supposed that one person could change his position in the room to such an extent and submit to so many blows.

Some of the victims were, before death, in positions along the east and south walls; others were nearer to the centre of the room. Several were hit while they were already lying on the floor.

The Russian royal family and members of the aristocracy, some of whom escaped from Russia at the time of the Revolution

2 Consider the following list of conclusions that might be drawn from Sokolov's account of what happened in Ipatiev House. Copy out the table and indicate in the columns 1 to 3 whether you think each conclusion is (1) definite, (2) possible, or (3) doubtful. If, for example, you think (a) is definite, put a tick in column 1, if possible in column 2, and if doubtful, in column 3.

	1	2	3
(a) The only evidence of violence was found in the basement room.			
(b) The room was badly damaged.			
(c) Several shots had been fired there.			
(d) Murder had taken place.			
(e) There had been more than one victim.			
(f) There were bloodstains in the room.			
(g) The murderers had lured their victims down from upstairs.			
(h) Nicholas II, his family and servants were the victims.			

Sokolov then examined a mine not far away, where numerous items of jewellery and clothing were found. In addition, there was the corpse of a dog, a set of false teeth, a human finger, two pieces of human skin, and some burnt splinters of mammal bones. Sokolov concluded:

(4) During the evening of 16 July, the imperial family, and those living with them were alive.

Early in the morning of 17 July, under cover of the darkness of the night, an auto truck carried their corpses to the mine in the tract of the Four Brothers.

On the clay area, at the open shaft, the corpses were stripped. The clothing was crudely removed, torn away, and cut with knives. . . .

The main purpose was to destroy the bodies. For this it was necessary, first of all, to dissect the corpses, to cut them up. This was done on the clay area. . . .

The dissected bodies were burned in the bonfires with the aid of gasoline and destroyed with sulphuric acid. . . .

The corpses, burned on the bare ground, gave up fat. Running out, it impregnated the soil.

3 (a) What is missing from Sokolov's investigation which would show beyond doubt that the Romanov family were murdered at Ekaterinburg?

  (b) How does Sokolov account for the absence of decisive proof?

Back from the dead?

(5) A defector from Communist Poland who was an informant for the Central Intelligence Agency said last night that he was Alexei, the only son of Nicholas II, the last tsar of Russia.

New York Times, 16 August 1964

The man concerned was known as Michal Goleniewski, a former colonel in the Polish Army Intelligence who crossed over to the West in 1960. He claimed that the murder story was a hoax and the whole family had escaped to Poland. His mother, he said, had died in 1924, his father in 1952, but that all his sisters were still living.

4 Using the information given in this chapter, and any other points that you consider relevant, suggest how it might be possible to investigate Goleniewski's claim.

The verdict

5 With a story as complicated as the fate of the Romanovs, it is not easy to arrive at a firm conclusion. There are three possibilities:
  1 all the family were killed
  2 all the family escaped
  3 some of the family were killed and some escaped.
  Which do you think is the most likely?
6 Whichever one you decide upon, somebody must be lying.
  In arriving at your verdict, you will have to question people's motives. What might either (a) the Soviet government in 1918, or (b) Michal Goleniewski, have to gain in giving false information?
7 How reliable are the findings of Sokolov's investigation?

7 Boom and slump in America

Prohibition and prosperity

On 17 January 1920 alcohol was outlawed in the United States. For the next thirteen years, it was illegal to drink wine, beer or spirits. This was the age of prohibition. It was also the age of the gangster who could supply Americans with what the law denied them. These were the 'bootleggers'.

Bootlegging was big business. In New York there were twice as many 'speakeasies' (illegal bars) after prohibition, as there had been licensed ones before. More people were convicted of drunkenness in Chicago than in the whole of England. With huge profits to be made in the sale of

Prohibition: beer being poured down the gutters

Al Capone goes fishing

drink, organised crime and corruption reached new heights. Notorious gangsters like Al Capone were very wealthy men. He drove in an armour-plated Cadillac and employed an army of men to gun down any rivals. Policemen, judges and politicians were bribed to ignore these gangland killings. When he was finally sent to prison, it was for not paying taxes.

Gangsters were not the only Americans who prospered in the 'Roaring Twenties'. Prices were low, wages were high and few people were out of work. Business was booming. Factories which had made guns and tanks for the war, now made cars and refrigerators. Before the war only the rich had been able to afford such things, but now every American family expected to own them. Money was easy to borrow, and hire-purchase became respectable.

Mass production meant that goods could be made more cheaply, so that more people could afford to buy them. This in turn meant that more people were needed to make the product. Henry Ford had shown how this method worked in making motor cars:

... work is planned on the drawing board and the operations sub-divided so that each man and each machine do only one thing. . . . The thing is to keep everything in motion and take the work to the man not the man to the work.

Mass production: one day's output from a Ford factory

His Model T Ford, the 'Tin Lizzie', was the best-selling car of all time. Other manufacturers copied his methods. By 1930 there were 23 million cars on American roads, three times as many as in 1920. Thirteen million homes had radio sets.

Not everybody shared in this prosperity. Some became steadily worse off during the 1920s. By 1929 half the families in America scarcely earned enough to live on. Farmers were particularly badly hit. During the war, American farmers had grown more crops to sell to European countries. Now this food was no longer needed. They could not make good their losses by selling at home, since the population was no longer increasing at the same rate. The government reduced the number of people allowed to emigrate to the United States in 1921. The increase in the number of motor cars was another blow to the farmer. More cars meant fewer horses and less need for fodder. Whilst industry boomed, farming steadily declined.

There was an even darker side to America in the 1920s. Prohibition was one example of intolerance; the Ku Klux Klan was a far worse one. First formed in the southern states in the nineteenth century and later disbanded, it now reappeared. Once again the Klansmen, with their

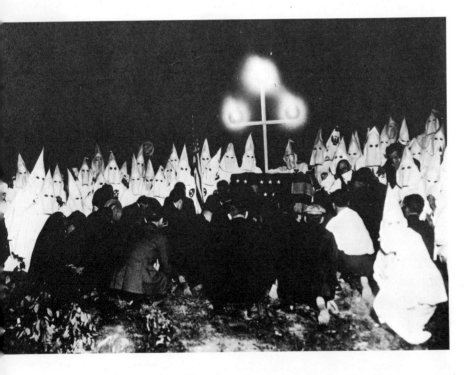

The dark side of America: a Ku Klux Klan initiation ceremony

long white robes, pointed hoods and mumbo-jumbo ritual, met around burning crosses in the middle of the night. They terrorised all those whom they considered were not one hundred per cent American – this included Negroes, Jews and Catholics. They communicated with each other in a code made up of the first letters of each word. 'Ayak' (are you a Klansman?) – 'Akia' (a Klansman I am). Maiming, branding, tar-and-feathering or killing were the methods they used against those who opposed them. For a time they had considerable influence in certain parts of America, particularly in the south. Although the movement had largely died out by 1930 as a result of various scandals, there are still some traces of it existing today.

Home of America's largest stock exchange: Wall Street, New York City

USA — lends money → Germany
repays war loans ↑ USA
Great Britain
France Belgium — pays reparations
repay war loans

Craze and crash on the stock market

In 1929 this booming prosperity came to a sudden halt in what is known as the Wall Street Crash. Wall Street is in the middle of New York City, and is the home of America's largest stock exchange. A stock exchange is a market where company shares are bought and sold. By buying shares in a firm like the Ford Motor Company for example, you, along with thousands of others, become a part-owner of it. If the firm makes a profit, you receive part of it. How large a part depends on the number of shares you have. If the firm continues to make a profit, then other people are anxious to buy your shares, and they become more valuable. On the other hand, if the firm makes a loss, then the value of your shares goes down.

If shares keep going up, people may start to buy them not for a share in the firm's profit, but just in order to sell them again for more than they paid. This is what happened in America. Buying and selling on the stock market became a craze. Thousands of Americans borrowed money to pay for shares hoping to 'get rich quick'. For a time many did. But, when nobody wants to buy, those who have borrowed suddenly find themselves heavily in debt. All they are left with are worthless pieces of paper.

Like crazes in clothes or records, the stock market craze came to an end almost overnight. In the last week of October millionaires became beggars. There was terrible panic. Some committed suicide rather than face ruin.

Money makes the world go round

The Wall Street Crash was like some great earthquake which sent tremors throughout the rest of the world. In chapter 5 you saw how Germany was saved by American money. Now, with the crisis at home, America was unwilling to lend dollars abroad. Germany found it increasingly difficult to pay reparations. Like the United States, the countries of Europe faced economic ruin.

'Brother, Can You Spare a Dime?'

'Brother, Can You Spare a Dime?' was a hit song of the 1930s, the period of the Depression. Desperate people fought to get their money out of the banks. Many banks ran out of money and people lost their life savings. Factories shut down. Lines of half-finished cars stood for years just as they had been left when the last shift ended. Men tramped the streets, or stole rides on freight trains looking for work. But there were no jobs. They lived on any scraps of food they could beg, steal or dig out of rubbish dumps. Hungry and angry men queued for free hand-outs of bread and soup.

Eleven hundred men standing in a Salvation Army breadline on 19 March, 1930, near the Bowery Hotel in Manhattan, descended upon two trucks delivering baked goods to the hotel. Jelly rolls, cookies, rolls, and bread were flung into the street, with the hungry jobless chasing after them. Joseph

Looking for work: an employment agency in New York in the 1930s

Drusin of Indiana Township, Pennsylvania, in November 1930 stole a loaf of bread from a neighbour for his four starving children. When caught, Drusin went to the cellar and hung himself.

When, like Joseph Drusin, the father was out of work, families had to leave their homes because they could no longer pay the rent. Thousands set up house in shacks built from old car bodies and packing cases. These shanty towns were called 'Hoovervilles' after the president who they felt had let them down.

Hooverville, USA

For the farmer, times which had been hard became even harder. Years later one farmer remembered that in the Depression in South Dakota the price of corn was minus three cents. 'If you wanted to sell 'em a bushel of corn, you had to bring in three cents.' Rather than do this farmers burned their crops in the fields. Cattle were slaughtered. Worst off were those who farmed in the Tennessee Valley. Here, years of cutting down trees and bad farming led to erosion. Fields were turned to deserts as the soil blew away in dust storms or was washed away by rivers. As their land disappeared, the farmers joined the homeless and unemployed on the road. By 1933, more than twelve million people, nearly a quarter of the labour force, were out of work.

When it seemed that nothing could save Americans and give them hope for the future, they elected a fifty-year-old man crippled from polio as the new president. Franklin Delano Roosevelt wore braces on his legs and had spent most of the past eleven years in a wheelchair. Now having conquered his own disease, he set about conquering America's.

'A New Deal'

At the start of his campaign for the presidency in 1932, Roosevelt had

President Roosevelt takes office; a cartoon by Miguel Covarrubias

addressed a wildly cheering audience in Chicago. Bracing himself against the reading desk, he had promised to give 'a new deal' to Americans. It was a phrase which people remembered. The actions which he took when he became president to try to lift the Depression are known as the New Deal. They had three aims – the three Rs – relief, recovery and reform.

To provide immediate relief for the poor, the government gave money to buy food and other bare essentials. There were no government pensions or insurance schemes for the old, the handicapped or the unemployed (though there were in Britain). The New Deal altered this. The Social Security Law of 1935 made sure that in the future, old people, those who were blind or crippled and those who were out of work, would receive some assistance.

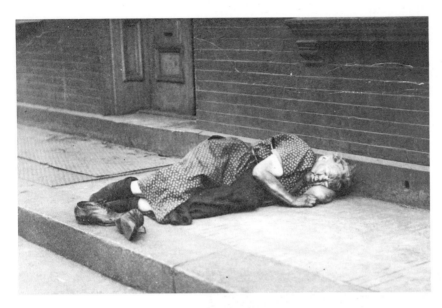

Before 1935 there were no government pensions or insurance schemes for the old

But above all, people needed jobs. Roosevelt set up government organisations to provide them. Young men under twenty-five joined the Civilian Conservation Corps to work in forestry for $30 a month. Other organisations employed men to build roads and schools, erect dams, write guide books and perform plays.

The Civilian Conservation Corps at work in Virginia

Recalling a visit to his home state, the President of the National Emergency Council wrote:

I saw old friends of mine – men I had been at school with – digging ditches and laying sewer pipe. They were wearing their regular business suits as they worked because they couldn't afford overalls and rubber boots.

But work of any kind did more than keep them from starving; it gave them back their pride. 'Do you know, Frank,' one of them said, 'this is the first money I've had in my pockets in a year and a half? Up to now I've had nothing but tickets that you exchange for groceries.'

Men who had money in their pockets could afford to buy the goods which industry produced. In this way industry would be helped to recover. This was also the aim of the National Recovery Administration. Firms were encouraged to agree to a set of rules which would put an end to unfair, cut-throat competition.

New York World Telegram,
4 January 1934

THE SOWER.

Farmers too, were helped. Because they were producing more food than people could afford to buy, the government paid them to produce less. To prevent their farms blowing away, schemes were set up to conserve the soil and make it richer.

A cartoon of 1934, called 'The Sower', shows Roosevelt striding across the fields under the lifting clouds of Depression, scattering seed. They were seeds of hope and confidence. Not all his measures were successful. Many of them were bitterly opposed, particularly by the wealthier businessmen who paid millions of dollars in taxes to pay for the reforms. But, through his 'fireside chats' on the radio, his energy and his new laws, he convinced Americans that things would get better. As one old man from Georgia said on the day Roosevelt died, 'He made a way for folks when there wasn't no way.'

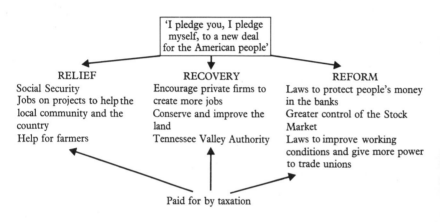

1920 Beginning of prohibition
1929 Wall Street Crash
1933 Roosevelt president of the USA
     'New Deal'
1935 Social Security Law

Using the evidence: riches to rags

(1) We in America today are nearer to the final triumph over poverty than ever before in the history of our land. The poor-house is vanishing from among us. Under these impulses, and the Republican protective system, our industrial output has increased as never before, and our wages have grown steadily in buying power. Our workers with their average weekly wages can today buy two or even three times more bread and butter than any wage-earner in Europe. At one time we demanded for our workers a full dinner pail. We have now gone far beyond that conception. Today we demand a larger comfort and greater participation in life and leisure.

President Hoover, 1928

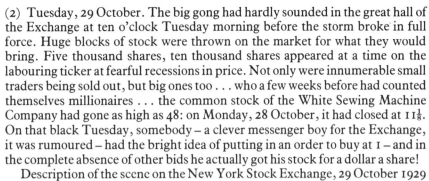

(2) Tuesday, 29 October. The big gong had hardly sounded in the great hall of the Exchange at ten o'clock Tuesday morning before the storm broke in full force. Huge blocks of stock were thrown on the market for what they would bring. Five thousand shares, ten thousand shares appeared at a time on the labouring ticker at fearful recessions in price. Not only were innumerable small traders being sold out, but big ones too . . . who a few weeks before had counted themselves millionaires . . . the common stock of the White Sewing Machine Company had gone as high as 48: on Monday, 28 October, it had closed at $11\frac{1}{8}$. On that black Tuesday, somebody – a clever messenger boy for the Exchange, it was rumoured – had the bright idea of putting in an order to buy at 1 – and in the complete absence of other bids he actually got his stock for a dollar a share!

Description of the scene on the New York Stock Exchange, 29 October 1929

(3) I talked to one man in a restaurant in Chicago. He told me of his experience in raising sheep. He said that he had killed 3000 sheep this fall and thrown them down the canyon, because it cost $1.10 to ship a sheep, and then he would get less than a dollar for it. He said he could not afford to feed the sheep, and he would not let them starve, so he just cut their throats and threw them down the canyon. . . . The farmers are being pauperised by the poverty of industrial populations and the industrial populations are being pauperised by the poverty of the farmers. Neither has the money to buy the product of the other; hence we have overproduction and under-consumption at the same time and in the same country.

Evidence given to a committee of the House of Representatives, 1932

How do we know?

In searching for answers, the historian may put forward suggestions based on his knowledge of the evidence, about what happened and why. That is, he makes hypotheses. These hypotheses are rather like a detective's hunches, and like hunches they have to be tested against further evidence. Some may be supported by other pieces of evidence, some denied and, in some cases, further evidence may simply not be available.

President Roosevelt talks to the people from his special train, 1936

Consider each of the following suggestions and, after looking at the evidence, decide whether it is (a) supported; (b) denied; or (c) neither supported nor denied (i.e. no evidence is available).

For example, the suggestion that the United States was a prosperous country in 1928 would be supported by Document 1.

(a) In 1928 American workers were better off than workers in Europe.

(b) During the Wall Street Crash the prices of shares rose.

(c) During the Depression American farmers could not produce enough food.

(d) Americans suffered more during the Depression than people in other parts of the world.

(e) President Hoover was confident that the United States would continue to prosper.

(f) Only the small traders lost money in the collapse of the Stock Exchange.

CIVIL WAR PLOT

MOSCOW ORDERS TO OUR REDS.

GREAT PLOT DISCLOSED YESTERDAY.

"PARALYSE THE ARMY AND NAVY."

AND MR. MACDONALD WOULD LEND RUSSIA OUR MONEY!

DOCUMENT ISSUED BY FOREIGN OFFICE

AFTER "DAILY MAIL" HAD SPREAD THE NEWS.

A "very secret" letter of instruction from Moscow, which we publish below, discloses a great Bolshevik plot to paralyse the British Army and Navy and to plunge the country into civil war.

The letter is addressed by the Bolsheviks of Moscow to the Soviet Government's servants in Great Britain, the Communist Party, who in turn are the masters of Mr. Ramsay MacDonald's Government, which has signed a treaty with Moscow whereby the Soviet is to be guaranteed a "loan" of millions of British money.

The letter is signed by Zinoviev, the Dictator of Petrograd, President of the Third (Moscow) International, and is addressed

paign of disclosure of the foreign policy of MacDonald.

ARMED INSURRECTION.

The IKKI [Executive Committee, third (Communist) International] will willingly place at your disposal the wide material in its possession regarding the activities of British imperialism in the Middle and Far East. In the meanwhile, however, strain every nerve in the struggle for the ratification of the Treaty, in favour of a continuation of negotiations regarding the regulation of relations between the S.S.S.R. and England. A settlement of relations between the two countries will assist in the revolutionising of the international and British proletariat not less than a successful rising in any of the working districts of England, as the establishment of close contact between the British and Russian proletariat, the exchange of delegations and workers, etc., will make it possible for us to extend and develop the propaganda of ideas of Leninism in England and the Colonies. Armed warfare must be preceded by a struggle against the inclinations to compromise which are embedded among the majority of British workmen, against the ideas of evolution and peaceful extermination of capitalism. Only then will it be possible to count upon complete success of an armed

Zinoviev, whose real name is Apfelbaum.

Daily Mail, 25 October 1924

These headlines appeared on the front page of the *Daily Mail* for 25 October 1924. They sent a shiver of fear and excitement through British homes: were the Communists really plotting revolution in Britain? After all, Britain had helped those fighting against the Communists in Russia after 1917. Might the tables now be turned?

'The new Gunpowder Plot'

The *Daily Mail* had obtained a copy of a 'very secret' 1200 word letter, signed apparently by Zinoviev, a leading member of the Russian government, and addressed to Communists in Britain. It called on them to act through the Labour Party to gain control of the armed forces and start a civil war in Britain.

The affair of the Zinoviev letter was one of the oddest episodes in the history of modern British politics. It is an intriguing story of forgery, foreign agents, secret pay-offs and deals in high places. As some claimed at the time, the letter has since been shown to be a fake. It was written not by Zinoviev, but by three White Russian exiles living in Berlin. Nevertheless, its effect was startling. It was, said Ramsay MacDonald, the prime minister, 'the new Gunpowder Plot'.

Governments Left, Right and Centre

Ramsay MacDonald was Britain's first Labour prime minister. As the chart below shows, his government depended on the support of the Liberals, and did not last long. But there were those who saw no difference between the Socialist Party and the Communists, and who

		Coalition	Conservative	Labour	Conservative	Labour	National	
	Election	1918	1922	1923	1924	1929	1931	1935
	Prime Minister	Lloyd George	Bonar Law	Ramsay MacDonald	Baldwin	Ramsay MacDonald	Ramsay MacDonald	Baldwin (succeeded by Chamberlain, 1937)
Government	Cons.	335	345		419		473	391
	Lab.	10		191		288	13	}41
	Lib.	133		159		59	35	}
Opposition	Lib.	28	116		40		33	20
	Lab.	63	142		151		52	154
	Cons.			258		260		

British governments between the wars. The figures show numbers of MPs

Stanley Baldwin

Ramsay MacDonald

The new National Government, August 1931. The prime minister handing out sprigs of lucky white heather to members of his Cabinet

were afraid of what might happen when they came to power. One aristocratic lady is reported to have telephoned a Labour MP to inquire if her throat would be cut. King George V wrote, in rather a surprised tone, of his new ministers:

I must say they all seem to be very intelligent & they take things very seriously. They have different ideas to ours as they are all socialists, but they ought to be given a chance & ought to be treated fairly.

MacDonald's particular interest was foreign affairs. As well as being Prime Minister, he was also Foreign Secretary. He succeeded in persuading France to agree to Germany paying more reasonable reparations. He was a strong supporter of the League of Nations, and attended its sessions. But his government's recognition of Soviet Russia, and especially the proposal that Britain should make a loan to Russia, caused an outcry. Coming on top of these actions, and four days before the voting in a General Election, the Zinoviev letter helped to make a change of government certain.

MacDonald's successor was the leader of the Conservative Party, Stanley Baldwin. Their backgrounds were very different. MacDonald was the illegitimate son of a Scottish farm-worker; Baldwin the heir of a wealthy industrialist. Between them, these two men held the office of prime minister for fourteen of the twenty years between the wars.

They did not remain on opposite sides in Parliament. If you refer to the chart again (page 99), you will see that for most of the 1930s there was a National Government in Britain. It contained members of the three major parties – Conservative, Labour and Liberal. Both MacDonald and Baldwin were in this government, with first one and then the other, leading it.

Such a government, drawn from more than one party, is unusual in modern British politics. In fact, as you can see, the Conservatives were the most powerful single group within it, and, for this reason, it was opposed by many socialists. Ramsay MacDonald and his supporters were regarded as traitors, and expelled from the Labour Party. 'We did not', wrote one of his former colleagues, 'desert the captain. It was the captain who brought in the pirates and deliberately scuttled the ship.' The two enemies which confronted the old captain and his new crew, were all-too-familiar in Britain between the wars – economic depression and unemployment.

Heroes on the dole

At the end of the Great War, Lloyd George had promised to make Britain into 'a fit country for heroes to live in'. For a time, it looked as if he might succeed. Products which had not been available during the war were now on sale again, and there were plenty of customers waiting to buy them. Ex-soldiers returning home from the trenches were able to find jobs easily. But this boom period was all-too-short. By the middle of 1921 more than two million people were out of work. You can trace

Unemployment in Britain between the wars

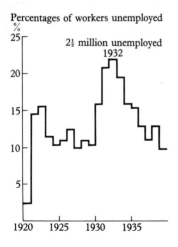

Percentages of workers unemployed

Unemployed men process down the Strand, November 1922

the rise and fall in their numbers from the graph on page 100. Although some years were better than others, you can see that after 1920 there were never fewer than one million unemployed in Britain before the Second World War.

For heroes who had been promised a better life, unemployment was a bitter experience.

> And this is England's gratitude
> To the men who fought and bled.
> They reward us with a medal,
> Then we're left to want for bread.

What went wrong? There is no simple answer to this question, but by piecing the evidence together, we can build up a picture of what happened.

The British Government, after the Armistice and the uncertain Peace, had behaved for a while as though victory had re-established her old strength. . . . They did not understand that the effects of war in Europe from the Rhine to the Volga, and beyond, had so lowered the purchasing power of the defeated peoples, the neutral countries and the new states, that Great Britain, for a long time to come, would lose many of her old markets for the export trade upon which her life depended, as well as the shipping of the world's merchandise from port to port which had been so great a source of her old wealth.

Sir Philip Gibbs, Ten Years After

Because Britain needed to import food and raw materials, she had to sell her own products abroad. Many of these overseas markets had disappeared as a result of the war. In addition, other countries had built up industries of their own, and no longer wanted British exports.

The hardest hit were the industries which had formed the backbone of British wealth in the nineteenth century – iron and steel, coal, cotton and shipbuilding.

Average annual exports	1911–13	1930–32
Coal (million tons)	90	61
Steel	4·7	2·3
Merchant ships (thousand gross tons)	410	54
Cotton yarn (million lbs)	226	137

Men without jobs employed on public works, 1921

The vast majority of people were not affected by unemployment: some of them at Ascot, 1925

Volunteer tram driver during the General Strike

The General Strike

The problems in the coal industry led in 1926 to a very serious situation. As the table shows, the amount of coal sold abroad fell considerably. Because of this, the mineowners wanted to cut miners' wages. The miners refused. Their slogan became 'Not a minute on the day, not a penny off the pay', and they appealed to other trade unions for support. This was given. On 3 May 1926, large numbers of workers joined the miners on strike.

1926: a food convoy protected by soldiers, 'despite the fact', according to a history of the Trades Union Congress, 'that from the beginning of the strike the TUC had made it clear that foodstuffs would be allowed free passage'. Why, then, did the government use troops?

Enthusiastic volunteers, many of them students, drove buses, and even tried, at great risk to themselves and their passengers, to drive railway locomotives. Armoured cars escorted lorries carrying food. There were no ordinary newspapers, but the government put out a special paper, the *British Gazette*, and ministers broadcast on the BBC. The trade unions replied in their own newspaper, *The British Worker*. As you can see, their views on the strike were very different.

Despite what many had feared, there was little violence. In Plymouth a team of strikers played the police at football. The strikers won 2–1. After nine days the General Strike collapsed. The miners were very bitter at what they considered to be a betrayal by their fellow workers. The miners' strike lasted for another six months before they too were forced to give in. Those who could still find work had to accept lower wages and longer hours. But for many, both in the mines and in other industries, there were no jobs, either then or later.

The thirties

In 1929 a Labour government came into office for the second time. They promised to reduce unemployment. But instead of getting better it got worse. As Britain was caught up in the world-wide slump which followed the Wall Street Crash, the number of men out of work more than doubled.

By 1931 the Labour government faced a crisis. They were under

PLEASE PASS ON THIS COPY OR DISPLAY IT.

The British Gazette

Published by His Majesty's Stationery Office.

No. 7. LONDON, WEDNESDAY, MAY 12, 1926. ONE PENNY.

ORDER AND QUIET THROUGH THE LAND.

Growing Dissatisfaction Among The Strikers.

INCREASING NUMBERS OF MEN RETURNING TO WORK.

850 Omnibuses In The Streets Of London.

MORE AND MORE TRAINS.

OFFICIAL COMMUNIQUE.

WHITEHALL, May 11.

The situation throughout the country shows a further improvement. The distribution of food supplies gives no cause whatever for apprehension. There have been a few reports of temporary local shortages in particular commodities, but on investigation it has been found that in the majority of these reports are inaccurate, and in the remaining cases the necessary steps have been at once taken to make the position secure. Especially large supplies of sugar were distributed yesterday.

The situation at the ports is entirely satisfactory, and there is a growing confidence among traders as to their ability to move goods consigned to them without the direct assistance of the Government.

The distribution of petrol is proceeding more rapidly than at any previous period of the General Strike.

There has been no interruption of the power services, and traffic on

WORK AS USUAL.

Tour Through Agricultural England.

FOOD FOR THE TOWNS.

(By a "British Gazette" Representative.)

A dash by road through the Eastern Counties of England brings home something of the magnitude of the task which has to be faced in feeding London. All through the day the rumble of great lorries is heard in this peaceful agricultural area, including the Counties of Norfolk, Suffolk, Cambridgeshire, Huntingdonshire and Essex, to feed the millions in the cities. In the evening the stream is reversed and this time the empty vehicles are radiating steadily from London to pick up more of their precious freight, and so it goes on.

In a run from London, via Cambridge and Ely to Hunstanton, I did not see a single breakdown or lorry held up for an accident, and considering the volume of traffic this is a remarkable achievement on the part of the drivers. It was a testimony to the remarkably high standard of driving. The lorries were, without exception, handled with great skill, and their drivers were always courteous in making way for faster traffic, so that the overtaking of a group of a dozen or more of these heavy vehicles held no terrors for the drivers of lighter and faster cars.

BUSY MARKET TOWNS.

The agricultural people of the district were carrying on their work in a normal manner, and everywhere I heard the opinion expressed that the trouble would soon be over. In Norfolk great droves of cattle were being driven along the roads to the

TO-DAY'S CARTOON.

By BERNARD PARTRIDGE

UNDER WHICH FLAG?

JOHN BULL: ONE OF THESE TWO FLAGS HAS GOT TO COME DOWN—AND IT WON'T BE MINE.

(By Courtesy of the Proprietors of "Punch.")

LEGAL ISSUE OF THE STRIKE.

Sir H. Slesser against Discussion.

THE TRADE DISPUTES ACT.

WESTMINSTER, Monday.

On the motion for the adjournment of the House of Commons, the legal aspect of the General Strike was raised.

Sir H. SLESSER referred to the speech made by Sir J. Simon, on Thursday evening last, on the subject of the law as it applied to trade disputes. He said that the legislature had decided that where a trade dispute existed, the procurement of a breach of contract was not in itself an illegal matter. Whether the act was lawful or unlawful depended on whether the trade dispute came within the definition of the Trade Disputes Act.

There was a matter to be decided by a court of law. Under the existing law, in the case of every trade union, no member could recover benefits at present.

He thought that it was most unfortunate that the legal question had been introduced at all at this juncture. He desired that the settlement, which he hoped would soon be achieved, in this matter, should not be prejudiced by anything that might ultimately be decided by a court of law.

Sir GEOFFREY COLLINS regretted that Sir J. Simon had not given notice to Sir J. Simon that he intended to raise the matter so that he could be present.

A SIGNAL CONTRIBUTION.

Sir DOUGLAS HOGG (the Attorney-General), who said he had only been given two minutes notice that the matter was to be raised, did not agree that it was unfortunate Sir J. Simon should have made the speech he did. His view was that Sir John's speech was a signal contribution to the knowledge of the public as to the true facts surrounding the present dispute, and that he did a great public service in stating in clear and unequivocal language what in his view was the law on the subject.

If he was not right, however, for him (Sir Douglas), holding the post he did, to say just what he believed to be the law in regard to the present position. It was his responsibility to advise the Government,

AMONG THE MINERS.

Uneventful Days in Yorkshire.

MEN ANXIOUS TO RETURN.

No Trouble Expected.

(By a "British Gazette" Special Representative.)

I have just returned to London after a week spent in Barnsley, the centre of the mining industry in the West Riding of Yorkshire and the headquarters of the Yorkshire Miners' Association.

I left London hastily by the first train after the declaration of the strike on May 1, anticipating trouble in this district; but it has been entirely uneventful—a week spent in the midst of people who are sorely distressed at the upheaval, but are anxious to preserve order and to return, as soon as possible, to normal working conditions.

The train by which I travelled north was well filled with people who were leaving for their homes at the first hint of trouble; but there was no panic. Barnsley was spending a quiet week-end, and it took the inhabitants some days to realise that a strike had been proclaimed, and they wandered happily enough about the town, filling the picture theatres and looking for the football results more eagerly than for the strike news.

At first there was a certain air of excitement throughout the town. But then were beginning to realise that there was little hope of a general

THE BRITISH WORKER

OFFICIAL STRIKE NEWS BULLETIN

Published by The General Council of the Trades Union Congress

No. 1.　　　WEDNESDAY EVENING, MAY 5, 1926.　　　PRICE ONE PENNY

IN LONDON AND THE SOUTH

Splendid Loyalty of Transport Workers

EVERY DOCKER OUT

" London dock workers are absolutely splendid," said an official of the Transport and General Workers' Union.

" So far as they are concerned, it is a 100 per cent. strike. There is no trouble and everything is going smoothly."

POLICE HELP REFUSED

At Swindon the railwaymen are obeying Mr. Cramp's injunction to remain steady and to preserve order. The Great Western works are, of course, closed, and no trains are running.

It was stated at a mass meeting of the N.U.R. that Mr. Collett (the

The General Council suggests that in all districts where large numbers of workers are idle sports should be organised and entertainments arranged.

This will both keep a number of people busy and provide amusement for many more.

chief mechanical engineer) had declined the oer of the police and the military to guard the railway works, saying he could rely on the strikers to preserve law and order.

Railway workshops at Wolverton, Crewe, and elsewhere are closed.

CHANNEL SERVICES

At Dover the whole of the tramways staff are out. The cross-Channel boat service is greatly curtailed, and a large number of passengers are awaiting the opportunity to cross.

NOT ENOUGH !

From 2½ to 3 million workers have ceased work.

The Government announced by yesterday's wireless that 30,000 volunteers had registered, expressing willingness to take the strikers' places. It doesn't seem enough!

Published for the General Council of the Trades Union Congress by Victoria House Printing Company, 2, Carmelite-street, London, E.C.4. Telephone (8 lines): 8210 City.

WONDERFUL RESPONSE TO THE CALL

General Council's Message : Stand Firm and Keep Order

The workers' response has exceeded all expectations. The first day of the great General Strike is over. They have manifested their determination and unity to the whole world. They have resolved that the attempt of the mineowners to starve three million men, women and children into submission shall not succeed.

All the essential industries and all the transport services have been brought to a standstill. The only exception is that the distribution of milk and food has been permitted to continue. The Trades Union General Council is not making war on the people. It is anxious that the ordinary members of the public shall not be penalised for the unpatriotic conduct of the mineowners and the Government.

Never have the workers responded with greater enthusiasm to the call of their leaders. The only difficulty that the General Council is experiencing, in fact, is in persuading those workers in the second line of defence to continue at work until the withdrawal of their labour may be needed.

WORKERS' QUIET DIGNITY

The conduct of the trade unionists, too, constitutes a credit to the whole movement. Despite the presence of armed police and the military, the workers have preserved a quiet orderliness and dignity, which the General Council urges them to maintain, even in the face of the temptation and provocation which the Government is placing in their path.

To the unemployed, also, the General Council would address an earnest appeal. In the present fight there are two sides only—the workers on the one hand and those who are against them on the other.

Every unemployed man or woman who " blacklegs " on any job offered by employers or the authorities is merely helping to bring down the standard of living for the workers as a whole, and to create a resultant situation in which the number of unemployed must be greater than ever.

The General Council is confident that the unemployed will realise how closely their interests are involved in a successful issue to the greatest battle ever fought by the workers of the country in the defence of the right to live by work.

MESSAGE TO ALL WORKERS.

The General Council of the Trades Union Congress wishes to emphasise the fact that this is an industrial dispute. It expects every member taking part to be exemplary in his conduct and not to give any opportunity for police interference. The outbreak of any disturbances would be very damaging to the prospects of a successful termination to the dispute.

The Council asks pickets especially to avoid obstruction and to confine themselves strictly to their legitimate duties.

SOUTH WALES IS SOLID !

Not a Wheel Turning in Allied Industries

' MEN ARE SPLENDID !'

Throughout South Wales the stoppage is complete, and everywhere the men are loyally observing the orders of the T.U.C. to refrain from any conduct likely to lead to disturbance.

So unanimous has been the response to the call of the leaders, that not a wheel is turning in the industries affiliated to the T.U.C.

MONMOUTHSHIRE

Complete standstill of industries in the eastern valleys. Absolute unanimity prevails among the rank and file of the affiliated unions, and not a single wheel is turning in the allied industries.

Monmouth Education Authority—which has a majority of Labour representatives—has arranged to feed the school-children where required.

ABERDARE VALLEY

All railway and bus services are at a standstill. The miners' attitude indicates that they are absolutely loyal to the advice of their leaders to refrain from anything in the nature of riotous behaviour.

NEATH

The workers have unanimously responded to the call in support of the miners, and the stoppage is complete.

With one exception, safety men are remaining at their posts. The behaviour of the men is splendid.

AMMAN VALLEY

Every industry and almost the entire transport services are at a standstill at Ammanford and throughout the populous Amman Valley.

GLAMORGANSHIRE

The men are obeying implicitly the instructions of their leaders not to create any disturbance. Crowded meetings of miners have registered their unanimous intention to stand by the T.U.C.

ABERTRIDWR

At the Windsor Colliery, Abertridwr, a deputation of the men and the management met and agreed to safety men being allowed to work.

A Trades Council, composed solely of branches affiliated to the T.U.C., has been formed to act as a Lock-out Committee for Abertridwr and Senghenydd.

PORT TALBOT

Perfect order is being maintained at Port Talbot, where all the industries are shut down.

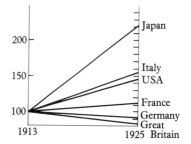

Index of manufacturing 1913–25

---

pressure to cut their spending – including unemployment benefits. Such a proposal was regarded with horror by most of the Labour Party, and by the trade unions, but finally accepted by Ramsay MacDonald. He remained as prime minister, but at the head of a National, not a Labour, government.

The vast majority of people in Britain in the 1930s were not affected by unemployment. For them it was a time of gradually increasing prosperity. It was in the shipyards of the north-east and Scotland, in the coal mines, and in the textile mills of Lancashire that unemployment was felt most keenly. To bring the country's attention to their plight some of the worst-off held rallies, staged demonstrations, and marched to London. The most famous of these marches was in 1936: the Jarrow Crusade. Because of the closure of the shipyard, over seventy per cent of the workers in Jarrow were unemployed. It was, in the words of the organiser of the march, 'like a workhouse without a wall round it'.

Alfred Smith

In its issue of 21 January 1939, the magazine *Picture Post* told the story of an unemployed Londoner, Alfred Smith.

He is a little man, thin, but wiry, with the pale face and bright eyes of a real Londoner. He wears a cloth cap and white muffler, old brown jacket and corduroy trousers. He talks animatedly, likes a joke, walks with his hands in his pockets, shoulders bent, head slightly forward. And he looks down as he walks – the typical walk of an unemployed man.

His face is lined, and his cheeks are sunken, because he has no teeth. He is only 35 years old.

Alfred Smith was married with four children. They lived in three rooms and a kitchen in a basement. The rooms were dark and they had been forced to sell most of their furniture.

Alfred Smith and family at home

Alfred Smith had been out of work for three years. Three mornings a week he went to the Peckham Employment Exchange. The rest of the time was spent tramping the streets, visiting factories and warehouses or reading the newspapers in the public library in an endless search for a job. On each visit to the employment exchange he had to report 'no work'. Every Friday he drew unemployment pay of £2.7.6 (£2.37½). If you compare this with the Smith family's weekly budget, you will see that, even if they spent this money carefully, the Smiths were permanently in debt. If they had to buy some additional item – shoes or blankets – the position became desperate.

	s.	d.
Rent	14	6
Clothes clubs	6	0
Insurance	1	8
Coal club	2	0
Coke	1	0
Lighting and fittings	3	0
Bread	6	0
Other food	16	0
	50	2 (£2 10s. 2d, or £2.51)

London was not an area of high unemployment. But this was no comfort to Alfred Smith.

He has kept his spirit through three long years of disappointment. But he is beginning to feel that perhaps there is no longer a place for him in our scheme of things, that he must change it or perish.

Eight months later the world was to change. Alfred Smith had been too young to be a hero in the First World War. Terrible though the remedy was, he was to be saved by the Second.

1921	End of post-war boom
1924	First Labour government
	Zinoviev letter
1926	General Strike
1931	National Government

Using the evidence: a local study

Many of the topics which are examined in this book are too remote for it to be easy to gain any first-hand evidence about them. There are some, however, which it is possible to explore for yourself. Britain during the period between the two world wars is one of these.
The work in this section is designed to show you:
 (i) what information to collect
 (ii) how to collect it
(iii) what use you can make of the information.
The work is divided into a number of different themes, but there may

well be others in your local area that you will wish to consider.

1 What physical remains are there of this period?

(a) Show on a map of your area:
(i) the parts which existed before 1920;
(ii) the parts which were built between 1920 and 1940, and which still exist;
(iii) parts which have been re-developed since 1940;
(iv) new parts which have been developed since 1940.
In order to make your map as accurate as possible, the area which you choose should not be too large. An example of how your map might look when it is completed is given in the diagram below.

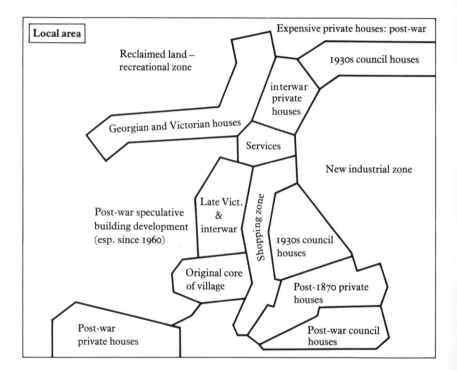

(b) Illustrate and briefly describe as many different types of buildings of the period as you can find. For example,
   (i) houses
  (ii) factories
 (iii) offices
 (iv) shops
  (v) schools
 (vi) hospitals
(vii) cinemas
(viii) public houses

1 Are there any distinguishing architectural features of buildings of this period?

An inter-war housing estate in Birmingham

2 What materials were used in building them?

3 Are any of these materials which had not been used in buildings before 1920?

4 What sorts of people probably lived in the different kinds of houses?

5 Do they tell you anything about people's leisure activities, in particular how, if at all, they differed from those of today?

Means of communication

(i) Show on the map you used for exercise (a) any main roads, railways, canals or airports.

(ii) Indicate any changes which have been made since 1940.

(iii) Try to obtain any bus or railway timetables from this period.

6 From the information which you have obtained, what conclusions can you draw about the transport system in your area fifty years ago?

2 What documentary evidence is there?

Local newspapers can be a very good source of evidence. You will usually find that the library keeps copies of back numbers.

(a) Find out how a major national event was reported (e.g. the General Strike of 1926). This is what one local paper had to say about preparations for a possible strike.

OMS, as some of our readers will remember, stands for the Organisation for the Maintenance of Supplies, which came into being some months ago. At present unofficial, but well prepared, the organisation is intended to be the official means of resisting any Labour attempt to paralyse the essential industries of the country. It is now appealing to all who believe in the maintenance of public order in England to enrol themselves as volunteers for whatever service they may be called upon to do, or may be able to perform.

Brighton Herald, 17 April 1926

1 Regular newspapers were not, of course, printed whilst the strike was on, but what was the attitude of the paper towards the strike once it had ended?

2 What local plans, if any, were made for dealing with any disruption caused by the strike? If none were made, why might this have been?

3 Were there any serious disturbances in your area during the strike, and if so, how were they dealt with?

(b) **What do the advertisements and articles published in the newspapers tell you about:**

(i) the kind of furnishings people had in their homes;

(ii) any new domestic appliances;

(iii) people's eating habits?

(c) Compare the advertisements in newspapers from a number of different years. Were there any changes in the prices of houses and goods?

(d) If the paper has an obituary column, work out the average ages of death for men and women. Remember that the larger your sample, the more accurate it is likely to be.

How do they compare with today's figures?

The latest fashions of 1932: the British Industries Fair at the White City

3 What do people still remember about this period?

There are many people still alive who have vivid memories of the twenties and thirties. Some of these have been published and can be read; but better still, see if you can find people who remember those times, and talk to them personally.

(a) My mother was on what they called 'the Parish', living on 4s.6d. (22½p) a week with two children. My father was a miner. He had a very nasty accident in the colliery when a roof-fall injured his head so badly he was taken away to a mental hospital. So I was a breadwinner when I was nine. I did odds and sods to get things by any means. There were about six men keeping pigs near our house, boiling stuff up to feed them. I used to take the spuds out of the pig meal at night and cleaned them up for us to eat.

A retired South Wales miner

(b) I'm perfectly certain a lot of women died through self-sacrifice. You could see them looking more haggard everyday, though they'd never admit it.

The middle classes didn't want to know about all this. There was certainly no attempt by the press to explain the poverty and the courage of the men and women of Wales. Their community spirit was very highly marked and the rougher the times the better the spirit. There's no question in my mind that in some ways people were actually happier then.

Organiser of a soup kitchen during the General Strike

(c) The well-to-do averted their eyes from the poor. They were too busy having a good time, they and the middle-class people generally. The upper-middle classes were top dogs. The City was a very busy place with invisible exports, insurance, banking and all that, all of which had very little to do with heavy industry. You could certainly make money and that was certainly done.

A politician, Lord Boothby

(d) Nobody knew what was really going on. It's quite simple to make people understand. First of all we had no wireless and *no one* read the newspapers. I had no idea until people marched in from Jarrow that anything was happening. People came back from the War and their only idea was to dance and get married . . . We were very poor. . . . Money meant a great deal. I had £50 a year to dress on and I didn't exceed it until I made money with my writing. My mother and I were left with £600 a year. . . .

My next job during the (General) strike was to go down the Harrow Road with a message and that was terrible. I saw how poor people were and I was terribly upset. . . .

I believe things are rather worse today than in the twenties and thirties.

A writer, Barbara Cartland

1 What evidence is there in these documents to show:
(a) the failure of the government welfare services;
(b) that the depression was more severe in some areas and some industries than in others;
(c) the 'gay twenties'?
2 What reasons are given for the failure of the middle class to understand the problems of the working class?
3 (a) How reliable is this kind of evidence?
(b) Which two extracts suggest that things were better then than they are now? Why might this claim be made?
(c) Compare these two parts of Document (d):
'I had no idea until people marched in from Jarrow that anything was happening.'
'My next job during the (General) strike was to go down the Harrow Road with a message and that was terrible. I saw how poor people were and I was terribly upset.'
In what way do they indicate some confusion in the mind of the speaker?

9 Communists and Nazis

Soviet Russia

The men who disappeared

This photograph claims to show three of the leaders of the new Soviet Russia at the Communist Party Congress of 1919. The familiar figure of Lenin is in the centre. Many photographs supposedly taken during this period show him in the same clothing, and the same pose. Apparently standing slightly in front of Lenin is a smiling Joseph Stalin. The third member of the group is Kalinin, one of Stalin's supporters in the Party.

Stalin, Lenin and Kalinin. In the struggle for power which followed Lenin's death, Kalinin supported Stalin. Refer to the beginning of chapter 9 and study this photograph carefully. It is supposed to show the three men at the Party Congress in 1919, but how genuine do you think it is?

But, if you look at it carefully, you will see that in some ways it is rather a strange photograph. There are signs that it has been tampered with. And, most significant of all, one person is missing from the group. Trotsky, the man who played a vital part in the success of the Revolution, does not appear. It could be, of course, that he was simply elsewhere when this photograph was taken. There is, however, another more likely and more sinister explanation.

Lenin had been aware of the struggle for leadership which would follow his death. There were two main rivals: Trotsky, the leader of the Red Army, and Stalin, the General Secretary of the Communist Party. Towards the very end of his life, Lenin had expressed his fear that 'Comrade Stalin has concentrated in his hands immeasurable power, and I am not sure that he will always know how to use that power with sufficient care.' He warned the party that they ought to 'consider ways of removing him'.

But Stalin was already too powerful. As General Secretary, he had been able to place his supporters in important positions. In the years after Lenin's death, Trotsky and those who supported him, disappeared from public life. He was removed first from the government, then from the party and finally, in 1929, from Russia. He spent the next eleven years escaping from Stalin's agents. They finally caught up with him in Mexico where he was hacked to death with an ice-pick.

Before he was killed, Trotsky had already officially ceased to exist.

He was cut out of photographs. In the history of the Revolution as it was rewritten in Stalin's Russia, there was no part for Trotsky and those whom Stalin considered to be his enemies. Remembering what her father was like at this time, Stalin's daughter, Svetlana, wrote: 'the past ceased to exist for him. He could wipe it all out at a stroke – and X would be doomed'.

The number of those who were doomed steadily increased. After 1935 it reached nightmare proportions in a series of great purges. Unknown millions were tortured, imprisoned, sent to labour camps or

'Soviet paradise': a cartoon in a French newspaper, 1935. The sign reads, 'We are very happy'

shot. No one was safe. Party officials, ministers, generals and members of Stalin's own family were eliminated. 'People vanished', Svetlana said, 'like shadows in the night.' It was not wise to inquire what became of them. In the end, only those who accepted Stalin's authority without question remained.

Plans and collectives

In the midst of the terror, great changes were taking place in Russia. The first of three Five Year Plans, introduced in 1928, called on all Russian workers to make a massive effort. Output in the heavy industries – coal, iron, steel, oil and machinery – was to go up three times. The output of electricity was to increase by six hundred per cent. The aim of the Five Year Plans was to turn Russia into one of the great industrial powers of the world. You can judge how successful they were, by looking at the figures below.

A poster announcing the first Five Year Plan

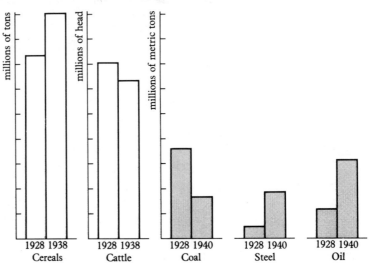

Results of Five Year Plans in Russia between the wars

As well as plans to increase output in the factories and the mines, there were schemes to improve agriculture. This was to be done by creating collective farms; that is, large farms owned by the state, rather than by individuals. To begin with, the government tried to encourage farmers to enter collectives. Money and machinery were provided to

Peasants applying to enter a collective farm, 1933

Industrial development: a tractor factory in 1933

make them attractive. Many of the poorer peasants, who had little or no land, did join. The better-off farmers, the kulaks, did not. By 1930, Stalin had decided that those who could not be persuaded would have to be forced. This was, he said, 'the new policy of eliminating the kulaks as a class'. It was a declaration of war. Rather than surrender, the kulaks burnt their crops, slaughtered their cattle and destroyed their farms. Millions of kulaks were sent to the labour camps in Siberia. Millions more died of starvation in the famine which overwhelmed parts of Russia as a result of the chaos on the land. There was no relief for the starving, as, according to the government, the famine did not exist.

In a train a Communist denied to me that there was a famine. I flung into the spittoon a crust of bread I had been eating from my own supply. The peasant, my fellow passenger, fished it out and ravenously ate it. I threw orange peel into the spittoon. The peasant again grabbed and devoured it. The Communist subsided. . . .

This was the experience of an Englishman travelling in Russia. Why do you think the Communist government took this attitude?

Despite the opposition, the amount of land farmed in collectives increased from four to ninety per cent during the ten years after 1929.

Communism outside Russia

Although the Communists seized power in Hungary for a few months in 1919, only Russia had a Communist government throughout the period between the wars. Elsewhere, both in Europe and beyond, the strength of the Communist parties varied greatly. In Britain, for example, despite the fears at the time of the Zinoviev letter, they had little real influence. In Germany, the Communist Party was, for a time, a powerful force. But there, they clashed with the National Socialist Party – the Nazis. It was literally a fight to the death.

Nazi Germany

The burning of the Reichstag

The crime

Putting my head through the open window of my car, I saw the great four-square mass of the Reichstag, a hundred yards to my left, surmounted by a ball of fire. Flames were leaping high through the glowing metal framework of the central cupola (dome); clouds of sparks and ashes rose into the air and were distributed by the wind. . . .

It was now about 9.30 p.m. Soon we heard from a policeman the rumour that a Dutchman had been taken inside the building.

Douglas Reed, a Times correspondent

On the evening of 27 February 1933, the Reichstag building in Berlin was burnt to the ground. This was the building where the German Parliament (Reichstag) met. For a year after the First World War, the Reichstag had met in the city of Weimar, where a new constitution had been drawn up. Thus Germany between 1918 and 1933 is usually known as the Weimar Republic.

Under the constitution, Germany was governed by the president, the chancellor and the Reichstag.

The Reichstag in flames

The president
Elected every seven years.
In 1932 the 85-year-old Field-Marshal von Hindenburg was elected for the second time.

The chancellor
Appointed by the president.
In January 1933, von Hindenburg appointed Adolf Hitler, leader of the Nazi Party. His proposals had to be passed by the Reichstag.

Old president and new chancellor, Hindenburg and Hitler

The Reichstag

After the elections in November 1932 the distribution of seats among the parties was

National Socialists (Nazis)	196 seats
Socialists	121
Communists	100
Others	166

The accused

This is the beginning of the Communist revolution! We must not wait a minute. We will show no mercy. Every Communist official must be shot, where he is found. Every Communist deputy must this very night be strung up.

Göring to Rudolf Diels (Gestapo chief)

The German Communist Party was founded at the end of December 1918. Two weeks later, its two leaders, Rosa Luxemberg and Karl Liebknecht, were brutally killed during a Communist uprising in Berlin. Communists and Nazis fought each other in numerous street battles.

The accusers

Before the ashes of the Reichstag building were cold the air waves were alive with Nationalist Socialist voices blaring forth details about the murderous, incendiary plans of the Communists, that had been frustrated just in time; SA men rushed about in trucks, drunk with victory and roaring threats at people; in the cellars of the SA barracks woollen blankets stifled the cries of the victims.

K. Heiden, *Der Führer*

The Nationalist Socialist German Workers' Party – the Nazis – had been a small political party when Hitler joined it in 1919. In 1923, they had tried, unsuccessfully, to overthrow the government in the Munich uprising (see chapter 5, page 71). When the Depression hit Germany in 1930, the Nazis became the second largest party in the country. The SA (*Sturmabteilung*) were the Nazis' private army, formed to keep order at their meetings and to fight their opponents. By 1932 the SA numbered 400 000 men, increasing to two million by the end of 1933.

The trial

Held in the Supreme Court in Leipzig, from 21 September to 23 December, 1933.
In the dock were:

van der Lubbe: a young Dutchman who had been found inside the burning Reichstag.
Torgler: leader of the Communist members of the Reichstag.
Dimitrov: a Bulgarian, and head of the Central European section of the Communist International.
Popov and Tanev: both Bulgarian Communists.

Van der Lubbe was found guilty, and sentenced to be executed by the axe. The other four were acquitted.

Who was responsible?

'I set fire to the Reichstag all by myself': Van der Lubbe on trial

I can only repeat that I set fire to the Reichstag all by myself. The others are in the trial, it is true, but they were not in the Reichstag. . . .

Van der Lubbe at the trial

It is established beyond any doubt that, given the brief time involved and the primitive means available to Lubbe, it would have been utterly impossible for any one man to set the building alight on this scale, let alone a man without knowledge of the premises and gravely handicapped, both mentally and physically, as Lubbe undoubtedly was.

R. Manvell & H. Fraenkel, *The Hundred Days to Hitler*, 1974

. . . the police found . . . instructions for a Communist–terrorist outbreak on Bolshevist lines . . . the discovery of this material has upset the plans for effecting a Bolshevist revolution. The burning of the Reichstag, however, was to have been the signal for a bloody uprising and civil war.

German government statement, 28 February, 1933

At a luncheon on the birthday of the Führer in 1942 the conversation turned to the topic of the Reichstag building. . . . Göring interrupted the conversation and shouted: 'The only one who really knows about the Reichstag is I, because I set it on fire!'

General Franz Halder, 1946

After the fire

Historians still argue about who was really responsible for the burning of the Reichstag. Did van der Lubbe, as he claimed, do it all by himself? If not, who helped him – the Communists or the Nazis? In the elections a week later, the Nazis increased the number of seats they held by thirty-seven. The Communists lost nineteen. Was the fire simply a lucky accident for the Nazis which enabled them to blacken their opponents? Or, was it too convenient to be an accident? What do you think?

When the new Reichstag met in the Berlin Opera House, the Communist Party was made illegal. Their members were not allowed to enter. This put the Nazis in an even stronger position. There was, said Hitler, a state of emergency, and he demanded that the Reichstag pass an Enabling Law giving him the power to pass any laws he liked. Only the socialists opposed it. But there were too few of them to prevent Hitler from taking almost his last step towards becoming the absolute ruler of Germany.

The Night of the Long Knives

Who could stand in Hitler's way now? Anyone who dared to oppose him was arrested. All political parties apart from the Nazis were abolished. Nazis controlled the trade unions. Only the army was strong enough to threaten him. They took their orders from the president and looked on the Nazi private armies, the SA and the SS as dangerous rivals. The chief of the SA, Ernst Röhm, wanted to control the army. Which should Hitler support – the Army or the SA? The ideas and methods of the SA were also unpopular with many of Hitler's new supporters, the rich and powerful industrialists. Finally he decided. In the early hours of 30 June 1934, 'the Night of the Long Knives', the leaders of the SA were rounded up and shot. A month later, the old president Hindenburg

The SA on the march through Nuremberg

died. There would be no more presidents. Instead, Hitler took the title of Führer (Leader) of Germany. The army took a new oath:

I will render unconditional obedience to the Führer, Adolf Hitler, Supreme Commander of the Armed Forces, and will be ready as a brave soldier to stake my life at any time for this oath.

Hitler was now supreme.

Hitler's Germany

In 1923 Hitler had tried and failed to seize power by revolution. Ten years later he had succeeded by legal means, by winning seats in the Reichstag. Once in power he had changed the laws and broken the opposition. But even this was not enough. It was not enough that the present generation of Germans should be controlled by the Nazis. Hitler was building a Nazi Empire which, he declared, would last for a thousand years – the Third Reich. He looked to future generations of Germans.

When an opponent declares 'I will not come over to your side', I calmly say, 'Your child belongs to us already.... What are you? You will pass on. Your descendants, however, now stand in the new camp. In a short time they will know nothing else but this new community!'

Schools and universities, textbooks and teachers, were all used to put forward Nazi ideas. In addition, there was the Hitler Youth. All non-Nazi youth organisations were banned. Parents who tried to prevent

Reveille at a Hitler Youth camp

their children joining risked imprisonment. Even so, about a third of Germany's young people were outside the movement when it became compulsory in 1938.

Boys entered the *Pimpfen* (Little fellows) when they were six; girls the *Jungmadel* (Young maidens) when they were ten. From then, until they joined the army or labour service at eighteen, boys and girls marched, drilled, camped, practised rifle-shooting and were instructed in Nazism.

Like Fascism in Italy (see chapter 10), Nazism was a message of force. In his book, *Mein Kampf* (My Struggle), in his speeches at the great Nazi rallies at Nuremberg, in his broadcasts, Hitler announced Germany's need for a powerful leader. The politicians of the Weimar Republic had been weaklings. They had accepted the humiliating terms of the Treaty of Versailles. Germany must grow and be strong again. Germans had a right to the lands taken away from them in 1919. They

'Your child belongs to us already': members of the Jungmadel

The Führer speaks: a Nuremberg rally in 1933

had a right to *'lebensraum'*, living space in the lands of eastern Europe. The right was theirs because the German race was superior to all other races on earth.

Above all Hitler preached hatred of the Jews. The Jewish race was evil, less than human. In his warped mind, the Jews alone were responsible for all that had gone wrong in Germany. For years he had poured forth his hatred. Now he could put his views into practice. The Nuremberg Laws took away from the Jews all their rights as citizens. They were not allowed to hold public office. Henceforth it was illegal for them to marry non-Jews. Jewish shops were looted, their synagogues burnt. Those who could, fled abroad. Those who remained faced beatings, imprisonment in concentration camps, and death. There was no place for them in the Third Reich.

1924	Stalin succeeded Lenin
1928	First of Russia's Five Year Plans
1933	Hitler Chancellor of Germany
	Burning of the Reichstag
1934	Night of the Long Knives
	Death of Hindenburg
	Hitler Führer of Germany
1935	Stalinist purges

Using the evidence: Adolf Hitler

How do we know?

A historian wrote recently: 'It is a rare thing, in history, to encounter a man as profoundly bad as his detractors say he is. It is hard to doubt that Adolf Hitler was such a man.'

Hitler has aroused greater feelings of revulsion than almost any other man in history. The obscene treatment of the Jews in the Germany of which he was absolute dictator, makes it difficult to regard him with feelings other than horror. But this should not prevent the historian from getting right the facts about him. It is on this basis that we should not only judge Hitler, but the reaction to him.

These extracts come from various sources – some from Hitler himself; others from those who were acquainted with him; and others from those writings about him at a later date.

(1) Hitler was a man about five feet ten inches tall, with blue eyes and, in his prime, brown hair and brown moustache. In private he could be affable and persuasive. His terrifying rages seem to have been simulated for a purpose – rather than the loss of self-control. One absurd legend has it that, when excited, Hitler was in the habit of chewing the carpet. This began in a British misunderstanding of the German term *Teppichfresser*; literally 'carpet eater', but really an idiom describing someone pacing up and down a room. . . .

Hitler's father Alois was, at the time of Hitler's birth, a senior official in the Austrian customs service, a man of some dignity in the various border towns to which he was assigned. . . . On his death the local newspaper gave him a generous obituary and reported that his passing left 'a great gap' in the community. . . .

Despite his father's death there was no question of poverty in the household. (The extreme poverty of Hitler's youth is a myth both he and his enemies fostered.). . .

There may well have been times in his Vienna years (from 1907 to 1913) when Hitler was hard-up. He may even have taken casual labouring jobs (if so this was the only time he could have been the housepainter of popular legend). Hitler later romanticised his 'poverty' in Vienna (and it suited his opponents to deride the Nazis for being led by a former 'tramp'). There *was* absolute poverty in Vienna at that time, as in every great European city. Human derelicts subsisted on charity. In winter many starved or froze to death. Hitler was not part of such misery. He remained fussy about his personal appearance. He

liked in those days to stress that he came from a 'respectable' family. His daily routine was that of a man of leisure.

The War Papers, 1977

(2) His father was an amorous peasant cobbler who became a minor government official in Austria through his wife's generosity. It was a strange family. Hitler was born of Alois's third wife, a maidservant who was a distant connexion of his. . . .

Of Hitler's relations with women there is no need to write. As was inevitable, the most scurrilous stories have spread in this connexion, and even the most serious biographies include accounts which have not the slightest evidence to support them . . . it is merely cheap . . . to spread the filthy libel that his niece committed suicide a few years ago as a result of Hitler's illicit attentions. There is not a tittle of evidence in any of these cases, nor is it reasonable that a man who is in every way a slave to his career should risk everything in scandals of this kind which even he could not weather. . . .

Nazi ministers take the salute: from left to right – Von Papen (Vice-Chancellor), Von Blomberg (Defence Minister), Hitler, Göring (Air Minister), Goebbels (Minister of Propaganda)

Apparently he never reads very much beyond official papers. Even in his agitating days he would never open a book. His personal room at the Brown House had no books, and none of the pictures taken at his chalet show any. It is doubtful if he has ever made a serious study of historical or philosophical works. . . . The written word has never had any appeal for him. Even in jail he would not read.

S. H. Roberts, *The House That Hitler Built* 1937

(3a) To me Vienna . . . represents, I am sorry to say, merely the living memory of the saddest period of my life.

Even today this city can arouse in me nothing but dismal thoughts. For me the name of this . . . city represents five years of hardship and misery. Five years in which I was forced to earn a living, first as a day labourer, then as a small painter; a truly meagre living which never sufficed to appease even my daily hunger.

(b) At that time (in Vienna) I read enormously and thoroughly. All the free time my work left me was employed in my studies. In this way I forged in a few years' time the foundations of knowledge from which I still draw nourishment today.

Adolf Hitler, *Mein Kampf*

(4a) It is probable that Hitler intended to marry his niece. Early party comrades who were close to him at that time subsequently told this author that a marriage seemed inevitable. That Hitler was deeply in love with her they had no doubt. . . .

Heiden (a writer who knew Hitler) tells of a letter which Hitler wrote to his niece in 1929 confessing his deepest feelings.... It fell into the hands of his landlady's son – with consequences which were tragic to more than one life.

Whatever it was that darkened the love between the uncle and his niece, their quarrels became more violent.... There was a scene between the two, witnessed by neighbours, when Hitler left his Munich apartment to go to Hamburg on 17 September 1931....

The next morning Geli Raubel was found shot dead in her room. The state's attorney, after a thorough investigation, found that it was suicide.

(b) ... I was having breakfast on the terrace of the Hotel Dreesen ... when Hitler strode past on his way down to the riverbank to inspect his yacht. He seemed to have a peculiar tic. Every few steps he cocked his right shoulder nervously, his left leg snapping up as he did so. He had ugly black patches under his eyes. He seemed to be, as I noted in my diary that evening, on the edge of a nervous breakdown. *'Teppichfresser!'* muttered my German companion, an editor who secretly despised the Nazis. And he explained that Hitler had been in such a maniacal mood over ... the last few days that on more than one occasion he had lost control of himself completely, hurling himself to the floor and chewing the edge of the carpet. Hence the term 'carpet eater'. The evening before, while talking with some of the party hacks at the Dreesen, I heard the expression applied to the Führer – in whispers of course.

W. L. Shirer, *The Rise and Fall of the Third Reich*, 1959

Questions and further work

1. How do the accounts given here about Hitler's family background differ?
2. Compare the descriptions of Hitler's life in Vienna given by historians, with Hitler's own account. What reason is suggested for doubting the accuracy of Hitler's?
3. Is Roberts correct in claiming that there is 'not a tittle of evidence in any of these cases'?
4. What two meanings of *Teppichfresser* are given? Which do you consider to be the most likely?
5. Which of the historians were obviously either acquainted with Hitler, or were alive at the time? Is this likely to make their accounts any more accurate?
6. Why is it often difficult to discover the truth about Hitler?

10 Aggression and appeasement

The Great War had been 'the war to end wars'. With great enthusiasm and high hopes the statesmen had created the League of Nations to keep the peace (see chapter 5). They had agreed to take firm action against any country which broke the rules. In the 1930s this decision was put to the test, when the authority of the League and world peace were threatened more than once.

Blackshirts in Italy

Although Italy had been among the victors, the war had left the country on the verge of ruin. Many Italians felt cheated. Some argued that Italy had not got all the territory she deserved in the peace settlement. Millions were without jobs and food. They were poor, angry and desperate. They joined groups of ex-soldiers who roamed the country in robber bands, or became Communists and set up local soviets. Others joined a new group – the Fascists.

The first *Fascio di Combattimento* (Fighting Group) had been formed in 1919 by a former teacher, soldier and journalist, Benito Mussolini. The word *fascio* means group or bundle: a bundle of rods formed the handle of the axe carried as a sign of authority in ancient Rome. Mussolini boasted that his men were bound together like these rods, to build a strong government for Italy. The Fascists in their black-shirted uniforms waged violent street battles against any rivals – particularly the Communists. Hundreds were killed. The king, Victor Emmanuel III, turned a blind eye to such methods, and did not use the army or the police to put down the Fascists, for he felt that the Communists were the greater threat.

So widespread was the unrest, and so numerous were the various political parties, that no government remained in power for long. In the four years after the war, there were five prime ministers. Mussolini promised that his army of Fascists would put an end to the chaos and restore order. Increasingly, his fellow countrymen, especially the better-off, who feared Communism as much as the king did, came to believe that Mussolini was the only man who could provide the leadership they wanted.

October 1922 was a turning-point both for Mussolini and Italy. The Fascists had made plans for a march on the capital to demand that they be given important posts in the government. In the event, most of those who took part in the 'March on Rome' went by train. It would have been a simple matter for the army to stop them. Instead the king asked Mussolini to become prime minister. By the time the Fascists arrived, their leader was already the new head of government.

But as yet, there were few Fascists in the Italian Parliament, or in the government. This changed in the election of 1924. By using their old methods of threats and violence, the Fascists made sure of victory. After 1924, although Victor Emmanuel still reigned in Italy, it was Mussolini who ruled. He became Il Duce, the Leader.

Fascism meant action, violence and the dictatorship of one man.

Il Duce, 1928

Action to build roads, develop industry and grow more food: violence to oppress opponents inside Italy, and impress foreigners with Italy's new fighting spirit: dictatorship which meant that Mussolini, and not the parliament, made the laws. Italians became accustomed to uniforms, parades, propaganda and censorship. They had gained a strong and stable government – Mussolini remained prime minister for twenty years – but they had lost the freedom to criticise.

Mussolini began to look for new glories, for ways of increasing Italian power. To cheering crowds he proclaimed that he would make Italy as powerful as in the days of the Roman Empire. Mussolini was looking for an overseas empire.

The Mukden Incident

The first challenge to the League of Nations came not from Italy, however, but from Japan. The South Manchurian Railway was owned by the Japanese. Although Manchuria was part of China, for many

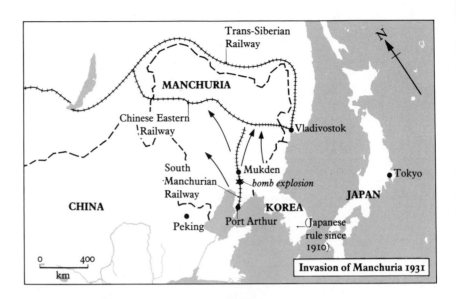

Planning to seize Manchuria: officers of the Japanese army in 1931

years the Japanese had had the right to station soldiers there to safeguard her property. But there was more than just a railway line to interest the Japanese in Manchuria. There were valuable raw materials for Japanese industries. There was land for her increasing population. Why not seize this answer to Japan's growing problems? It seemed to many Japanese army officers that their government's failure to do so showed that the politicians in Tokyo were too weak and soft. They determined to take action themselves.

On the night of 18 September 1931, there was an explosion near the city of Mukden. According to the Japanese account it destroyed part of the down line, 'creating a gap in the line of 80 centimetres'. This did not prevent the southbound express from reaching Mukden on time, although it was seen by Japanese soldiers 'to sway and heel over to the side' as it leapt the gap at full speed.

The army acted quickly. They occupied first the city of Mukden, and, within five months, the whole of Manchuria. The country was re-named Manchukuo. China appealed to the League for support against Japanese aggression. Japan in turn accused China of starting the fighting by blowing up the railway.

The League investigates

The League of Nations sent an investigating team to Mukden, in an attempt to discover what had actually happened. These extracts are from their report. They have been rearranged to show how the two versions of what took place differed.

The explosion

(a) *Japanese version*
On arrival at the site of the explosion, the patrol was fired upon from the fields on the east side of the line. Lieutenant Kawamoto immediately ordered his men to deploy and return the fire. The attacking body, estimated at five or six, then stopped firing and retreated northwards. The Japanese patrol at once started in pursuit and, having gone about 200 metres, were again fired upon by a larger body, estimated at between three and four hundred.

(b) *Chinese version*
On the night of 18 September, all the soldiers of the 7th Brigade, numbering about 10 000, were in the North Barracks ... the west gate in the mud wall surrounding the camp which gave access to the railway had been closed. ... At 10 p.m. (of the 18th) the sound of a loud explosion was heard, immediately followed by rifle fire.

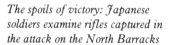

The spoils of victory: Japanese soldiers examine rifles captured in the attack on the North Barracks

Although his force was then only 500, and he believed the Chinese army in the North Barracks numbered 10 000, Lieutenant-Colonel Shinamoto at once ordered an attack on the Barracks.... The attack was vigorously contested by the Chinese troops within, and there was fierce fighting for some hours ... by 6 a.m. the entire barracks were captured at the cost of two Japanese privates killed and twenty-two wounded.

As instructions had been received ... that special care was to be taken to avoid any clash with Japanese troops in the tense state of feeling existing at the time, the sentries at the walls of the Barracks were armed only with dummy rifles.... As soon as the attack began, the chief of staff ... again reported to General Wang I-Cheh by telephone. The latter replied that no resistance was to be offered.

Almost the only point on which the two accounts agree is that there was an explosion. But, according to the Chinese, it was none of their doing. The investigators were inclined to agree. They doubted that it had caused any damage – what was there to make them suspicious about this?

There are also some odd points in the Japanese account of the attack on the Barracks. If five hundred men attack a force twenty times larger, and there is fierce fighting for a number of hours, they might be expected to lose more than two dead and twenty-two wounded. What do you think probably happened at Mukden?

The League of Nations team decided that 'the military operations of the Japanese troops during this night ... cannot be regarded as measures of legitimate self-defence'. Their verdict had no effect. The League took no further measures. Japan resigned from the League of Nations, and in 1937 her armies attacked China once more.

Il Duce v the Lion of Judah

The next test which the League faced was in Africa. The ancient kingdom of Abyssinia was one of the few African countries which were

The Lion of Judah and his family

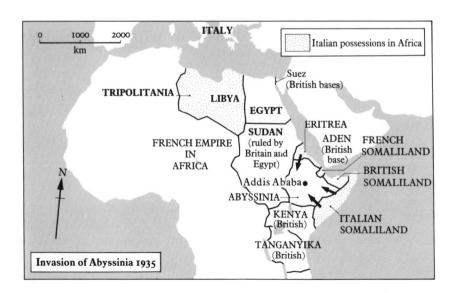

Invasion of Abyssinia 1935

ITALY

Italian possessions in Africa

Suez (British bases)

TRIPOLITANIA — LIBYA

EGYPT

SUDAN (ruled by Britain and Egypt)

ERITREA

FRENCH EMPIRE IN AFRICA

ADEN (British base)

FRENCH SOMALILAND

BRITISH SOMALILAND

Addis Ababa

ABYSSINIA

KENYA (British)

ITALIAN SOMALILAND

TANGANYIKA (British)

N

0 1000 2000 km

not ruled by Europeans. It was a poor country, about four times the size of Great Britain, surrounded, as you can see on the map on page 130, by European colonies.

For forty years, Abyssinia had been under threat from Italy. When Mussolini said that he would make Italy as powerful as in the days of the Roman Empire, the Abyssinians knew very well how he intended to do it. But, both countries were members of the League of Nations. Emperor Haile Selassie, the Lion of Judah, did not believe that the League would let him down if his country were attacked.

As in Manchuria, matters came to a head with an 'incident'. Wal Wal was a tiny town near the border with Italian Somaliland, where desert herdsmen watered their cattle. In December 1934, there was a small-scale battle there between Italian and Abyssinian troops. Abyssinia

Hopelessly outmatched: some of Haile Selassie's troops

claimed that she had been attacked, but as it was not clear quite where the border between the two countries lay, the Italians claimed that they had every right to be there. The League of Nations was asked to settle the dispute. In Geneva, the question was discussed for nine months. Finally a decision was reached. Italy was in the wrong, and should withdraw her troops immediately or face the consequences.

Mussolini had no intention of obeying. Whilst the discussions had dragged on, he had been building up an army of invasion, equipped with machine-guns, tanks, aeroplanes and mustard gas. The Abyssinians, on the other hand, were armed with spears and rifles which were fifty years out of date. In October 1935 Italian armies crossed the northern and southern borders, and advanced steadily on the capital, Addis Ababa.

In May 1936, Addis Ababa fell to the Italians. Haile Selassie's troops, brave but hopelessly outmatched, had been unable to stop them. The severe measures which the League of Nations had promised turned out to be little more than threats. Although the members agreed not to sell some goods to Italy, these did not include the ones which would have really hurt Mussolini's plans – oil and steel; and no military aid was given to Abyssinia. Il Duce added it to his empire, and the Lion of Judah fled abroad. The hope that the League of Nations could keep peace in the world died: even as the Italian occupation of Abyssinia began, fighting was breaking out elsewhere.

'Guernica will not die'

In the spring of 1937, the mayor of a small town broadcast over the Spanish radio. His voice breaking with emotion, he said:

As I stand before this microphone to tell the world what my eyes have seen in what was once Guernica, I call God to witness that I speak the absolute truth.

The ruins of Guernica

The events which he described had taken place a week earlier in the mountain town of Guernica in northern Spain. On Monday, 26 April, market day, Guernica had been destroyed. It was, he swore, the work of German aeroplanes, which bombed the houses and machine-gunned the inhabitants. 'Guernica has been burnt,' the mayor said, 'but Guernica will not die.'

Exactly what took place in Guernica that day, like much that was happening in Spain at that time, is still argued about. For almost a year there had been civil war. The war had started when a group of army officers led a revolt against the government. As countries outside Spain became involved, the fighting grew fiercer and bloodier. General Franco, the leader of the Nationalist rebels, asked Hitler and Mussolini

Nationalist leader: General Franco in 1938

for help. They sent troops and aeroplanes. The government forces, the Republicans, were supported by Russia and the International Brigades of foreign volunteers. For those who volunteered, like the English writer George Orwell, it was a chance to fight Fascism. To the Nationalist supporters, it was a war against Communism.

The mayor's story was supported by journalists who visited the still-burning ruins of Guernica shortly afterwards. *The Times* for 28 April reported:

The bombardment ... occupied precisely three hours and a quarter, during which a powerful fleet of aeroplanes consisting of three German types, Junkers and Heinkel bombers and Heinkel fighters, did not cease unloading on the town bombs weighing from 1000 lb. downwards and, it is calculated, more than 3000 two-pounder aluminium incendiary projectiles.

But the Nationalists denied that German planes had caused the destruction. Guernica, they claimed, had been dynamited by Republican soldiers in order to gain support and sympathy for their cause. There are still those who believe this.

You have already discovered that in the confusion and propaganda of war, the truth is often lost. In the light of later events, it was not hard to believe that the German air force used Guernica to practise their tactics. By 1939, when the Nationalists had won, and General Franco was the ruler of Spain, Europe was on the edge of an even greater crisis.

Versailles overthrown

Since 1933 Hitler had been steadily overthrowing the terms of the Treaty of Versailles, as he had always said he would.

Article 42: Germany is forbidden to maintain or construct any fortifications either on the left bank of the Rhine or on the right bank to the west of a line drawn fifty kilometres to the east of the Rhine.
Article 43: In the area defined above ... military manoeuvres of any kind ... are in the same way forbidden.
On 7 March 1936, German troops marched into the Rhineland. The

The hope that they could keep peace in the world died. A meeting of the Council of the League of Nations in 1936

133

much larger French Army did not try to stop them. Hitler later said that these were the most nerve-racking hours of his life.

Article 80: Germany acknowledges and will respect strictly the independence of Austria. ...

On 12 March 1938, Germany invaded Austria, the country where Hitler had been born. Austria became part of the German Empire.

Article 81: Germany ... recognises the complete independence of the state of Czechoslovakia. ...

In October 1938, after meetings between the leaders of Germany, Italy, France and Britain, Germany occupied the Sudeten area of Czechoslovakia. In March of the following year, Germany took over most of the rest of the country.

Article 87: Germany ... recognises the complete independence of Poland. ...

On 23 August 1939, Nazi Germany and Soviet Russia signed an agreement: Russia would not go to war against Germany. In a secret clause, they agreed to divide Poland between them.

In 1936 Hitler and Mussolini had made the 'Axis' agreement. Now in August 1939, whilst Mussolini hesitated, Hitler was ready to go to war.

1922	Mussolini prime minister of Italy
1931	Mukden incident
	Japanese occupation of Manchuria
1935	Italian invasion of Abyssinia
1936	Beginning of Spanish Civil War
	'Axis' agreement between Italy and Germany
	German remilitarisation of the Rhineland
1938	German occupation of Austria
	German occupation of Sudetenland
1939	German occupation of remaining part of Czechoslovakia
	Nazi–Soviet Pact

Using the evidence: peace – at any price?

How do we know?

The historian often knows, after the event, what happened. This can be both an advantage and a difficulty, but it does usually mean that he has more information than was available to people at the time.

The British government and the prime minister, Neville Chamberlain, have been much criticised for coming to terms with Hitler over Czechoslovakia in 1938. Germany was weaker than she appeared, Hitler was bluffing, and anyway could not be trusted. Chamberlain should, therefore, have stood up to him, gone to war if necessary, and rid Europe of a great evil.

It is now easy to say that Chamberlain was wrong, and his critics were right. But was it so obvious at the time? In this exercise, you are asked to consider how things appeared in that September of 1938, and what people's attitudes were then.

'Peace in our time'

(1) The summer of 1938 was passing with the usual news of holiday crowds and cricket matches, but by August the difficult-looking word 'Czechoslovakia' had begun to appear daily in the newspaper columns. Little was known of this place except as a country which apparently exported cheap gloves, glassware, and boots. Newspaper readers now learned with interest that it was a democratic country near Austria which had come into being as a result of the Peace of Versailles. ... Soon they learned more: the Sudeten German minority, encouraged by the Nazis, was claiming autonomy (independence) from the Czechoslovakian government. ... Hitler was letting it be clearly understood that the future of the Sudeten Germans was the exclusive concern of the Third Reich. ...

Yet on the whole the British were encouraged by the press to remain blindly optimistic. The *Sunday Express*, for example, on 4 September 1938: 'Crisis Off Till a Week Tomorrow. No Sensations Expected! ...'

Nobody except the extreme Left felt quite sure why Britain should go to war, if at all. 'Who are these *Sizzeks*, anyway?' as country people asked. What right had 'Sizzeks' to rule over Germans (it was overlooked that the Sudetens had never formed part of Germany), and why should they not make concessions? ... The *Daily Express* asserted complete faith in Chamberlain. ... 'The policy of this journal is to be sympathetic with those in trouble and at the same time to look after our own affairs. ... For us, in Britain, in the midst of these troubled times, it is the duty of all, every man and woman, to stand behind the prime minister, to support his deeds, to ratify his acts, to uphold his position.'

Robert Graves and Alan Hodge, *The Long Week-end*, 1940

In the 1930s newsreels were watched regularly by about half the population. This is what the writer George Bernard Shaw had to say in one of them. He is commenting on Hitler's decision to rearm Germany in March 1935.

(2) Well, you may take it from me that the news from Germany is the very best news that we have had since the war. Ever since 1918 we, like all the other powers, have been behaving just as badly as we possibly could. Well now,

when Germany was defeated, when Germany fell, they went and they sat on Germany's head and they kept sitting on Germany's head, although it was quite positive, quite evident to any sensible person, that they couldn't go on like that forever. Then there came a very intelligent gentleman named Adolf Hitler and he, knowing perfectly well that the powers would not fight, he snapped his fingers at the Treaty of Versailles. Just exactly as if we in England had been in the same position. As if the powers had beaten us and sat on our head. Then the first man who had the gumption to see that we might get up on our legs and defy all those old treaties, he would be the most popular man in England. There can be no peace in the world until there is peace between England, France, Germany, Russia, the United States and all the big powers of the West. Now take that home and think about it and don't be frightened anymore about the Germans.

(3) When I think of those four terrible years, and I think of the 7 000 000 of

We, the German Führer and Chancellor and the British Prime Minister, have had a further meeting today and are agreed in recognising that the question of Anglo-German relations is of the first importance for the two countries and for Europe.

We regard the agreement signed last night and the Anglo-German Naval Agreement as symbolic of the desire of our two peoples never to go to war with one another again.

We are resolved that the method of consultation shall be the method adopted to deal with any other questions that may concern our two countries, and we are determined to continue our efforts to remove possible sources of difference and thus to contribute to assure the peace of Europe.

Neville Chamberlain

September 30. 1938.

Signing away the Sudetenland: Chamberlain, Mussolini, Hitler and Daladier sign the Munich Agreement in 1938

Anglo-German agreement: Hitler's signature is above Chamberlain's

young men who were cut off in their prime, the 13 000 000 who were maimed and mutilated, the misery and the suffering of the mothers and the fathers, the sons and the daughters, and the relatives and the friends of those who were killed, and the wounded, then I am bound to say again what I have said before, and what I say now, not only to you, but to all the world – in war, whichever side may call itself victor, there are no winners, but all are losers. It is those thoughts which have made me feel that it was my prime duty to strain every nerve to avoid a repetition of the Great War in Europe.

Neville Chamberlain, speech to Conservative Party members, 1938

(4) First of all I must say something to those who have written to my wife or

The bearer of peace: Chamberlain returns from Munich

myself in these last weeks to tell us of their gratitude for my efforts and to assure us of their prayers for my success. Most of these letters have come from women – mothers or sisters of our own countrymen. But there are countless others besides – from France, from Belgium, from Italy, even from Germany, and it has been heartbreaking to read of the growing anxiety they reveal and their intense relief when they thought, too soon, that the danger of war was past. . . .

I shall not give up the hope of a peaceful solution, or abandon my efforts for peace, as long as any chance for peace remains. I would not hesitate to pay even a third visit to Germany if I thought it would do any good. But at this moment I see nothing further that I can usefully do in the way of mediation. . . .

For the present I ask you to await as calmly as you can the events of the next few days. As long as war has not begun, there is always hope that it may be prevented, and you know that I am going to work for peace to the last moment. Good night.

Broadcast by the prime minister, 27 September 1938

Daily Express

Fleet-street, London
CENtral 8000
September 30, 1938

PEACE

BE glad in your hearts. Give thanks to your God.

The wings of peace settle about us and the peoples of Europe. The prayers of the troubled hearts are answered.

People of Britain, your children are safe. Your husbands and your sons will not march to battle.

A war which would have been the most criminal, the most futile, the most destructive that ever insulted the purposes of the Almighty and the intelligence of men has been averted.

It was the war that nobody wanted. Nobody in Germany. Nobody in France. Nobody, above all, in Britain, which had no concern whatever with the issues at stake.

No war for us

Oh, farewell
Pride, pomp and circumstance
of glorious war.

FAREWELL, a long farewell, we trust. For its pride does not fill our hearts. Its pomp has vanished. And its glory is ashes. Farewell, then, to its gnawing anxieties, its endless blind horror, its fantastic folly.

Through the black days, this newspaper clung to belief that peace would prevail, that common sense would triumph.

Over and over again we said it: "There will be no European war involving Britain this year, or next year either."

Now, in the moment when our persistent faith is justified, it is no time to estimate who has emerged the victor from the long controversy. Peace is a victory for all mankind.

To him the laurels

IF we must have a victor, let us choose Chamberlain. For the Prime Minister's conquests are mighty and enduring—millions of happy homes and hearts relieved of their burden. To him the laurels!

And now let us go back to our own affairs.

We have had enough of those menaces, conjured up from the Continent to confuse us.

From 1914—and on

IN 1914 Germany menaced us on the seas, threatening to interfere with our ocean highways. That was the story.

In 1920 Bolshevism was the menace. It was imperative, so we were told, that we should fight Bolshevism lest it destroy us. We must exterminate that monstrous power.

Such was the cry of those who urged us on to a holy war against the infidels.

Today's bogey!

NOW, in 1938, there is a new menace. Some undefined threat in Europe. Against this threat we must take up our arms in defence of our lives and liberties.

All these frightening pictures are very vague in outline. The meanings of these manifestations are hard in truth for the human mind to conceive.

Our biggest menace

BUT one menace is concrete enough. The greatest of all menaces to our society, our stability, the happiness of our people. The menace of Unemployment.

It was with us in 1914. It returned, more severe in form, in 1920. And in 1938 it is a real burden upon our shoulders.

Comfort

THERE is one thing about it. Although it is a menace, it also represents to us a potential source of strength. The hands that are not working. The muscles that are not in use. The brains that are idle.

Unemployment is a reservoir of national power, unused, going to waste, but capable of adding immensely to our strength in the world. For, of course, the best possible use to which we can put our workless thousands is in preparing our defences.

We can do it. We have the gold. We have the engineering skill. We have the land—countless acres of land which can be brought into fuller production, supplying food for the people.

We have the raw materials, all we need, at home or in the territories of the Empire.

And we have the men.

Get busy

WITH these resources, these vast reserves of power, we can and we should make ready to defend ourselves.

We can weld the men, the money and the materials into an overwhelming array of weapons, a mighty curtain of defence between the Empire and any who might think of challenging its peace.

When that is done our Prime Minister can say, like Herr Hitler, "Our fortifications are fully effective for defence."

Questions and further work

1 What different sources of information, available to the mass of people in 1938, are given in the extracts? Rank them in the order in which you think they had most influence.

2 If you had had no further information to go on, what would you have learnt about:
Hitler;
Czechoslovakia;
Germany's right to the Sudetenland;
Britain's concern in the Czechoslovak problem;
Chamberlain's attitude towards war;
the attitude of the majority of people in Britain and Europe towards the Czech crisis?

3 Shortly after Chamberlain's return from his third visit to Germany, a Public Opinion Poll was held in Britain.
Copy out the table and answer these questions as you might have answered them at the end of September 1938, and again as you might have answered them at the end of September 1939.

	1938		1939	
	Yes	No	Yes	No
The treaty of Versailles penalised Germany unfairly.				
Hitler has no more territorial claims in Europe.				
Germany wants peace.				
The people of Britain should give their full support to the Government.				
Britain should not risk war over problems on the Continent of Europe.				
Britain has not got the military strength to stand up to Germany.				

4 In Document 4, Chamberlain refers to the many letters he had received. If you had been one of those letter-writers, what would you have said to the prime minister?

5 There were people who strongly criticised the Munich Agreement. Write a letter to a popular newspaper of the time, opposing Chamberlain's policy, and giving the grounds on which you oppose it. (Remember that you can only use information which was generally available in September 1938.)

11 The war in Europe

It was barely twenty-one years since the slaughter on the Western Front had stopped. Yet the war which began with Germany's invasion of Poland in September 1939 was to develop on an even more world-wide scale than the conflict of 1914–18. When it ended with the surrender of Japan in August 1945, few parts of the world had not been affected. Millions of people, in Eastern Europe, in Japan, in German concentration camps, had suffered hideously before meeting brutal and horrifying deaths. Some of its results are still with us.

At sea, German U-boats struck at British convoys in what Churchill in 1941 called 'the Battle of the Atlantic'. Not until 1943 was this serious threat to Britain's vital supply lines overcome. In the air, Germany's early superiority brought sweeping successes. After 1942 massive raids on German cities by British and American bombers sought to bring Germany to her knees.

The events of those seven years are outlined in chapters 11 to 13. They are illustrated by some of the vast amount of contemporary evidence which is available to historians studying this period.

1939

In the early morning of 1 September, German forces crossed the frontier into Poland. They attacked swiftly, using tanks and armoured vehicles. German fighters and bombers destroyed the Polish air force before it could get off the ground. This was *Blitzkrieg*, lightning war.

On 3 September, Britain and

A week before the invasion, Hitler told his generals of his plans. He did not expect Britain and France to try to stop him.

Our strength lies in our quickness and brutality. . . . I have given the command and I shall shoot everyone who utters one word of criticism, for the goal to be obtained in the war is not that of reach-

Blitzkrieg: German Stukas

France declared war on Germany, but they could do nothing to help the Poles. German troops reached the capital, Warsaw, within a week.

ing certain lines but of physically demolishing the opponent. And so for the present only in the east I have put my death-head formation in place with the

Russian armies began their attack from the east on 17 September. By the end of the month, Poland was defeated.

After his success in Poland, Hitler offered peace to Britain and France. It was refused. Even before this refusal, Hitler wrote to his army commander-in-chief that Germany's aim remained 'the destruction of our western enemies'. Whilst this was being planned, the Allied French and British armies sat in France waiting for something to happen. These were the months of the 'phoney war'.

command relentlessly and without compassion to send into death many women and children of Polish origin and language. ...

I experienced those poor worms Daladier and Chamberlain in Munich. They will be too cowardly to attack.

At 11.15 a.m. on 3 September, the British prime minister broadcast to the nation.

This morning the British Ambassador in Berlin handed the German government a final note stating that unless we heard from them by eleven o'clock that they were prepared at once to withdraw their troops from Poland a state of war would exist between us. I have to tell you now that no such undertaking has been received and that consequently this country is at war with Germany.

1940

On 9 April the 'phoney war' suddenly ended. Germany attacked Denmark and Norway. Denmark was occupied in the first day. Norway, with the help of Allied troops, held out for longer. When events in France forced their withdrawal, Norway surrendered.

Hitler's original plan of attack on the west was the same as Germany's in 1914. At a conference on 23 November 1939, he told his generals: *My decision is unchangeable. I shall attack France and England at the most favourable and earliest moment. Breach*

DAILY SKETCH   WEDNESDAY, APRIL 10, 1940.—Page 7

SPECTRE OF IDLE ARMS FACTORIES

GERMANY

IRON ORE

NORWAY

NARVIK

CLIVE UPTTON

INDIGESTION 'NECESSITY KNOWS NO LAW' - - - By CLIVE UPTTON

What does this cartoon suggest Hitler hoped to gain?

Behind their massive defensive system, the Maginot Line, the French felt that they were safe from German attack.

of the neutrality of Belgium and Holland is of no importance. No one will question that when we have won. We shall not justify the breach of neutrality

They were wrong. On 10 May, Germany struck against Belgium, Holland and Luxembourg. But the main weight of their attack came elsewhere. As Allied troops moved north, German *Panzer* divisions went round the Maginot Line through the wooded hills of the Ardennes, where nobody had thought their tanks could move.

Within a week they had reached the Channel. The British and French

as idiotically as in 1914.

HITLER IS FOLLOWING THE SCHLIEFFEN PLAN

Headline in the *Evening Standard*,
10 May, 1940

This was what Hitler wanted people to think. The original plan had been altered so that the main attack came where it was least expected.

Three months before the collapse, Hankey and I had made a tour of the French front. When we reached the ill-famed

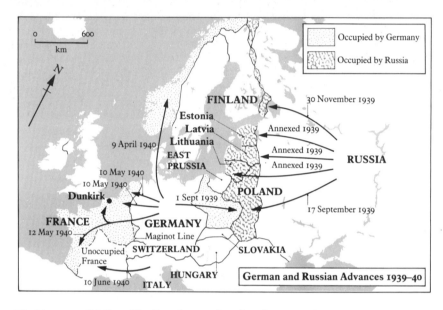

German and Russian Advances 1939–40

Rescued from the beaches of Dunkirk

The bitterness of defeat. The French were forced to sign the surrender in the same railway carriage in which the armistice of 1918 had been signed by the Germans

forces in the north were cut off and squeezed into the area around Dunkirk. In the last days of May, when all seemed lost, a third of a million men were rescued from the beaches by a fleet of small boats. But nothing could save France.

Hitler was now the master of western Europe. Since Britain still stubbornly refused to come to terms, plans for Operation Sea Lion, the cross-Channel invasion, got under way.

First, the *Luftwaffe* would gain control of the air. This was the Battle of Britain. In the summer sunshine, German bombers on their way to attack the airfields of southern England, and their fighter escorts, battled with the Spitfires and Hurricanes of the RAF. Both sides suffered heavy losses.

On 7 September, the *Luftwaffe* turned away from the airfields, and bombed London. Ten days later, although the bombs continued to fall on British cities, Hitler postponed his invasion plans. His attention switched to other battlefields on the far side of Europe and in the deserts of North Africa.

section of Sedan, General Corap, commanding the ninth French army corps, had taken us to the Meuse and shown us the wooded banks and rushing waters. 'Look at the terrain,' *he had said to us, 'no German army can get through here.'*
Viscount Templewood, *Memoirs*

Führer's Headquarters
August 1 1940
TOP SECRET
Directive No.17 for the Conduct of Air and Naval Warfare against England.

In order to establish the conditions necessary for the final conquest of England, I intend to continue the air and naval war against the English homeland more intensively than heretofore.

To this end I issue the following orders:
1 The German air force is to overcome the British air force with all means at its disposal and as soon as possible. . . .
2 . . . Attacks on the harbours of the south coast are to be undertaken on the smallest scale possible, in view of our intended operations. . . .
3 The Luftwaffe *is to stand by in force for Operation Sea Lion.*
4 I reserve for myself the decision on terror attacks as a means of reprisal.
5 The intensified air war may commence on or after August 6. . . .
ADOLF HITLER

The remains of an air battle over Kent, September 1940

1941

Hitler's agreement with Stalin had saved Germany from fighting a war on two fronts. Now, he had nothing to fear from the west, and could turn his attention to the vast lands of the east. Whilst his bombers were droning nightly over Britain, Hitler planned his master-stroke – Operation Barbarossa – the invasion of Russia.

Yugoslavia and Greece, where Mussolini was finding glory hard to come by, were bombed into surrender in a month. Then, on 22 June, the full might of the German *Blitzkrieg* was launched against Russia. Within a few weeks it had struck deep into the country. The Russians fell back, burning and destroying as they went. Nothing which might be of use to the enemy was left standing.

In the event that invasion (of England) does not take place, our efforts must be directed to the elimination of all factors that let England hope for a change in the situation. . . . Britain's hope lies in Russia and the United States. If Russia drops out of the picture, America, too, is lost for Britain, because the elimination of Russia would greatly increase Japan's power in the Far East. . . . Russia's destruction must therefore be made a part of this struggle. . . . The sooner Russia is crushed the better. . . . if we start in May '41, we will have five months in which to finish the job.

Hitler to his commanders-in-chief, July 1940

Russian territory captured by Germans by Dec. 1941

N

0   200   400
km

L. Ladoga
Leningrad
BALTIC SEA
Moscow
Smolensk
GERMANY
Kiev
Rost
HUNGARY (German ally)
SWITZERLAND (neutral)
RUMANIA (German ally)
YUGOSLAVIA (occupied by Germany)
Sevastopol
ITALY (aided the invasion of Russia)
BULGARIA (German ally)
BLACK SEA
ALBANIA (occupied by Germany)
TURKEY (neutral)
MEDITERRANEAN SEA
GREECE (over-run by Germany 1941)
Operation Barbarossa 1941
CRETE

In the north, Leningrad was surrounded. It was the start of a siege which was to last for nine hundred days in which one million people died. In December the leading German units caught sight of the spires of Moscow. This was the nearest they came to taking the capital. In the coldest winter for a century, the Russians counter-attacked. The German armies, ill-equipped for conditions in which a mug of boiling soup froze solid in under a minute, could advance no farther. Large areas of western Russia were still in their hands, but Moscow was saved.

2 January 1942

... Faces one sees in the street are either unnaturally drawn and shiny ... or green and lumpy. There is not an ounce of fat under the skin. And these desiccated skeletons are being gnawed by frost. (As I write these words I can hear a mouse, crazy with hunger, rummaging in the wastepaper basket, into which we used to throw crumbs. We call her Princess Myshkina. She hasn't even the strength to rejoice that all the cats have been eaten.)

Vera Inber, *Leningrad Diary*

The icy cold, the lack of shelter, the shortage of clothing, the heavy losses of men and equipment, the wretched state of our fuel supplies – all this makes the duties of a commander a misery, and the

Russian troops fight to save Moscow

1942

In the spring, they tried again. The main thrust now was in the south, towards the city of Stalingrad. Success here would open the way to the precious oil of the Caucasus and the Middle East. The battle for Stalingrad was one of the bloodiest and most brutal of the war.

After months of bitter hand-to-hand fighting, a quarter of a million Germans were trapped in the ruins of the city. Hitler ordered them to fight to the last man. Those who were still alive finally surrendered in January 1943.

Stalingrad was not Germany's only defeat in 1942. For a year, British, Italian and German armies had battled for control of North Africa. In October, the forces led by two of the best-known generals of the war,

longer it goes on the more I am crushed by the enormous responsibility I have to bear.

Diary of General Guderian, German tank commander, 1941

And imagine Stalingrad; eighty days and eighty nights of hand-to-hand struggles. The street is no longer measured by metres but by corpses. . . . Stalingrad is no longer a town. By day it is an enormous cloud of burning, blinding smoke; it is a vast furnace, lit by the reflection of the flames. And when the night arrives, one of those scorching, howling, bleeding nights, the dogs plunge into the Volga and swim desperately to gain the other bank. The nights of Stalingrad are a terror for them. Animals flee this hell; the hardest stones cannot bear it for long; only men endure.

A lieutenant of XXIV Panzer Division

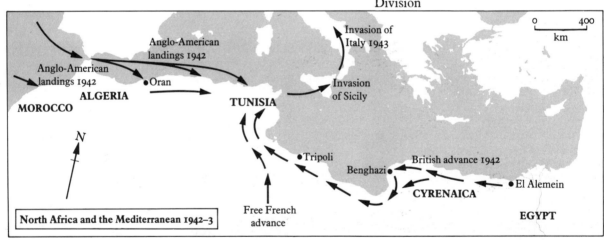

North Africa and the Mediterranean 1942–3

Rommel and Montgomery, clashed near the tiny Egyptian town of El Alamein. Montgomery's tanks broke through Rommel's defences, and sent his army retreating along the coast. In Tunisia they met an Anglo-American army moving eastwards, and surrendered.

The victor of El Alamein: General Montgomery (centre) and two of his commanders

1943

From Tunisia, the Allies crossed the Mediterranean and landed on the coast of Italy. Mussolini was overthrown by his former supporters, and the new government made peace. But they did not control the whole of the country. The British and Americans held the south; the Germans the north. In a daring raid on the mountain-top hotel where he was held, Mussolini was rescued by German commandos, and put at the head of a German-controlled state in northern Italy.

For the rest of the year, and well into 1944, the Allied advance could make only slow progress.

2 September 1943
1 Having captured Sicily as our first slice of the Italian home country, the time has now come to carry the battle on to the mainland of Italy.
2 To the Eighth Army has been given the great honour of being the first troops to land on the mainland of the continent of Europe.
We will prove ourselves worthy of this honour. . . .
3 Forward to Victory!
Let us knock Italy out of the war!
4 Good luck. And God bless you all.
Personal message from General Montgomery to the officers and men of the Eighth Army

The advance into Italy: American troops entering Naples, October 1943

1944

It was through France rather than Italy, however, that the fatal blow against Germany was to be struck. On D-Day, 6 June, thousands of soldiers waded ashore in Normandy at the start of Operation Overlord.

After four years, British troops were back on the beaches of France. This time they were not driven back into the sea, despite the formidable defences of Hitler's 'Fortress Europe'.

Gradually, village by village, city by city, the occupying army was

. . . the next combination of moon, tide, and time of sunrise that we considered practicable for the attack occurred on June 5, 6, and 7.
. . . When the conference started the first report given us by Group Captain Stagg and the Meteorologic Staff was that the bad conditions predicted the day before for the coast of France were actually prevailing there and that if we had persisted in the attempt to land on 5 June a major disaster would almost surely have resulted . . . by the following morning a period of relatively good

Back on the beaches of France: supplies being unloaded in Normandy shortly after D-Day

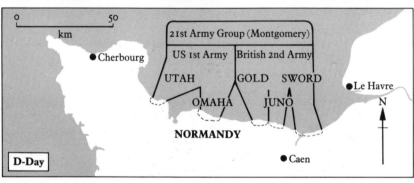

21st Army Group (Montgomery)

US 1st Army | British 2nd Army

UTAH | GOLD | SWORD

OMAHA | JUNO

NORMANDY

Cherbourg

Le Havre

Caen

N

D-Day

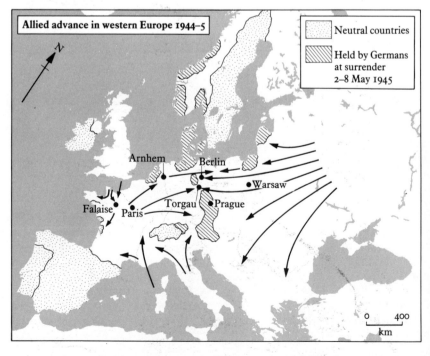

Allied advance in western Europe 1944–5

Neutral countries

Held by Germans at surrender 2–8 May 1945

Arnhem

Berlin

Warsaw

Falaise

Paris

Torgau

Prague

N

forced to give way. In August, General de Gaulle, the Frenchman who had refused to surrender in 1940, marched in triumph through the streets of Paris. By December the Germans were desperately defending the frontiers of the fatherland itself. They counter-attacked fiercely in the Ardennes, the scene of former glory, and for a time the Allied advance was held. But it was too late. With the Russians closing in from the east, the final collapse could not be far off.

weather ... would ensue, lasting probably thirty-six hours. ...

I quickly announced the decision to go ahead with the attack on 6 June ... each went off to his respective post of duty to flash out to his command the messages that would set the whole host in motion.
General Eisenhower, Supreme Allied Commander, *Memoirs*

Soldiers of the western front!
... I expect you to defend Germany's sacred soil ... to the very last! ...
Heil the Führer!
VON RUNSTEDT
Field-Marshal

1945

In March the river Rhine, the last big obstacle on the way to Berlin, was crossed. A month later, American and Russian soldiers shook hands at Torgau.

As Russian guns pounded the capital, Hitler killed himself rather than face capture. His corpse, as he had ordered, was burned.

On 8 May, the victorious countries celebrated the end of the war in Europe.

How did Hitler die? According to his orderly:
... I went into the Führer's quarters. He was sitting on the couch. He had fired a 7.65 bullet into his right temple – not into his mouth, as has often been said. The revolver had fallen at his feet and his blood had poured on to the carpet. Beside him, half-lying on the couch, was his wife: she had preferred to take poison.
Hitler's remains were examined by Russian doctors. According to one of them:
No matter what is asserted today, our commission could not detect any traces of a gunshot on 8 May 1945. Hitler poisoned himself.

Last days of the Third Reich: Hitler inspects a group of young soldiers

Planning the war

The Allied leaders met on various occasions to plan the conduct of the war and discuss strategy. On many points there was agreement, on some there was not. From the beginning the Americans had decided that they would concentrate on defeating the Axis powers in Europe, before turning the full weight of their military power against Japan. At Casablanca in 1943, Churchill persuaded Roosevelt that the Allies should first seek success in southern Europe by invading Italy. The more difficult operation, striking at Germany through France, should be postponed until 1944. It was not a decision which pleased Stalin. He insisted that his British and American allies should open up a second front against Germany in order to relieve pressure on Russia. It was not enough that they should send supplies to Russia. At the Teheran Conference, held at the end of 1943, he argued strongly in favour of a cross-Channel invasion of France. Churchill was still anxious to strike at Central Europe, but Roosevelt supported Stalin.

Despite the differences, the alliance survived. By the time the leaders met at Yalta in February 1945, Germany was close to defeat. The question for the Allies to answer at Yalta was not how to win, but how Europe was to be settled once victory had been achieved.

Using the evidence: the Nuremberg trials

How do we know?

When judging people's actions, it is not enough for the historian to be aware of what they knew. He must also understand how they felt. In this chapter and the next, the evidence sections look at two events about which the people of 1945 felt very strongly. Whether these events should have taken place has been questioned ever since. Although we may not agree with the decisions made thirty years and more ago, it is important to understand why they were taken.

1 The Nuremberg trials raise a number of important and difficult questions:
   (a) Is it possible for the losers in a war to receive a fair trial from the victors?
   (b) Should the leading Nazis have been executed without a trial?
   (c) As you saw in chapter 5, Germany was judged to be guilty of starting the 1914–18 war. Why, then, was there a war trial in 1945, but not in 1918?
   (d) Was it right to single out a number of individuals, or were all the German people equally guilty of a crime against humanity?

Nazis on trial

(1) The remaining intimate collaborators of Hitler lived a bit longer. I went down to Nuremberg to see them. I had often watched them in their hour of glory and power at the annual party rallies in this town. In the dock before the International Military Tribunal they looked different. Attired in rather

shabby clothes, slumped in their seats fidgeting nervously, they no longer resembled the arrogant leaders of old. They seemed to be a drab assortment of mediocrities. It seemed difficult to grasp that such men, when last you had seen them, had wielded such monstrous power, that such as they could conquer a great nation and most of Europe.

William L. Shirer, *The Rise and Fall of the Third Reich*

On 20 November 1945, the trial of twenty-two leading Nazis began at Nuremberg. Only twenty-one actually appeared in the dock. Martin Bormann, Hitler's deputy, was missing. Whether he was alive or dead nobody knew for certain. He was tried in his absence.

The accused were tried on four counts:

(i) crimes against peace – carrying out wars of aggression;

(ii) war crimes – ill-treatment of prisoners of war and civilians;

(iii) crimes against humanity – extreme brutality against whole groups of people;

(iv) conspiracy – plotting together to commit the other three crimes.

The record of the trial runs into several thousands of pages. Hundreds of witnesses were heard, including the former commandant of the Auschwitz concentration camp.

(2) I commanded Auschwitz until 1 December 1943, and estimate that at least 2 500 000 victims were executed and exterminated there by gassing and burning, and at least another half-million succumbed to starvation and disease, making a total dead of about 3 000 000. This figure represents about seventy per cent or eighty per cent of all persons sent to Auschwitz as prisoners, the remainder having being selected and used for slave labour in the concentration-camp industries. Included among the executed and burnt were approximately 20 000 Russian prisoners of war (previously selected and taken out of prisoner-of-war cages by the Gestapo) who were delivered to Auschwitz in *Wehrmacht* transports operated by regular *Wehrmacht* officers and men. The remainder of the total number of victims included about 100 000 German Jews, and great numbers of citizens, mostly Jewish, from Holland, France, Belgium, Poland, Hungary, Czechoslovakia, Greece, or other countries. We executed about 400 000 Hungarian Jews alone at Auschwitz in the summer of 1944.

On the ninth day of the trial, a film of the concentration camps, made at the time they were liberated by the Americans, was shown. The reactions of the prisoners were noted by an American psychiatrist.

(3) Schacht objects . . . turns away. . . . Fritzsche already looks pale and sits aghast as it starts with scenes of prisoners burned alive in a barn . . . Keitel wipes brow, takes off headphones . . . Hess glares at screen. . . . Neurath has head bowed, doesn't look . . . Funk covers his eyes, looks as if he is in agony. . . . Göring keeps leaning on balustrade, not watching most of the time. . . . Funk swallows hard, blinks eyes, trying to stifle tears. . . . Funk now in tears. . . . Seyss-Inquart stoic throughout. . . . Speer looks very sad, swallows hard . . . Raeder watches it without budging. . . Papen sits with hand over brow, looking down, has not looked at screen yet. . . . Schirach, watching intently, gasps, whispers to Sauckel. . . . Funk crying now. . . . Dönitz has head bowed, no longer watching. . . . as human skin lampshade is shown, Streicher says, 'I don't believe that'. . . . Fritzsche, pale, biting lips,

really seems in agony. . . . Frick shakes his head incredulously at speech of female doctor describing treatment and experiments on female prisoners at Belsen. . . . Funk, crying bitterly, claps hand over mouth as women's naked corpses are thrown into pit.

The case for the defence, Göring:

(4) **Maxwell Fyfe:** You heard what I read you about Hitler, what he said to Horthy and what Ribbentrop said, that the Jews must be exterminated or taken to concentration camps. Hitler said the Jews must either work or be shot. That was in April 1943. Do you still say that neither Hitler nor you knew of this policy to exterminate the Jews?

Göring: For the correction of the document——

Maxwell Fyfe: Will you please answer my question. Do you still say neither Hitler nor you knew of the policy to exterminate the Jews?

Göring:. As far as Hitler is concerned, I have said I do not believe it. As far as I am concerned, I have said that I did not know, even approximately, to what degree this thing took place.

Göring replies to questioning

Kaltenbrunner:

(5) I had no idea of the existence of these Action Groups or commandos described by Ohlendorf. Later on I heard they existed. . . . As I have already said once, I have never had authority to sign on my own initiative a so-called order for execution, that is to say a death sentence. Apart from Hitler, nobody in the whole Reich had such authority except Himmler and the Reich Minister of Justice.

Frank:

(6) **Defence Counsel:** Witness, did the concentration camps in the Government General come under you, and did you have anything to do with their administration?

Frank: Concentration camps were entirely a matter for the police and had nothing to do with the administration. Members of the civilian administration were officially prohibited from entering the camps.

Counsel: Have you yourself ever been in a concentration camp?

Frank: In 1935 I participated in a visit to the Dachau concentration camp, which had been organised for the Gauleiters. That was the only time that I have entered a concentration camp.

Counsel: Did you ever participate in the annihilation of the Jews?

Frank: I say yes, and the reason why I say yes is because having lived through the five months of the trial, and particularly after having heard the testimony of the witness Hoess, my conscience does not allow me to throw the responsibility solely on these small people. I myself have never installed an extermination camp for Jews or supported the existence of such camps; but if Adolf Hitler personally has laid that dreadful responsibility on his people, then it is mine too, for we have fought against Jewry for years; and we have indulged in the most horrible utterances; my own diary bears witness against me. Therefore, it is no more than my duty to answer your question in this connection with 'yes'. A thousand years will pass and this guilty side of Germany will still not be erased.

Questions and further work

1 In the evidence presented, what points did the defendants make in their defence?
2 Is there any evidence to suggest that the defendants genuinely regretted what had happened?
3 Which of the reactions to the verdicts quoted on this page do you agree with?
4 Write either a prosecution or a defence speech for those on trial at Nuremberg.

What The Judges Said of Them

HERE are some of the highlights from what the judges said of the guilty—and the innocent—men:

Ribbentrop: He played an important part in Hitler's "solution" of the Jewish question. The court dismissed his attempt to wash his hands of complicity by sheltering behind Hitler.

Hess: Hitler's closest confidant until his flight to Britain No evidence that he was not completely sane at the time of his crimes

Keitel: Ordered the execution of prisoners; signed the order that troops should use terrorism. Nothing to be said in his mitigation.

Bormann: No conclusive evidence of his death In his absence found guilty of responsibility for the lynching of Allied airmen.

Papen: To carry through his plan to undermine Austria for the Nazis

he engaged in bullying and intrigue, but such offences were not criminal under the Nuremberg Charter.

Schacht: He helped the rearmament of Hitler's Germany, but he opposed aggression and resigned when he realised Hitler was bent on war

Fritsche: Merely an underling of Goebbels, whose orders he carried out or passed on.

Jodl: The arch-planner of the war He signed the order to shoot Commandos and war prisoners.

Streicher: He infected the German mind with the virus of anti-Semitism.

Raeder: The idea of invading Norway was his before it occurred to Hitler He tried to dissuade the Fuehrer from attacking Russia, and urged war on Britain as "our main enemy."

The reactions

12 The world at war

You read in chapter 10 how Japan took control of Manchuria from China in 1931. Japanese leaders continued to look for ways of increasing their country's empire, and in 1937 they launched a full-scale invasion of China. A year earlier, Japan had made an agreement with Germany and Italy to resist Communism, but she did not immediately join Germany when the war in Europe began. The war in the Pacific did not begin until 1941 and it remained, to a large extent, a separate conflict. Although Germany and Japan were allies, their soldiers did not fight alongside each other, as did Britons and Americans. Britain and the USA were involved in the fighting both in Europe and the Pacific; Russia only declared war on Japan towards the very end.

The Pacific war

Pearl Harbor and after

At breakfast time on Sunday, 7 December 1941, Japanese aeroplanes swooped on the United States Naval base of Pearl Harbor in Hawaii. They had taken off from six aircraft carriers, 450 kilometres to the north.

Pearl Harbor: USS California *on fire*

Japanese troops advance into Burma. The main bridge had been destroyed in a vain attempt to halt their progress

Salute to the Rising Sun —Japanese troops on the border between Indo-China and Burma

In a devastating surprise attack, a large proportion of the American Pacific Fleet was destroyed or crippled. Nearly two hundred American planes were lost, most of them before they could get off the ground.

Four days later, Germany and Italy declared war on the United States. After two years of neutrality, America was now in the war with a vengeance. But nothing, it seemed, could halt the Japanese onrush.

YEAST-VITE
TONIC TABLETS
The Lightning Pick-Me-Up
For HEADACHE, NERVES, INDIGESTION, ETC.
7 o...1/4, 3/3 and 5/4 (including matchless tax)

BLACK-OUT
ZERO
HOUR
TO-NIGHT
UNTIL 8.34 A.M.
MOON 10.27 MOON 7.45
RISES AM SETS PM

Daily Express

No. 12,971   Saturday, December 20, 1941   One Penny

THE JAPS •
GO FORWARD •

BRITISH GARRISON ON INVADED HONGKONG ISLAND REPORTED TO BE MAKING LAST STAND AT VICTORIA PEAK, FORTIFIED PICNIC RESORT. PENANG ISLAND, MALAYA, EVACUATED; JAPS ADVANCE ON MAINLAND.

• RUSSIANS TAKE THREE MORE TOWNS
  FRONT, THREATEN GERMAN FLANK /
• BRITISH IN LIBYA TAKE DERNA AIRFIEL
  AXIS FORCES IN PORT OF DER

HONGKONG GARRISON
FIGHT TO THE LAST

'Final stand' at picnic mountain turned into a Gibraltar

HONGKONG, FIGHTING TO THE DEATH WITH SWARMS OF JAPANESE WHO LANDED YESTERDAY AT MANY POINTS ON THE ISLAND, REJECTED WITH SCORN A THIRD OFFER OF SURRENDER TERMS, AND THEN CAME SILENCE.

Late last night it was officially announced in London :—

"The report from Japanese sources that Hongkong has been in Japanese hands since this morning cannot be confirmed or denied, as no communication has been received from the colony since early this morning."

Berlin, quoting Tokyo reports, said the Japanese flag had been hoisted in the port of Hongkong, and that points of final British resistance were being broken.

Tokyo announced last night that the re

JAPS CLAIM A CAPITAL CITY

IN messages from Kow loon, the Japanese claim to have "occupied Victoria, the capital of Hongkong island."... The city extends along the coast for about 5 miles. The harbour of Hongkong Island covers an area of 10 square miles.

7,000,000 U.S. MEN TO MARCH

Express Staff Reporter

NEW YORK, Friday.
SEVEN million Americans will march to war during the next year.

That was the expectation in Washington tonight as the Senate and House of Representatives agreed to call men aged 20 to 44 inclusive into military service.

Throughout December, and on into the new year, they struck blow after blow. The extent of the Japanese success can be seen from the map below. For the Americans and British it was a diary of disaster.

This was the high point of Japanese success. They had now over-run American, British and Dutch possessions in Asia and had advanced rapidly across the Pacific. They were now the masters of South East Asia. But it was a mastery they found difficult, and in the end impossible, to maintain.

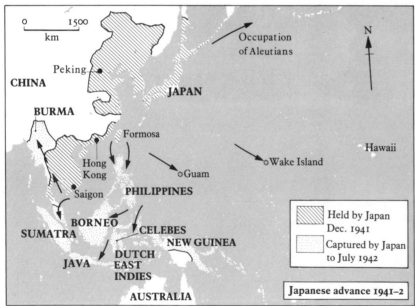

The battle of Midway and the Allied offensive

The turning-point came in two naval battles fought in May and June 1942. First in the Coral Sea and then more disastrously at Midway Island, the previously unbeatable Japanese navy was defeated. Thereafter, despite fanatical resistance, the Japanese were forced to retreat.

As the map below shows, there were three main thrusts in the Allied attack. American forces carried out a series of amphibious landings, island-hopping across the Pacific. Meanwhile, Australian, British and Indian troops were fighting a very different kind of war in the jungles of New Guinea and Burma.

Not even the efforts of the *kamikaze* pilots could halt the steady advance. They considered it an honour to die flying their planes packed

General MacArthur

One of a series of amphibious landings: American landing craft approach Guam

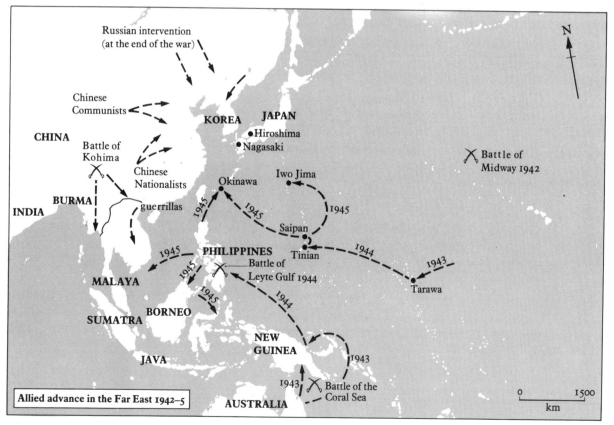

Allied advance in the Far East 1942–5

with high explosive on to the decks of enemy ships. But it was an act of
desperation against an enemy that was too powerful.

Admiral Ohnishi, the originator of the *kamikaze* attacks, wrote this
on the evening before he committed suicide in the traditional Japanese
manner of *hara-kiri*:

I wish to express my deep appreciation to the souls of the brave special
attackers. They fought and died valiantly with faith in our ultimate victory. In
death I wish to atone for my part in the failure to achieve that victory and I
apologise to the souls of these dead fliers and their bereaved families.

They had first been used at the beginning of 1945 in the defence of the
islands close to Japan. Here the Americans hoped to establish bases
from which to launch massive air strikes against the Japanese home-

*Kamikaze pilots receive a ceremonial
cup of sake from Admiral Ohnishi*

land. The islands of Iwo Jima and Okinawa finally fell, but not without long and bitter resistance by the defenders. More than 100 000 Japanese sacrificed themselves in the three months' battle to save Okinawa. American losses totalled about 13 000. If the Japanese were prepared to put up such a fight to defend Okinawa, what kind of resistance might the Allies expect to meet in an invasion of Japan itself? It was questions like this which led to one of the most fateful decisions of the war.

The machinery of war

The machinery of war: The dive bomber and the tank, main elements in Blitzkrieg, made possible the German Army's rapid advances in Europe

Radar, developed in Britain, added a new dimension to warfare

Hitler's secret weapons, the V1 bomb and the V2 rocket. Although they came too late to save Germany, they caused much damage in southern England

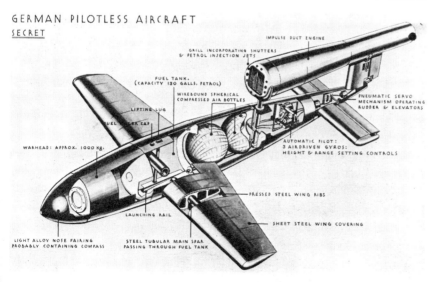

The machinery of war: The aircraft carrier and the landing craft were the chief weapons in America's fight-back against Japan in the Pacific. As in the First World War, German submarines were responsible for heavy losses amongst merchant shipping in the Atlantic

Landing Craft
BRITISH AND AMERICAN

L.C.P. (L)
LANDING CRAFT
PERSONNEL (LARGE)

L.C.A.
LANDING CRAFT ASSAULT

L.C.S. (M) Mk. I
LANDING CRAFT
SUPPORT (MEDIUM)

L.C.T. (5)
LANDING CRAFT
TANK

L.C.T. (4)
LANDING CRAFT TANK

L.C.T. (3)
LANDING CRAFT TANK

L.C.F. (3)
LANDING CRAFT FLAK
(THREE)

Using the evidence: the bomb that changed the world

DAILY EXPRESS

No. 14,094   Lighting-up: 9.39 pm to 4.33 am   TUESDAY AUGUST 7 1945   Weather: Cool, showers   One Penny

Smoke hides city 16 hours · after greatest secret weapon strikes

THE BOMB THAT HAS CHANGED THE WORLD

Japs told 'Now quit'

20,000 tons in golf ball

THE Allies disclosed last night that they have used against Japan the most fearful device of war yet produced—an atomic bomb.

It was dropped at 20 minutes past midnight, London time, yesterday on the Japanese port and army base of Hiroshima, 190 miles west of Kobe.

The city was blotted out by a cloud of dust and smoke. Sixteen hours later reconnaissance pilots were still waiting for the cloud to lift to let them see what had happened.

The bomb was a last warning. Now leaflets will tell the Japanese what to expect unless their Government surrenders.

So great will be the devastation if they do not surrender that Allied land forces may be able to invade without opposition.

ONE atomic bomb has a destructive force equal to that of 20,000 tons of T.N.T., or five 1,000-plane raids. This terrific power is packed in a space of little more than golf ball size.

Experts estimate that the bomb can destroy anything on the surface in an area of at least two square miles—twice the size of the City of London.

When it was tested after being assembled in a farmhouse in the remote desert of New Mexico, a steel tower used for the experiment vaporised; two men standing nearly six miles away were blown down; blast effect was felt 300 miles away.

And, at Albuquerque, 120 miles away, a blind girl cried "What is that?" when the flash lighted the sky before the explosion could be heard.

This was the first the world knew of the atomic bomb. With the destructive force of 20 000 tonnes of TNT, the bomb, which had taken scientists five years to produce, had been dropped on the Japanese city of Hiroshima the day before. The devastation it caused had been greater than even its makers anticipated. Were the Allies right to unleash such a horrifying weapon on mankind?

(1) Most of Hiroshima no longer exists. The impact of the bomb was so terrific that practically all living things, human and animal, were literally seared to death by the tremendous heat and pressure engendered by the blast. Buildings were crushed or wiped out. Those outdoors were burned to death and those indoors killed by the indescribable pressure and heat. The city is a disastrous ruin. The destructive force of the new bomb is indescribable, as is the terrible devastation caused. The dead were burned beyond recognition. The authorities are unable to obtain a definite check-up on casualties.

Radio Tokyo (overseas service)

(2) Outside the gate of the park, Father Kleinsorge found a faucet [tap] that still worked – part of the plumbing of a vanished house – and he filled his vessels and returned. When he had given the wounded the water, he made a second trip. This time, the woman by the bridge was dead. On his way back with the water, he got lost on a detour round a fallen tree, and as he looked for his way through the woods, he heard a voice ask from the underbrush, 'Have you anything to drink?' He saw a uniform. Thinking there was just one soldier, he approached with the water. When he had penetrated the bushes, he saw there were about twenty men, and they were all in exactly the same nightmarish state: their faces were wholly burned, their eyesockets hollow, the fluid from their melted eyes had run down their cheeks. (They must have had their faces upturned when the bomb went off; perhaps they were anti-aircraft personnel.) Their mouths were mere swollen, pus-covered wounds, which they could not bear to stretch enough to admit the spout of the teapot. So Father Kleinsorge got a large piece of grass and drew out the stem so as to make a straw, and gave them all the water to drink that way. One of them said: 'I can't see anything.' Father Kleinsorge answered as cheerfully as he could, 'There's a doctor at the entrance to the park. He's busy now, but he'll soon come and fix your eyes, I hope.'

J. Hersey, Hiroshima, 1946

Of those who survived the heat and the blast, many died later from the effects of radiation. Over thirty years after the event people are still dying.

(3) It was a secret perfectly kept.

Then when success was assured it was months before President Truman decided to use the bomb.

The inventors told Truman early in May that they were ready. The military wanted to use the missile at once.

Truman hesitated. Finally he asked Jimmy Byrnes, now Secretary of State, to make a study.

Byrnes went away for six weeks, and travelled to all the secret depots where the bomb was being assembled.

He returned to Washington with his recommendation. It was: Do not use it.

What caused them to change their mind is not known.

Daily Express, 7 August 1945

(4) I had realised, of course, that an atomic bomb explosion would inflict damage and casualties beyond imagination. On the other hand, the scientific advisers of the committee reported, 'We can propose no technical demonstra-

tion likely to bring an end to the war; we see no acceptable alternative to direct military use.' It was their conclusion that no technical demonstration they might propose, such as over a deserted island, would be likely to bring the war to an end. It had to be used against an enemy target.

The final decision of where and when to use the atomic bomb was up to me. Let there be no mistake about it. I regarded the bomb as a military weapon and never had any doubt that it should be used. The top military advisers to the president recommended its use, and when I talked to Churchill he unhesitatingly told me that he favoured the use of the atomic bomb if it might aid to end the war.

All that remained of Hiroshima   President Truman

Japanese victim of radiation

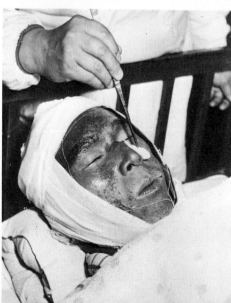

The question was asked in the early autumn of 1945: 'Did you approve or disapprove of the use of the atomic bomb?' In the United States eighty-five per cent of those sampled registered approval; in other countries the vote was as follows:

	Canada	Britain	France
	%	%	%
Approval	77	72	85
Disapproval	12	21	10
No opinion	11	7	5

Questions and further work

In discussing whether or not the Allies were right to use the atomic bomb against Japan, consider the following questions.
1 Was it necessary to drop the bomb on a populated area? Would a demonstration of its power, on some deserted area for example, have been as effective?
2 Could the Allies have been fully aware of the effects of atomic warfare?
3 Need a second bomb have been dropped?
4 Did the bombs used on Hiroshima and Nagasaki cause greater damage than the fire-storms created by incendiary bombs in some German cities?
5 Would the Allies have succeeded in defeating Japan without using them?
6 If so, did the bombs bring about a much earlier Japanese surrender?
7 Would the atomic bomb have been used against Germany if it had been ready in time?
8 Does the account given by the *Daily Express* of the way the decision was made agree with President Truman's recollections?

13 The Home Front

Waiting for the 'all clear' in a public air-raid shelter in London

As in 1914–18, the strains of war fell on civilians and fighting men alike. But, in the Second World War, the fighting was more widespread, the weapons more deadly, the treatment of conquered people more brutal. The final cost in human lives is unknown. In Europe alone it was not less than thirty-five million, of which the greater number were civilians. Once-great cities lay in ruins. Palaces, cathedrals, factories and railways were reduced to rubble. In parts of Germany ninety-three per cent of the houses had been destroyed by bombing. A new phrase was used to describe the thousands of refugees who were left without homes, families or even countries. They were 'displaced persons'.

'The bomber will always get through'

In Britain, over sixty thousand people were killed in bombing raids.

Bad though this was, it was far less than many experts had forecast. German bombers had been expected to attack in massive force immediately war was declared, killing and injuring millions of the population. It was feared that there would be widespread panic and uncontrollable disease amongst those who survived this onslaught. Plans were made to save as many lives as possible. Civil defence workers – firemen, ambulance drivers and ARP (Air Raid Precautions) wardens – were recruited and trained. Public air raid shelters were built. Specially-designed family shelters which could be erected in a garden were produced. With memories of the poison gas used in the trenches in the First World War, gas masks were issued to everybody in the country. There were different models for babies, children and even animals. Above all, there was a scheme to move children out of the cities to safer areas in the

How to make your shelter more comfortable. The Anderson shelter was designed to protect families from the effects of bombing

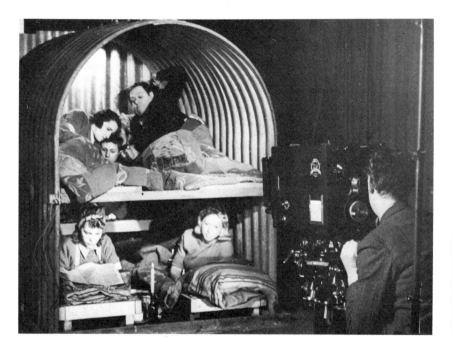

country. In the three days before war broke out, one and a half million children were evacuated. Carrying a gas mask, a day's food supply and a large luggage label tied round their neck, they set out by road and rail, to be dropped off along the route. It was often several days before their parents knew where their children were.

Babies had their own type of gas mask

I know that we rehearsed the evacuation every morning for a week. Each morning my sister and I would leave home with our packed sandwiches and clothes. We would say goodbye to our parents. Our labels were pinned on and I felt sick. We were not told the date of the real departure in case the Germans bombed the train . . . but at that time people seemed to find spies under their beds every night. So we had to leave home without knowing if we would return that day or not. We went through this awful ritual of goodbye every morning for a week. Every morning I felt sick and kissed my parents and felt I was leaving my name and identity with them.

Evacuation: London schoolchildren leave for safer areas

Women at war (1): members of the WAAF, and their mascot, prepare to hoist an anti-aircraft balloon

Women at war (2): a group of ATS volunteers learn the mysteries of an anti-aircraft gun

For this seven-year-old boy, and for many others, evacuation was a terrifying experience. Where were they going? If they ever returned, would they find their homes destroyed, their parents killed?

Scarcely had the prime minister finished telling the nation that war was declared, when the air-raid warning sirens sounded in London. This was it. Londoners filed into the shelters and waited for the bombs to fall. But nothing happened. The lone aeroplane which had been

spotted over the Channel turned out to be friendly, and the 'All Clear'
was given.

Where is the enemy?

King George VI wrote in his diary for 3 March 1940:

We have been at war for six months today.

Most people in this country, including the govt., have been surprised that
we have not suffered from air raids as was predicted. In the meantime, govt.
policy of the child evacuation scheme, so carefully worked out, has not been a
great success owing to lack of danger, & many children have returned to their
homes in cities & towns.

Bombs had fallen – faraway in the Orkneys in October. The first

*'Dig for Victory' takes on another
meaning: bomb damage in London,
January 1941*

civilian casualty was killed there in the middle of March. But the first bombing raid of the war on the mainland of Britain did not take place until 9 May 1940, near Canterbury. As a result, despite government warnings of the dangers, there had been a steady movement of evacuees back to more familiar surroundings. By Christmas, three-quarters of the children had returned. Evacuation had made many people aware for the first time of the conditions in which children from the cities normally lived. Large numbers of them were found to be in poor health, undernourished and verminous. There were frequent complaints about their unruly behaviour. The amount of money the government gave for their upkeep was felt to be far too small, and there were few regrets when they went back home.

For the population of Britain, as for the army in France, these were the months of the 'phoney war'. Far more deaths resulted from the complete night-time blackout which had been imposed at the beginning of September, than from enemy action. The restrictions were eased, although street lighting was still very dim and car headlights had to be masked. The total ban on theatres, cinemas and football matches was lifted. Few people continued to carry their gas mask. 'Hitler,' Chamberlain said, 'has missed the bus.' He was soon proved wrong.

London's burning

Far from having missed the bus, Hitler was simply waiting for the moment to strike. As Scandinavia was overrun and German forces swept into France, it was Chamberlain who was felt to have failed. Winston Churchill replaced him as prime minister. There was, he declared, to be no question of surrender.

We shall defend our island, whatever the cost may be, we shall fight on the beaches, we shall fight on the landing grounds, we shall fight in the fields and in the streets, we shall fight in the hills. . . .

With the fall of France, Britons prepared to do just that. Gun emplacements were built and anti-tank ditches dug. Place names were painted out and signposts removed. A citizens' army, the Local Defence Volunteers, had been formed in May. Renamed the Home Guard, it now stood ready to hurl itself against German tanks and paratroopers.

But it was in the air, not on land, that the German advance was halted. At first, the bombing raids were part of Hitler's invasion plan. When that was called off, they continued in an effort to destroy docks, railways, factories and morale. On both sides, there were those who believed that civilian populations would be so overwhelmed by the devastation caused by bombing, that they would lose the will to fight. In 1940 and 1941, it was the turn of the people of London and other British cities to suffer as the inhabitants of Warsaw and Rotterdam had suffered earlier. In the last three years of the war, British and American bombers wreaked even greater havoc on the cities of Germany.

The first of the big raids on London began at five o'clock on the

Dockland Family Is Bombed Five Times

BY "DAILY HERALD" REPORTERS

THE family of Mr. Jack Crawley, of Wapping, E., has been bombed five times.

Besides Mr. Crawley and his wife there are Kate, aged 28, Irene 23, Helen 16, Joe 9, and Grannie, who is 70.

They are all homeless and destitute.

The first time they were bombed they were on the stairway at their home. The house rocked like a rocking horse.

For the next raid they went to a shelter. An aerial torpedo followed them and made a crater outside the gates of the dock.

Their house was demolished in this raid.

So they decided to leave Wapping—and the raiders caught them in the open streets. Bombs fell near but they escaped.

Another bomb fell on them when they reached their destination and next night, when they had moved on again, they were bombed again.

"Look Out, Ref"

"LOOK out, ref., here's a bomber," shouted the goalkeeper at a football match in the suburbs of a South-East coastal town on Saturday.

Without waiting for the whistle the players ran for cover.

Within a few seconds 12 bombs dropped, one near the football ground, some on private houses and others on allotments.

It is believed that the raider, a Heinkel, was eventually brought down by A.A. fire.

The three casualties were all allotment workers.

Party Hit

BOMBS broke up an open-air party in a North-West town. Children were buried under the wreckage of a recreation ground pavilion in which they were having tea.

Rescue workers released everybody in half an hour.

It is believed that the bomb was aimed at a neighbouring greyhound track, where a meeting was in progress.

An eye-witness said: "The whole thing was over in 20 seconds.

"The bomber dived out of the clouds to about 500 feet, dropped two bombs, and then shot into the clouds again."

Wedding Goes On

MISS GLADYS GARRARD and Mr. Frank Harvey were being married in the centuries-old church of St. Margaret's, Ipswich, when the church windows were blown in.

A heavy calibre bomb had exploded a few feet from the porch.

The vicar whispered to the bridegroom, "What would you like to do?"

Frank looked at Gladys, said, "Carry on."

The two beribboned bridal cars were buried under rubble and the couple, followed by guests, set out on foot for the reception a couple of miles away.

He Just Dropped In

ONE British sergeant-pilot baled out over a London district yesterday and landed at the back of a house where a Press Association reporter has his home.

The pilot's first words to the reporter, after learning of his identity, were: "My father is your correspondent in Liverpool. Could you please try to let him know that I am safe after baling out?

"I got a Jerry before he got me," he added.

The pilot was surrounded by a cheering crowd as he landed. Regardless of the fact that a raid was still in progress dozens rushed to shake his hands.

His parachute was torn to shreds by people determined to have souvenirs of the event. Finally he was rescued from his admirers by soldiers.

Cows Lick Bomb

WHEN a German plane crashed across a lane near a village in South-East England wreckage was scattered over two fields.

Bombs rolled across one field and grazing cows began licking them.

Three of the crew baled out. Two were captured by Home Guards and the third was killed. His parachute failed to open.

London 1944: the results of one of the first flying-bomb attacks

difficult. Anti-aircraft guns forced the bombers to fly at a height which made it even more difficult. Public shelters, Anderson shelters and underground stations provided places of refuge. For these reasons, there were fewer deaths than had been thought likely. But, perhaps best remembered, is the work of the various Civil Defence organisations in saving lives.

In a booklet published in 1942, the Ministry of Home Security explained how this worked (see opposite page). The ARP warden reported the falling of a bomb, an 'incident', to the Control Centre for the area. If there was a fire, he also informed the local Fire Control. These controls ordered out the parties needed to deal with the incident. They could call on assistance from other centres within the region, if there were too many incidents for them to handle.

There were instances of panic and confusion, of people fleeing from the cities, of shops and homes being looted. But the period of the Blitz was also a time when people showed extraordinary courage, endurance and generosity. Neither in 1941, nor in the flying bomb attacks of 1944, was morale broken.

The effects of bombing

Despite the suffering it caused, it is doubtful whether the mass bombing of cities played a vital part in deciding the final outcome. On 14 November 1940, the centre of Coventry was largely destroyed in what was then the heaviest attack of the war. Yet trains and buses were running almost normally within a matter of days. Factories were soon back to something like full production. In July 1943, the RAF attacked the port of Hamburg. They dropped so many incendiaries that fire storms, with winds reaching 240 kilometres an hour, were created. The loss of life and destruction of houses was immense. But the effect of this and similar raids on German war production was small.

Rationing

Although the heaviest period of bombing ended in the middle of 1941, people's problems were by no means over. Britain still faced shortages. German U-boats were sinking large numbers of merchant ships in the Battle of the Atlantic. Factories were busy turning out the goods needed to fight the war. There were few luxuries, and even the necessities of life were often hard to come by. Food, petrol and clothing were rationed. Furniture was in short supply. People were urged to kill off the 'squander-bug' who would eat into the war effort.

Food rationing began in January 1940. It was at its most severe eighteen months later. If you compare a week's allowance then, with the amount that you eat in a week, you will see that it was not very generous. There was little more than a single decent helping in a week's supply of basic foodstuffs.

To help both the family diet and the country, people were encouraged to 'Dig for Victory'. Lawns, parks, patches of waste-land, all were used to grow vegetables. Carrots, which were said to help you to see in the blackout, formed the main ingredient in numerous recipes published by the Ministry of Food. Woolton pie, named after the Minister, was particularly popular. Hens, rabbits, even pigs, were fed on waste and raised in yards and gardens. By these means, although there were shortages, there was no starvation. Indeed, in many cases, people's diet was better balanced during the war than it had been before, and the general standard of health actually improved.

A week's food allowance was adequate but far from generous. It varied during the war years but in a typical week each person was allowed one shilling's worth (5p) of meat. Other food was rationed by weight: sugar, 225 g; fat, 225 g; jam or honey, 115 g; cheese, 85 g; coffee, 55 g; liquid milk, 1185 g. In addition, there was on average one real egg a fortnight

Wartime poster

A time of change

It was not just the bombs and the shortages that affected people's lives. Far more even than in the First World War, everyday life was controlled by government regulations. Conscription into the armed forces was introduced from the beginning. Britain was the only country to apply this to women also. Most of the half million women in the services at the end of the war were volunteers, however. As in the earlier war, the number of women employed in industry, agriculture and the civil service rose considerably. This helped to strengthen their demand for equal pay, much as that previous experience had strengthened the demand for the vote. Both men and women workers were directed into jobs where they could make the biggest contribution to the war effort. Similarly, the demands of war boosted industries like aircraft manufacture and electronics, where Britain had been falling behind.

As well as hardship and terror, the war also brought some benefits. Better health was one. Higher earnings was another. Average weekly

RAF Operations Room, Coastal Command Headquarters

earnings rose by about eighty per cent between 1938 and 1945. Thanks largely to government food subsidies, the cost of living rose by less than half of this. Unemployment, the great problem of the inter-war period, largely disappeared. In particular, far-reaching proposals were put forward to improve the future lot of those who had been called upon to make such sacrifices. The Beveridge Report of 1942 set down the basis of the welfare state which was put into effect after 1945. Even before the war ended, the 1944 Education Act set out to provide free and better schooling for all children.

The end of barbarism

Although the people of Britain faced much suffering and danger during these years, they were spared some of the horrors that confronted civilians elsewhere in Europe. Of the United Kingdom, only the Channel Islands were occupied. To live in an occupied country was to live in

A new Dark Age: concentration camp prisoners working in the clay-pits at Sachsenhausen

fear. Fear of being transported to a slave labour camp. Fear of being killed merely on suspicion of resisting the occupier, or simply out of revenge. Above all, there was the concentration camp, and the extermination of millions of people for no reason other than that they were Poles, or Russians, or Jews.

After the war, a German engineer described how he saw the massacre of 5000 Jews in a town in the Ukraine. They were driven out to a number of pits on the edge of the town.

An old woman with snow-white hair was holding a one-year-old child in her arms and singing to it and tickling it. The child was cooing with delight. The parents were looking on with tears in their eyes. The father was holding the hand of a boy about ten years old and speaking to him softly; the boy was fighting his tears. The father pointed to the sky, stroked his head and seemed to explain something to him.

At that moment the SS man at the pit shouted something to his comrade. The latter counted off about twenty persons. . . . They went down into the pit, lined themselves up against the previous victims and were shot.

The end of the war marked the end of what Churchill described as a 'new Dark Age'.

Using the evidence: the Blitz

The attack on the Arms Towns

Dates of main raids	Estimated enemy planes engaged	Total civilians killed in all raids to end of 1941		Estimated enemy planes engaged	Total civilians killed in all raids to end of 1941
Coventry			Bristol (and Avonmouth)		
14 November	400		24 November	50	
8 April	300	1236	2 December	100	
10 April	200		6 December	50	1159
			3–4 January	150	
Birmingham			16 March	150	
1 November	–		11 April	150	
19 November	350				
22 November	200	2162	Sheffield		
3 December	50		12 December		
11 December	200		15 December		
9–10 April	250		(2 nights)	300	624
			Manchester (with Salford and Stretford)		
			22–23 December (2 nights)	150	1005

Questions and further work

British newspapers described the bombing raids in great detail. But, as well as giving information, they were also used to boost civilian morale.
1 In what ways do the extracts on page 171:
   (a) show a light-hearted side to the bombing;
   (b) show that people remained cheerful and unafraid;
   (c) show that the fight against the effects of bombing was being won?
2 Imagine that you are a newspaper editor in 1940–41.
   Produce the front page of your newspaper:
   (a) describing one of the raids listed above.
   (b) including suitable photographs selected from those accompanying this chapter, with appropriate captions, and
   (c) a personal account of the raid by a member of one of the families in the photographs on pages 169 and 171.

14 Co-operation and conflict

New hopes

For two months in the middle of 1945 the representatives of fifty countries gathered in San Francisco. They came to consider plans for a new international organisation to take the place of the League of Nations. From their deliberations in the San Francisco Opera House emerged the United Nations. In the opening words of the Charter solemnly signed on 26 June, they were 'determined to save succeeding generations from the scourge of war, which twice in our lifetime has brought untold misery to mankind'.

As at Versailles twenty-five years previously, the statesmen who signed the Charter of the United Nations were optimistic. But they were

THE GENERAL ASSEMBLY

Administrative Tribunal

UN Emergency Force
UN Relief and Works
Agency

Committees,
subsidiary bodies

International
Court of Justice

Trusteeship Council

Security Council

Economic and Social
Council

Military Staff
Commission

Special bodies:
UNICEF (Children's Fund)
Commissioner for Refugees

International Atomic
Energy Agency

Disarmament
Commission

Regional Economic
Commissions

SECRETARIAT

Specialised
agencies

Commission on Co-ordination
Technical Assistance Board

The opening session of the General Assembly of the United Nations, October 1946

The United Nations

anxious not to repeat earlier mistakes. This time international peace and co-operation must be more than pious hopes. The organisation of the United Nations was intended to make it more effective in preventing war than the League had been. In addition to this major purpose, various specialised agencies were formed or taken over by the United Nations. Their aim (expressed in Article 1 of the Charter) was,

To achieve international co-operation in solving international problems of an economic, social, cultural, or humanitarian character, and in promoting and encouraging respect for human rights and for fundamental freedoms for all without distinction as to race, sex, language, or religion.

New conflicts

A month after the San Francisco meeting, the world's three most powerful politicians met in a former royal palace in Potsdam, not far from Berlin. They were the leaders of the alliance which had defeated Germany and which, a few weeks later, was to defeat Japan. Two of them, Stalin and Churchill, had met at various times before, most recently in February at Yalta in Russia. The third, President Truman of the United States, was a newcomer. Formerly vice president, he had become president on the death of Roosevelt, three months earlier. Halfway through the Potsdam Conference, Churchill was replaced by Clement Attlee, who became prime minister of Britain when the Labour Party won the General Election in July 1945. Of the Big Three who had planned the downfall of Hitler's Germany, only Joseph Stalin, dictator of Russia, remained in power during the years immediately after the war.

But neither death nor the ballot box were responsible for the break-

Churchill, Roosevelt, Stalin and their military advisers at the Yalta Conference, February 1945

up of the victorious alliance. As the war drew to a close, Britain and America on the one hand, and Russia on the other, became increasingly suspicious of each other. Russian armies were encamped in large areas of eastern Europe which they had occupied as the Germans retreated. They had pushed forward into the heart of Germany itself. Would Stalin be willing to surrender this opportunity of expanding Russian Communist influence? For his part, Stalin was wary of America's military and industrial strength. On the day after his arrival at Potsdam, Truman received a telegram from Washington. The world's first atomic bomb had been successfully detonated in the New Mexico desert. The United States was the only country in the world to possess such a devastating weapon. Once the common enemies had been defeated, how safe would Russia be? Such uncertainties explain the shift from co-operation to conflict between the former allies, in what was to be labelled the 'Cold War'.

As a result, the meetings at Potsdam were often stormy. Even so,

Churchill   Attlee

Truman

Stalin

The victors meet at Potsdam

agreement was reached on a number of points. Truman secured Stalin's promise that Russia would join the fighting against Japan; a promise which was duly kept. The final decisions on the fate of Germany and the recently-freed countries of Europe were made. President Truman returned home. He had gone to Potsdam anxious to maintain friendly relations with Russia. 'But,' he wrote later, 'the personal meeting with Stalin and the Russians . . . enabled me to see at first hand what we and the West had to face in the future. . . . Force is the only thing the Russians understand.'

The iron curtain

During the next few years divisions between Communist and non-Communist governments both in Europe and elsewhere, became more serious. They are divisions which still exist. As both sides accused the other of seeking to increase its influence, the threat of war was never very far away. The events of these years are fairly simple to relate. But, as you will see, very different accounts have been given of why they occurred.

In a speech he made in March 1946, Winston Churchill said:

From Stettin in the Baltic to Trieste in the Adriatic, an iron curtain has descended across the Continent. Behind that line lie all the capitals of the ancient states of central and eastern Europe.

Churchill gave this speech in Fulton, Missouri. By this time most American troops had returned home from Europe. Both the British and American armies had been greatly reduced, but Churchill wanted to warn his listeners of a new danger facing Europe. At Yalta it had been agreed that the Russian frontier should be moved westwards. The Russians, however, were also using the power of their army to set up Communist governments outside these areas. Churchill saw the growth of Communism as a threat to peace. The iron curtain was a barrier which shut off the peoples of eastern Europe from freedom.

Wary of America's military and industrial strength, Joseph Stalin in 1946

There is another way of looking at Stalin's actions after the war. That is to see them not as the beginnings of a Communist takeover, but as part of a policy of ensuring Russia's safety. If Russia was surrounded by friendly countries, any invasion from the west, like that of Hitler in 1941, would be less likely to succeed.

Whatever Stalin's motives were, within two years he had established a block of countries in eastern Europe dominated from Moscow. There were two exceptions. In Czechoslovakia a Communist government did not come to power until 1948. And in Yugoslavia, although there was a Communist government led by Marshal Tito, it did not accept Russian control.

The Truman Doctrine

Russian expansion had been formidable. Where would it stop? To the south lay Greece, Turkey and Persia. Through them Russia could gain access to both the Mediterranean and the Indian Ocean. Russian troops had remained in Persia after the war. In Greece the government was fighting a civil war against strong Communist-backed forces. None of the three was capable of resisting Russian influence alone. It was only as a result of Anglo-American pressure in the United Nations that the Russian troops were withdrawn from Persia, whilst both Greece and Turkey relied heavily on military and economic aid from Britain.

This was aid that Britain could ill afford. In February 1947 the American government was informed that British assistance to Greece and Turkey could no longer be continued. The United States, it seemed, would either have to take Britain's place, or accept yet more Communist governments. President Truman decided that not only must America give aid to Greece and Turkey, but they must also give

'Force is the only thing the Russians understand': President Harry Truman

active support and leadership to the non-Communist parts of the world. This policy became known as the Truman Doctrine.

As with much else in this period of history, the Truman Doctrine has been seen as both saving and threatening world peace. To the question 'Who threatened whom?' different answers have been given from either side of the iron curtain.

The seeds of totalitarian regimes are nurtured by misery and want. They spread and grow in the evil soil of poverty and strife. They reach their full growth when the hope of a people for a better life has died.

We must keep that hope alive. The free peoples of the world look to us for support in maintaining their freedoms.

If we falter in our leadership, we may endanger the peace of the world – we shall surely endanger the welfare of our own nation.

President Truman, 12 March 1947

The following opinion is taken from an article by a Russian historian.

The next step along the road of worsening relations with the USSR was the 'Truman Doctrine', which meant in reality the rearmament of Greece and Turkey and building bases in these countries for American strategic bombers. These actions were screened, of course, by pompous pronouncements about defending democracy and peace.

Re-building in West Germany under the Marshall Plan

The Marshall Plan

It was not just to Greece and Turkey that the United States offered help. Throughout Europe the recovery from the devastation of war was slow and painful. To help in the rebuilding, the American government was prepared to give men, money, machinery and materials to those countries which asked for them. This scheme was called the Marshall Plan after the American Secretary of State who first put it forward. The offer was open to all European countries, but Russia and her friends in eastern Europe declined to accept. In the end, fourteen countries received aid amounting to some twelve billion dollars through the Marshall Plan. It was a considerable boost to economic recovery.

Our policy is directed not against any country or doctrine but against hunger, poverty, desperation, and chaos. Its purpose should be the revival of a working economy in the world so as to permit the emergence of political and social conditions in which free institutions can exist.

George Marshall, 5 June 1947

However, Russian historians have interpreted American policy rather differently:

Thus the Marshall Plan, widely advertised as a plan 'to save peace', was essentially aimed at uniting the bourgeois countries on an anti-Soviet basis. Even right-wing politicians and publicists saw the Marshall Plan as the nucleus of a new Holy Alliance against Communism.

The Berlin Airlift

The reaction to the Marshall Plan was another sign of the growing split between the two groups of countries. In the middle of 1948 came the most serious clash between them thus far. It was in Germany. At the end of the war, the country had been divided into four occupation zones, controlled by the USA, the USSR, Britain and France. The capital, Berlin, which lay 160 kilometres inside the Russian zone, was divided in the same way, and linked to the western zones by recognised

Berlin divided: the border between the Russian and British zones

road, rail and air routes. In June 1948, the Russians closed all the land routes into Berlin from the west. It was, they claimed, necessary because the western powers had changed the currency in use in their zones. The Russians had not, and refused to allow the new money into Berlin. America, Britain and France, on the other hand, saw this as a move to try to force them to abandon Berlin. Their answer was to transport all supplies into Berlin by air.

Berlin Airlift: the millionth sack of coal being delivered from an American aeroplane

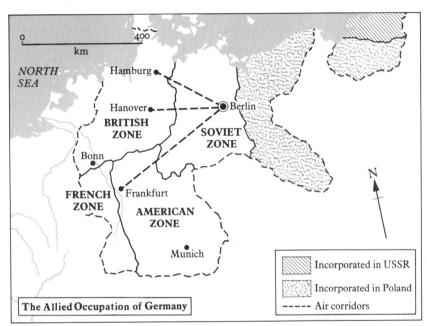

The airlift lasted for eleven months. During that time more than two and a quarter million tonnes of food and supplies were flown in by over a quarter of a million flights. Finally the land routes were reopened. The immediate crisis was over, but Berlin was to remain at the centre of the Cold War.

When we refused to be forced out of the city of Berlin, we demonstrated to the people of Europe that with their co-operation we would act, and act resolutely, when their freedom was threatened.

President Truman

Alternatively, the Russian view:

The Soviet authorities were ready to provide food and fuel for the population of the whole of Berlin, but the Western occupying powers deprived the inhabitants of West Berlin of the possibility of obtaining any help from Eastern Germany, and tried to represent the situation thus created as a blockade. . . .
The USA organised a so-called 'airlift' to supply West Berlin by air. . . .
This stunt served the purposes of propaganda and was also bound to intensify the 'Cold War'.

NATO

Even before this latest clash, the non-Communist countries had discussed the possibility of working more closely together. The Berlin crisis and the coming to power of a Communist government in Czechoslovakia made these discussions more urgent. On 4 April 1949 the document bringing the North Atlantic Treaty Organisation (NATO) into being was signed in Washington. The USA and Canada joined ten European countries in agreeing that 'an armed attack against one or more of them in Europe or North America shall be considered an attack against them all'. It was the most powerful military alliance there had ever been in peacetime.

Four months later the first Russian atomic bomb was exploded. The need for NATO to defend the West appeared even more obvious. But, after 1949, the conflict was no longer limited to Europe. (See chapter 17.)

The parties to this treaty reaffirm their faith in the purposes and principles of the Charter of the United Nations and their desire to live in peace with all peoples and all governments. They are determined to safeguard the freedom, common heritage and civilisation of their peoples, founded on the principles of democracy, individual liberty and the rule of law.

The North Atlantic Treaty

The Russians, however, denounced NATO:

The Soviet government did everything it could to save the world from being split into two military blocs. It appealed to the countries that might participate in the proposed organisation to hold back from joining an anti-Soviet alliance ... the Soviet Union issued a special statement analysing in detail the grave consequences affecting the entire international situation that would follow from the establishment of a military alliance of the Western powers.

All these warnings failed, however, and the North Atlantic Alliance came into being.

The end of Stalinism

On 5 March 1953 Stalin died. It was, as his daughter described it, a horrifying end.

For the last twelve hours the lack of oxygen was acute. His face altered and became dark. His lips were black and the features grew unrecognisable. The last hours were nothing but a slow strangulation. The death agony was terrible. He literally choked to death as we watched.

You can judge Svetlana's own view of her father by her comment that 'God grants an easy death only to the just'.

Stalin had held Russia in an iron grip for almost thirty years. Out of the struggle for power which followed his death emerged a very different kind of ruler – Nikita Khrushchev. It was hoped that under his leadership there would be not only an improvement of conditions inside Russia, but also some easing of tension in the world. There were hopeful signs. The activities of the secret police lessened. Their former chief, Beria, was the only one of Khrushchev's rivals to 'disappear' after being removed from power. The Eastern bloc countries were allowed greater independence. Whereas Stalin in his later years had scarcely travelled, even inside Russia, Khrushchev visited a number of countries either side of the iron curtain. Most startling of all, at a meeting of the Russian Communist Party in 1956, he accused Stalin of having made many mistakes. It was the beginning of a process of de-Stalinisation throughout the Communist world.

But, although there were changes, the difficulties were by no means ended. The Warsaw Pact of 1955 organised the countries of eastern Europe into a defensive system similar to that of NATO. In Hungary, a movement to remove the leaders imposed by Stalin, quickly became a revolt in favour of a complete break with Russia. It was crushed with great ferocity by Russian tanks. About 25 000 people were killed, and some 200 000 Hungarians fled abroad. There was to be no letting-go of the gains made in 1945.

A very different kind of ruler: Nikita Khrushchev in 1956

1945	Charter of the United Nations signed in San Francisco
	Potsdam Conference
1946	Churchill's 'iron curtain' speech
1947	Withdrawal of British aid from Greece and Turkey
	Truman Doctrine
	Marshall Plan
1948	Communist government in Czechoslovakia
	Berlin airlift
1949	NATO formed
	Russians exploded their first atomic bomb
1953	Death of Stalin
1955	Warsaw Pact formed
1956	Hungarian Revolution

Using the evidence: the Hungarian rising, 1956

(1) ... after the war the situation became even more complicated. Stalin became even more capricious, irritable and brutal; in particular his suspicion grew. His persecution mania reached unbelievable dimensions. ... Stalin's mania for greatness ... suspicion and haughtiness not in relation to individuals in the USSR but in relation to whole parties and nations. ...

Extracts from Khrushchev's speech to the Russian Communist Party,
25 February 1956

(2) I have no objection to saying in open session what I have said before: namely, that we shall never have a secure peace or a happy world so long as Soviet Communism dominates one-third of all the peoples that there are, and is in the process of trying at least to extend its rule to many others. These people who are enslaved are people who deserve to be free, and who, from our own selfish standpoint, ought to be free because if they are the servile instruments of aggressive despotism, they will eventually be welded into a force which will be highly dangerous to ourselves and to all the free world.

Therefore, we must always have in mind the liberation of these captive peoples. Now liberation does not mean a war of liberation. Liberation can be accomplished by processes short of war.

John Foster Dulles, US Secretary of State, 15 January 1953

Hungarians trample on a broken statue of Stalin

(3) People are jumping up at the tanks, throwing hand grenades inside and then slamming the driver's windows. The Hungarian people are not afraid of death. It is only a pity that we can't stand for long. . . .

Hungarian news agency report, 4 November 1956

(4) Ten years ago today, the Hungarians rose briefly against the men behind their masters. It was a spontaneous gesture in favour of change. The rising was put down by foreign troops. Some of the leaders who had tolerated or sympathised with the rising were murdered by the foreign authorities. . . .

The nation that endured and survived this shattering disappointment has recovered. . . . I would dare to set out their attitude like this. . . .

1 I am proud to be Hungarian – enormously, continuously, excitedly proud. I share in any success of this country, no matter who or what has engineered it.

2 I have no time for this government. I suppose I would join the party if it were necessary as a means of getting a good job. . . .

5 Life here is not bad, I'd like more books and newspapers from the West.

I'd like more freedom of discussion and criticism. . . .

7   I believe that Western foreign policy is completely wrong. . . . Colonialism and imperialism are wicked and still flourish.

Patrick O'Donovan, Hungary Ten Years After, 1966

(5) The Voice of America and other agencies would begin to stir up the resistance spirit behind the iron curtain, letting the Poles, Czechs and others know that they had the moral backing of the US government.

Next, he said, resistance movements would spring up among patriots. . . .

Report of a speech by Dulles, New York Times, 27 August 1952

(6) WARSAW PACT AND UNIFIED COMMAND ACCORD
May 14 1955

In accordance with the pact of friendship, co-operation and mutual assistance between the People's Republic of Albania . . . the Hungarian People's Republic . . . the Union of Soviet Socialist Republics and the Czechoslovak Republic, the signatory states have decided to set up a unified command of armed forces. . . . the contracting parties . . .

Taking into consideration at the same time the situation which has arisen in Europe . . . the formation of a new military alignment in the form of the West European Union with the participation of Western Germany, which is being remilitarised, and her inclusion in the North Atlantic bloc, which increases the danger of a new war . . .

The Illustrated London News, 3 November 1956

(Left.)
RUSSIA, THE WEST, AND THE SATELLITE COUNTRIES IN A MAP WHICH THROWS MUCH LIGHT ON THE SITUATION IN EASTERN EUROPE. A POINT OF GREAT INTEREST WHICH EMERGES IS THE RELATIVE STRENGTH OF THE RUSSIAN AND NATIVE FORCES IN VARIOUS COUNTRIES, AS AT OCT. 23. IN THE EVENT OF POLAND AND HUNGARY COMPLETELY THROWING OFF THE RUSSIAN YOKE, THE IMPORTANCE OF CZECHOSLOVAKIA AS THE ONLY PHYSICAL LINK BETWEEN RUSSIA AND EAST GERMANY IS MUCH INCREASED.

Portraits of Rakosi are burnt in the streets of Budapest. During Stalin's lifetime, Rakosi had been the feared and hated dictator of Hungary

Have decided to conclude the present treaty of friendship, collaboration and mutual assistance. . . .

(7) The world knows that in the past three days Soviet forces in Hungary have been ruthlessly crushing the heroic resistance of a truly national movement for independence, a movement which, by declaring its neutrality, proved that it had been no threat to the security of the Soviet Union.

Letter from the British prime minister to the Soviet premier,
6 November 1956

(8) First, we must understand that Russia is just as frightened of attack by the Western Alliance as we are of attack by her. She therefore has *her* deterrent. Part of her overall security is the belt of satellite nations in eastern Europe. Any move by the Western nations which suggested that they might help the satellite countries to regain their freedom would meet with instant counter-action by Russia. Similarly on our part, if Russia should bring pressure to bear on any part of the NATO area.

Field-Marshal Montgomery, Memoirs

Questions and further work

1 Many students took took part in the uprising.

Referring to the evidence in Documents 1–4, consider these arguments that might have been raised in a discussion between students for and against joining in the revolt. Prepare both a case in favour of rebellion, and one against.

(i) Khrushchev's speech has shown that the Russians are prepared to make changes in Eastern Europe;

'It is only a pity that we can't stand for long': Budapest citizens and Russian tank

(ii) Khrushchev's speech was an attack on Stalin's personality, not on his policy;

(iii) We cannot possibly hope to defeat Russian troops;

(iv) The Western powers have said that they will support us;

(v) I am prepared to wait for changes to take place gradually;

(vi) The United States has said that she is not prepared to go to war in order to help us gain our freedom;

(vii) A Hungarian should be proud to risk his life in order to free his country from foreign rulers;

(viii) Both Russia and the Western countries are equally as bad – they both have colonies;

(ix) The existence of the AVO (the Hungarian secret police) cannot be tolerated any longer;

(x) There is massive support for the rebellion;

(xi) Provided we are brave, and our tactics are right, even civilians can gain some success against tanks;

(xii) The important thing is to be proud of our country, and not to worry about who governs it;

Are there any other points which you feel should be raised in this discussion?

What would your final decision be?

2 You saw in this chapter how Russian historians have given a different interpretation of events during this period, from the one generally accepted in the West.

Write an account of the revolt in Hungary as it might be written by a historian justifying Russia's actions, using the following points as a guide:

(i) The West had been stirring up anti-Russian feeling in Hungary;

(ii) Hungary had treaty obligations to Russia;

(iii) Russia was prepared to allow Hungarians greater freedom than they had before 1953;

(iv) Russia was threatened by NATO;

(v) After 1955 Russia and Eastern Europe were faced with a new danger from an old enemy;

(vi) Hungary was trying to withdraw from her treaty obligations;

(vii) Hungary was vital to the defence of Russia;

(viii) The Western powers would have reacted in precisely the same way.

Use the evidence contained in Documents 5 – 8, and any other evidence you consider relevant, to support your case.

15 The end of empires

The saint, the statesman and the soldier

It was late in the afternoon of 30 January 1948. A tiny, frail, old Indian came out of a house in Delhi. He wore the plain white cotton clothes of a peasant. Supported by his two young grand-nieces, he made his way slowly to the wooden platform where he was to conduct evening prayers. A crowd of some five hundred people waited to greet him. As he reached the platform, a young man stepped from the crowd, pulled out a revolver, and shot him three times. Half an hour later, Mohandas Karamchand Gandhi, revered by millions of Indians as 'Mahatma' or 'Great Soul', was dead.

A year earlier, a 38-year-old teacher and lawyer had returned to his home in the British colony of the Gold Coast, after studying in the United States and Britain. His few possessions were packed in a cardboard suitcase. In 1951, whilst he was serving a prison sentence, the political party which he now led won a general election. Released from prison, he became prime minister, then president, and finally 'Osagyeto' ('Redeemer') of his country. It was no longer the Gold Coast, but Ghana, the first black African colony to gain independence. Kwame Nkrumah was its first leader. On 24 February 1966, whilst the 'Redeemer' was in an aeroplane on his way to Peking, the leading

The saint, Mahatma Gandhi

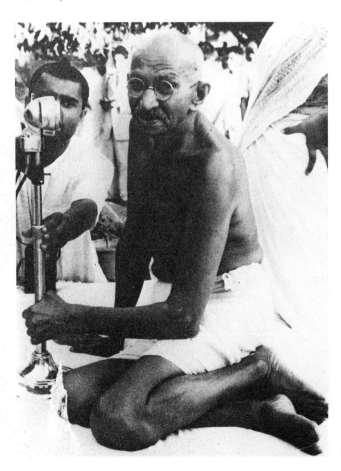

The statesman, Kwame Nkrumah on a visit to Britain in 1

generals in his army back home seized power. Nkrumah had been an energetic but spendthrift ruler. The man who had arrived with one suitcase went into exile with a fortune estimated at £2½ million.

Colonel Jean Schramme, nicknamed 'Black Jack' in spite of his fair hair, was the commander of a band of mercenaries. Mercenaries are soldiers who hire themselves out to fight for whoever can afford to pay them. In the 1960s there were many mercenaries fighting in the Congo, the vast area in the centre of Africa most of which had once belonged to Belgium. Schramme, himself a Belgian, had lived there since he was fourteen. Now 37, his knowledge of local languages was greater than his knowledge of military matters. In 1967 he and the 150 men of his No. 10 Commando were besieged in a small town by the Congolese Army. A journalist who managed to slip into the town described the mercenaries he met.

The 'cowboy' image was strong – almost obligatory. They bristle with arms – some actually carrying two pistols slung low around the hips in the true *Bonanza* style – they delighted in dressing up, often with looted clothes; and their jeeps were loaded with drink as well as arms and ammunition. They walked with a swagger.

Most of them, he reported, 'had not the remotest idea what was going on'.

The soldier, Colonel 'Black Jack' Schramme

These three men – Gandhi, Nkrumah and Schramme – had little in common. But they were all deeply involved in the break-up of the European empires in Asia and Africa. Their lives illustrate the successes and the failures, the idealism and the violence that were part of that upheaval.

The jewel divided

For two centuries India had been the 'brightest jewel' in the crown of the British Empire. But, as you read in chapter 1, there were many Indians who yearned for independence, even before the First World War. Congress, the Indian Nationalist Party, had held its first meeting as early as 1885. But it was fifty years later, in 1935, that the Government of India Act was passed, which looked forward to the day when India would be self-governing.

The years between had been far from peaceful, and one incident in particular raised an outcry not just in India, but throughout the world. In April 1919 a British officer, Brigadier-General Dyer, had ordered his men to open fire on a public meeting in the city of Amritsar; 379 people were killed and 1200 others were wounded. There had earlier been serious riots in Amritsar; four Europeans had been killed and public meetings banned. Even so, the action taken by Brigadier-General Dyer in ordering his troops to fire into an unarmed crowd was, as Winston Churchill described it in the House of Commons, 'a monstrous event'. Churchill's words came too late, however, and after the massacre at Amritsar, support for Mahatma Gandhi spread.

Gandhi was fiercely opposed to British rule in India. He became leader of the Congress Party, but the method he preached was civil disobedience – resistance, but non-violent resistance. Not all Indians, however, even some who claimed to be followers of Gandhi, were willing to use peaceful means. The last thirty years of British India were marked by large-scale rioting, killings and bombings.

Some of the most violent fighting took place not between Indians and the forces of British rule, but among Indians: between Moslem and Hindu. Some eighty million Moslems lived in India. They feared what might happen to them if the British were to hand over power to a Hindu-dominated Congress. Thus was born the idea of a separate Moslem state to ensure their safety. With increasing vigour, Muham-

Lord Mountbatten addresses the Pakistan Parliament; Muhammad Jinnah is sitting on his left

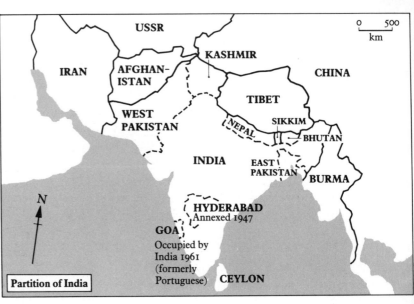

Partition of India

mad Jinnah, leader of the Moslem League, pressed for partition. The country should be divided – India for the Hindus, and a new state for the Moslems.

Not only Congress, but the British government also, resisted the Moslem League's demands. If there was to be self-government, it must be for a united India. The new viceroy, Lord Mountbatten, quickly recognised that such a policy simply would not work. When the transfer of power took place on 15 August 1947, two countries – India and Pakistan – emerged.

In an attempt to overcome some of the problems, Pakistan was divided into two blocks – West and East Pakistan (the latter is now Bangladesh). But no amount of care could prevent several million people from finding themselves on the wrong side of the frontier. In the two-way rush of Hindus to India and Moslems to Pakistan, there were scenes of utter confusion, destruction and wholesale slaughter. Although Gandhi's presence was a calming influence in Bengal, one danger area, there was nothing he could do to prevent the butchery in the Punjab, or the Indian capital, Delhi. The beginnings of independence were marked by the massacre of countless thousands. The murder of Gandhi by a Hindu fanatic was part of this tragic story.

Freedom for Africa

Shortly after the ending of the Second World War, a conference was held in Manchester. It met in a small, dreary hall. Amongst the two hundred delegates to this fifth Pan-African Congress, was Kwame Nkrumah. The assistant secretary was Jomo Kenyatta, later to become President of Kenya, but then a farmworker in Sussex. He was so little

The Pan-African Congress meets in Manchester, November 1945

known that in an article published by *Picture Post* he was described as being from Abyssinia.

Although the British press paid little attention to the conference, it was an important step on the road to African independence. In their speeches and resolutions, delegate after delegate called for equality and freedom for Africans. Some thought that force was the only way. Other speakers were less violent. But the message on the placards was clear: 'Freedom For All Subject Peoples'.

The Second World War played an important part in the movement to free Africa. By 1945, countries like Britain and France, which had large colonies in Africa, had neither the strength nor the wealth to hold on to their colonies against the will of the populations there. Africans had fought alongside Europeans in the war. They came to feel that, like the people conquered by the Nazis, they too had lost their freedom. As one future African leader wrote:

... World War II taught the African most powerful ideas. During the war the Allied Powers taught the subject peoples (and millions of them!) that it was not right for Germany to dominate other nations. They taught the subject peoples to fight and die for freedom. . . .

Educated men like Kwame Nkrumah returned to their countries determined to end colonial rule. The example of India made them even more determined.

The success of the independence movement in Africa can be measured by comparing these two maps, showing the areas under white control.

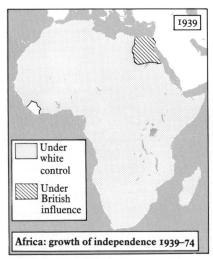

Key:
- Under white control
- Under British influence

Africa: growth of independence 1939–74

For the most part, it was a peaceful process. But there were some exceptions. Kenya was one. Between 1952 and 1955 a movement known as the Mau Mau attacked the farms of white settlers, burning and killing where they struck. Kenyatta was accused of leading the guerrillas, and although that was never proved, he was imprisoned.

British troops were used to combat the attacks. Kenya finally became independent in 1963. In the early 1970s, Portugal fought a long drawn out struggle against guerrilla freedom fighters in the colonies of Angola and Mozambique, both of which became independent in 1975.

Problems of freedom

The history of African countries after independence, however, has not always been peaceful. Freedom has produced its difficulties as well as its triumphs.

Many problems arose because the frontiers drawn by nineteenth-century European politicians on the map of Africa were often quite artificial. For one thing, they paid little attention to such natural boundaries as lakes or rivers. One odd exception to this was the border between Kenya and what used to be Tanganyika. Until 1919 Tanganyika was ruled by Germany. Kaiser Wilhelm II asked his grandmother, Queen Victoria, for a favour. Would she agree to the boundary being drawn so as to give Germany the honour of ruling over the highest mountain in Africa, Kilimanjaro? As a result, the boundary had a strange kink.

More seriously, the frontiers paid no heed to the boundaries which existed between tribes. Tribes were split between one country and another. A single country could contain members of several tribes who might have been enemies for centuries. At best, they would speak different languages and come from different backgrounds.

Not surprisingly, it has often been difficult to create a sense of unity,

Putting the finger on a Mau-Mau suspect

Chaos in the former Belgian Congo

a sense of being part of a country. Age-old tribal rivalries have flared up into bloody civil wars. One of the worst was in Nigeria in 1967, when one part of the country attempted to break away and form the separate state of Biafra. The three-year war which followed was brutal and vicious. To the Ibos of Biafra it was a war to avoid extermination. They would win, their leader Colonel Ojukwu said, because:

The enemy believes that lead will win this war, but lead does not win wars. It is the heart that wins wars. They have no heart, they've got a lot of lead. We have heart and very little lead and are using both to very great advantage.

Despite Nigeria's superiority in men and weapons, the Biafrans were not easily crushed.

Mercenaries mopping up in Stanleyville in the Congo

Similar violence took place in the Congo, in which Schramme and his mercenaries were involved. There were some 140 tribes in the Congo, speaking some thirty different languages. But there the problem was not caused just by tribal conflict. When the Belgians withdrew in 1960, they had made few preparations for the new nation's independence: they had made no attempt to train the people for self-government. The chaos which followed lasted for almost ten years.

A Commonwealth of Nations

A happier story has been the development of the British Commonwealth. As the former British colonies became independent, the majority of them joined with Britain to form the Commonwealth. This is held together by ties of friendship, rather than by formal treaties or alliances. The prime ministers of the Commonwealth countries meet at a conference held every year in London. Here they discuss problems and try to reach acceptable solutions. It does not always work. What is perhaps surprising is that with so many different countries represented, it works at all!

Using the evidence: apartheid in South Africa

How do we know?

The treatment by the government of South Africa of the black African population has aroused bitter argument. Their policy of 'separate development' – apartheid – is fiercely condemned by many other countries, and jealously defended by South Africa. In such a situation, it is not always easy to separate fact from fiction; statements designed to mislead, from those seeking to inform.

It is important for the historian to be able to distinguish between:
(i) matters of *fact* about which everybody would agree; and
(ii) matters of *judgement* about which people might disagree.
For example, compare these two statements:
(a) This car has a 1500 c.c. engine.
(b) This car is better than that one.
Statement (a) is a matter of fact; and statement (b) is a matter of judgement.

Separate development or racialism?

Before reading the evidence, you should find out the meanings of –

Afrikaan, Bantu, Bantustan, Bushman, Hottentot. You may also need to refer to this datelist:

1652	Dutch settlement at the Cape of Good Hope
1814	British took over government of Cape Province
1833	Dutch settled in Orange Free State and Transvaal
1910	Union of South Africa joined British and Dutch areas under one government
1948	Policy of apartheid began
1950	Population divided into four groups according to race – Bantu, white, coloured and Asiatic
1959	Government decided to establish Bantustans (the first of these, Transkei, was set up in 1962)
1961	South Africa was forced to leave the Commonwealth

(1) More than three hundred years ago two population groups, equally foreign to South Africa, converged in rather small numbers on what was practically an empty country. Neither group colonised the other's country or robbed him by invasion and oppression. Each settled and gradually extended his settlements, and in the main each sought a different part in which to dwell. There were clashes and frontier wars, and border areas were conquered, but since then the white man has added, and is adding, more land to the Bantu areas from that portion which he himself settled and intended to be his own.

The first point is, therefore, that there was no colonialism, only separate settlement by each group, nearly simultaneously, and each had the chance for more than 300 years to develop his country to serve his growing population group.

Information Service of South Africa, *Progress through Separate Development: South Africa in Peaceful Transition*

South African winner of the Nobel Prize for Peace: Albert Luthuli, a former Zulu chief, receives the prize in 1961

(2) The Dutch formed their first settlements at the Cape about the middle of the seventeenth century, and have been in South Africa ever since. There are, in fact, several Afrikaans myths that need exploding: perhaps the most virulent one is that there was no one at the Cape on their arrival. It is quite true that the Bantu peoples were coming south and had not reached the Cape when the Dutch arrived, although they seem to have been farther south than the Boers today claim. But to say that the place was empty was to overlook a lot of Bushmen and a very great many Hottentots. . . . Between being systematically exterminated and interbreeding with the Dutch to form the present-day 'coloured' population of South Africa, the Hottentots have all but disappeared and the Bushmen are fast disappearing. The Dutch. . . met the Bantu coming south and fought some bloody wars with them.

Paul Bohannan, *African Outline*

Separate development in Johannesburg

(3) The policy [of apartheid] will aim at concentrating, in so far as it is possible, the main . . . groups and sub-groups of Bantu in their own separate territories, where each group will be able to develop into a self-sufficient unit.

Dr Verwoerd, Minister of Native Affairs, 1948

(4) All the Bantu have their permanent homes in the Reserves and their entry into other areas and into the urban areas is merely of a temporary nature and for economic reasons. In other words, they are admitted as work-seekers, not as settlers.

Dr Eiselen, Secretary of the Department of Bantu Administration and Development, 1959

(5) Everyone's infected. I visited an African man dying in hospital. He has suffered greatly under apartheid. His face is stretched and beautiful, his real self very far away. But the machinery of his personality feebly grinds out racist nonsense about the tribal inferiority of the other patients.

Pat Williams (white South African), *Return to Unease*, 1966

(6) *The Rand Daily Mail* (28/7) reported a meeting addressed by Chief P. R. Mphephu, Chief Councillor of the Venda Territorial Authority during the prime minister's visit. The chief said in the course of his speech of welcome that his people appreciated what the government was doing and would do in

'*They are admitted as work-seekers*': recruits to the gold-mines undergo a medical examination. They will then be issued with a pass book which they must carry when they enter white areas

the future, and that they intended developing step by step with government guidance and not hurriedly. His words were greeted with laughter and expressions of shock. He was greeted by more laughter when he said a film he had seen recently depicting a nation which got into trouble because it received independence before it was ready for it, proved that his territory would get into trouble if it were granted self-rule now. There were murmurs from the audience when Chief Mphephu said his people were going to help the government fight terrorists whom he described as troublemakers.

Africa Digest, 1971

(7) The government . . . have no intention of creating African areas which are genuinely self-supporting. . . . If such areas were indeed self-supporting where would the Chamber of Mines and the Nationalist farmers get their supplies of cheap labour? . . .

. . . To anyone who knows these poverty-stricken areas (the Reserves), sadly lacking in modern communications, power-resources, and other needed facilities, the idea of industrial development seems far-fetched indeed. The beggarly £500 000 voted to the so-called 'Bantu Investment Corporation' by Parliament is mere eyewash: it would not suffice to build a single decent road, railway line, or power station.

Nelson Mandela, *No Easy Walk to Freedom*

(8) Population of South Africa today (millions)

Bantu	10·9
white	3·1
coloured	1·5
Asian	0·5

Questions and further work

1 Copy out this table and tick each of the statements which you consider to be true:

Europeans first settled in South Africa in the middle of the seventeenth century.

Europeans were the first people to live in the area near the Cape of Good Hope.

Relations between the Dutch and the Bantu were peaceful.

After 1959, black South Africans were not allowed to work outside the Bantustans.

After 1959, black South Africans were not allowed to settle outside the Bantustans.

All white South Africans support the policy of apartheid.

Some Bantu leaders support the policy of the government.

---

2 With each of these pairs of statements, decide which is a fact, and which is a judgement:

(a) The Europeans grew crops and developed those areas of South

Africa where they settled.

The Europeans have a right to keep those areas they developed for themselves.

(b) The policy of apartheid is the best way of ensuring that people of different races live in harmony.

Apartheid is a policy of separate development.

(c) There have been civil wars in some African countries after independence.

Black Africans are incapable of establishing peaceful governments.

(d) White Africans are superior to black Africans.

Some people believe that people of different races are inferior.

3 Look at each of these pairs of judgements about the situation in South Africa, and write out the one which you support:

(a) Africans are allowed outside the Bantustans so that they may share in the prosperity of South Africa.

Africans are allowed outside the Bantustans in order to provide a labour force in white South African areas.

(b) The Bantustans will eventually become sufficiently prosperous to provide for all the needs of their populations.

The Bantustans do not possess sufficient resources ever to become prosperous.

(c) Apartheid is the fairest policy for all South Africans.

Apartheid means that some sections of the population of South Africa can never become as well-off as others.

(d) The relationship between the size of the various racial groups in South Africa and the areas of land they possess is unjust.

The amount of land a racial group possesses should depend not on their numbers, but on the degree of effort they put into developing it.

16 Sun, Chiang and Mao

Above left Sun Yat-sen was born in 1867, the son of a peasant family. He was educated in Hawaii and the USA, finally training as a doctor in Hong Kong

Above right Chiang Kai-shek was born in 1887, into a wealthy family of landowners. He trained as an army officer in Japan. Later he joined Sun Yat-sen and the Kuomintang

Right Mao Tse-tung in 1938. Like Sun he came from a peasant family. He quarrelled with them and left home to go to high school and college; one of the first members of the Chinese Communist Party

Fall of the Manchus

Since the seventeenth century, China had been ruled by the Manchu emperors. They resisted any attempts at change and were despised by revolutionaries like Sun Yat-sen. In the twelve years after 1899 he tried ten times to overthrow them. None of these efforts succeeded, but support for Sun's movement was growing.

On 9 October 1911, whilst Sun was in the United States, a bomb exploded accidentally in Hankow in a workshop used by the revolutionaries. The uprising had been planned for a week later, but such was the disturbance caused by the unexpected explosion that it began the following day. This time the revolution was successful. Within four months the last of the Manchu emperors, a boy of six, had abdicated. Sun returned to become the first president of the new republic of China.

The republic in difficulties

Sun's first period in office was short. The revolutionaries had been forced to rely on a powerful general, or warlord, Yuan Shi-kai, to help overthrow the Manchus. When Yuan insisted that he be made president, the day after the republic officially came into existence, Sun's supporters were not powerful enough to resist. They could only hope that Yuan would continue the work of the revolutionaries and try to improve conditions for the great mass of the Chinese people, make the country more democratic and free from foreign interference. But Yuan had no intention of doing anything of the sort. At first he simply took no notice of the wishes of the national assembly in which Sun's Kuomintang (Nationalist) Party had most of the seats, and he expelled all but his own supporters. Those that were left elected him president for life. Yuan's next step was to try to become emperor.

He very nearly succeeded. The republic for which Sun had struggled for so long seemed on the point of disappearing almost before it had started. It was saved by the actions of the Japanese, who threatened to seize control of China. Yuan's failure to stand up to the Japanese demands lost him much support, and in 1916 he died. His illness was brought on, it was said, by his disappointment at not becoming emperor.

But his death plunged China into even greater chaos. With nobody to keep the hundreds of warlords in check, each one set himself up as the ruler of as big an area as he could control, using his private army to terrorise the local population. Sun Yat-sen was once more chosen as president by the assembly, to which the Kuomintang members had returned, but he had little real power. His government ruled only a small area of southern China, and even there it depended on the protection of a warlord.

Sun looked for help outside China. Only one country was prepared to support him, a country which was also without friends – Soviet Russia.

Soviet advisers went to Canton and helped to make the Kuomintang stronger by reorganising it and by training an army. They also helped to start the Chinese Communist Party in 1921. Three years later the two parties joined, and Sun's position looked more promising. He was on the point of starting an expedition against the warlords of the north in 1925, when he died. It was left to his friend, brother-in-law and lieutenant, Chiang Kai-shek, to embark on the northern expedition in the following year.

The warlords overcome

Chiang's forces swept triumphantly northwards, taking over armies as they advanced. By the time he reached Shanghai at the end of March 1927, no opposition remained in southern China. However, Chiang suspected, with good reason, that once the warlords had been finally defeated, the Communists would try to seize control of the Kuomintang, and he determined to strike first. In April all the Communists that could be found in Shanghai were slaughtered on Chiang's orders. The

China in 1926. A group of workers accused of strike-breaking being tried by their fellow workers in Canton

WITH WRISTS BOUND BY CORDS : CHINESE WOMEN AND MEN, CHARGED WITH STRIKE-BREAKING, BEFORE A TRIBUNAL OF STRIKERS AT CANTON.

killings continued in other cities. Those who escaped were forced to seek refuge in the mountains. Confident that the Communists were no longer a threat, Chiang resumed his march north. By 1928 he had captured Peking, and for the first time since the fall of the Manchus, almost the whole of China was united under one ruler.

Communists in hiding

In the mountain wilderness of south-central China, the remaining Communists set up the Kiangsi-Hunan soviet, under the guidance of Mao Tse-tung. For six years this small state survived repeated attacks from Chiang's much larger forces. Four times his army advanced, and four times they were forced to retreat, defeated by Mao's guerrilla tactics and the difficulties of the mountains. Rather than face Chiang's

Chiang Kai-shek's soldiers set off on one of their unsuccessful campaigns to drive the Communists from the Kiangsi-Hunan soviet

Four times the Kuomintang army advanced into the mountains, and four times they were forced to retreat

armies in a pitched battle where sheer weight of numbers would have made them unbeatable, Mao's orders to his troops were: 'when the enemy advances we retreat, when he halts, we harry him, when he retreats we pursue'. On the fifth occasion in 1934, Chiang, having by now learnt his lesson, adopted a new strategy. By surrounding the Communists and cutting off their vital supplies and reinforcements, he hoped to starve them into surrender. It was a plan which almost worked.

The Long March

As the situation inside the Communists' stronghold became increasingly desperate, they decided on the one scheme which gave any hope of survival. Those who were fit enough broke through the besiegers to find safety in the north. It was a fearsome journey across some of the highest mountain ranges in the world, seemingly impassable rivers, and the terrible swamps of the grasslands. There are many still alive in China who remember the grasslands.

They spread, an immense sombre shoreless ocean of mud, a desert of water; swamps which sucked us down; with clumps of bushy grass here and there, and little bits of firm land; there was only one trail. Those that went forward marked it by a white rope of goat's hair. And the one day it snowed, we could not find the rope again. We moved snow with our bare hands for hours. The rope was our lifeline.

The marchers faced constant attacks from Chiang's Nationalists and Tibetan tribesmen. When there was nothing else, they boiled and ate their leather belts. Only one-fifth of the 100 000 who had set off survived the 10 000 kilometre march.

A year after leaving Kiangsi, the Communists established the Yenan soviet in this desolate region of northern China. The Long March was over.

The grasslands: a tapestry showing the Communists on the Long March

The Japanese threat

Chiang's protests had failed to dislodge the Japanese from Manchuria in 1931 (see chapter 10). It was clear that they were only waiting for the right moment to strike at China proper. For Chiang the Japanese were less of a danger than the Communists. They were, he said, 'a disease of the skin', whereas the Communists were 'a disease of the heart'. Not all of Chiang's generals agreed with him. One in particular, the one Chiang had chosen to lead the campaign against the Communists, refused to go on fighting them any longer. When Chiang furiously tried to force the soldiers to continue the campaign, they made him their prisoner. Chiang was only set free when he agreed to call off the campaign, and join the Communists in fighting the Japanese.

In July 1937 the Japanese struck. Well-trained and well-armed, they brushed aside all opposition. The Chinese could not resist the weapons of modern warfare. They died in their hundreds of thousands. In ten days in December, the population of the city of Nanking was reduced from 1 100 000 to 250 000. By the end of 1938 most of northern and eastern China was in Japanese hands. Chiang had retreated into the mountains around Chungking where the Japanese motorised columns could not pursue him. There he stayed, largely inactive, for the next six years.

Meanwhile Mao turned the guerrilla tactics which he had used so successfully against Chiang against the Japanese. By enlisting the aid of the people in the countryside, the Communists came to control large areas of Japanese-occupied territory by the end of the war. After Pearl Harbor, Chiang received supplies and equipment from the United States. Mao seized his from the Japanese. Both knew that the final

China 1931–9

▨	Japanese territory 1930
⦂	Japanese occupation 1931–9
◀---	The Long March 1934–6

Japanese soldiers fighting their way along a street in Shanghai

Japanese troops enter the Forbidden City in Peking, July 1937

SUN, CHIANG AND MAO 207

reckoning between the Kuomintang and the Communists had yet to come.

Civil war

In 1945, as both sides raced each other to accept the surrender of Japanese forces in North China, the American government tried to get Mao and Chiang to agree. It was a vain hope. Even during the war their armies had clashed. Now that the Japanese threat had disappeared, the Americans were able only to postpone the conflict for a year.

Troops of Mao Tse-tung's army advance against the Nationalists in northern China, 1948

Shanghai, December 1948: with paper money almost worthless, thousands queued for the gold allowance distributed by the Kuomintang government. Ten people were crushed to death

Civil war broke out in earnest in 1947. At the outset, the Nationalists appeared the stronger; but the balance was soon to change. Although fewer in number, the Communist troops were much better-led and their morale was far higher. They had the support of the overwhelming majority of peasants, and as their successes mounted, their numbers

Mao Tse-tung proclaims the People's Republic of China

were swollen by the thousands who deserted the Kuomintang. Despite American aid, the Nationalist cause began to crumble.

At the end of 1948, the two armies, each of half a million men, met at Hsuchow in the most decisive battle of the war. The last of Chiang's best troops were overwhelmingly defeated. Within months, he had fled to the island of Formosa (Taiwan) with the remains of the Kuomintang. On 1 October 1949, Mao Tse-tung became chairman of the new People's Republic of China. The Communists had triumphed.

1911	Manchu emperor overthrown
1921	Founding of the Chinese Communist Party
1925	Death of Sun Yat-sen
1926	Chiang Kai-shek's northern expedition
	Massacre of Communists in Shanghai
1934	Start of the Long March
1935	Yenan soviet established
1937	Japanese invasion
1947	Beginning of civil war between Kuomintang and Communists
1949	Mao Tse-tung declared the People's Republic of China

Using the evidence: all Mao's children

Until his death in 1975, Mao Tse-tung directed all the efforts of the government and the people towards creating his vision of a Communist China. In plays and films, from posters and huge portraits of Chairman Mao, the people were urged to work for the new China. In factories, in agricultural communes, and in the army, the thoughts of Chairman Mao, contained in *The Little Red Book*, were read and put into practice. In schools, even the youngest children learned them by heart. Education, which in traditional China had been for the privileged few, became the means of training all in the ideals of Mao's Communism.

(1) *The Foolish Old Man who Removed the Mountain*
The Foolish Old Man's house faced south and beyond his doorway stood two great peaks, Taihang and Wangwu, obstructing the way. He called his sons, and hoe in hand they began to dig up these mountains with great determination. Another greybeard, known as the Wise Old Man, saw them and said derisively, 'How silly of you to do this! It is quite impossible for you four to dig up these two huge mountains.' The Foolish Old Man replied, 'When I die, my sons will carry on; when they die, there will be my grandsons, and then their sons and grandsons, and so on to infinity. High as they are, the mountains cannot grow any higher and every bit we dig they will be that much lower. Why can't we clear them away?' Having refuted the Wise Old Man's wrong view, he went on digging every day, unshaken in his conviction. God was moved by

this, and he sent down two angels, who carried the mountains away on their backs.

(2) Chia Cheng was mad with rage at the sight of his erring son. He shouted to the attendants, 'Gag his mouth and beat him to death.' They laid Pao-yu on a bench, tied him to it and began to beat him with a heavy rod. Chia Cheng seized the rod himself and beat Pao-yu with all his might.

Suddenly the Matriarch's [grandmother] voice was heard. Chia Cheng hurried out to meet his mother. He fell on his knees and said, 'Your son disciplined his son because he had the honour of the family at heart.'

The Matriarch dismissed Chia Cheng, saying, 'Of course a son should be disciplined, but you should know when to stop.'

Eighteenth-century Chinese novel

(3) Dear comrade editor,
On all festive occasions, my father burns some joss paper for dead ancestors. I say to myself that, while it is right for us poor peasants to show remembrance for our dead family members, the burning of joss paper is a superstitious act, and should be opposed. So I persuade my father not to do that, but he is very stubborn in his thought and insists on burning the joss paper. A dispute has thus arisen.

I discussed the matter with my fellow students at school and asked their opinions. Some said, 'With regard to your father's superstitious thoughts, you must persuade him slowly and let him change gradually. You must not rush things and hope to rid him of all his superstitious thoughts overnight.' I disagreed.

I feel that slow persuasion shows a lack of a firm proletarian stand and is an act of bowing to feudal superstitious thoughts. I am a member of the Communist Youth League. I don't care who he may be. If he has incorrect thoughts I will struggle firmly against him. I will make no exception, even for my own parents.

Comrade editor, is there anything wrong with the way I think and act?
Lo Hua
Middle School No.49
Chungking

Letter to the editor of China Youth, 16 April 1965

(4) *The Story of Nien Ssu-wang*
December 31 1966. Dusk was falling as Nien Ssu-wang hurried back from the town of Tatung to the army barracks for the New Year's Eve party. As he came to a railway bridge, he heard a train approaching and, at that very moment he spotted a suspicious figure on the lines ahead. He ran forward and saw a large rock lying across the rails. 'Saboteur!' he shouted. He sprang on the fellow and grappled with him. The train kept on. Nien Ssu-wang saw that it was only about thirty metres from the rock.

At this instant, Chairman Mao's teaching, 'When we die for the people it is a worthy death,' flashed through his mind. With all the class hatred in his being concentrated in his fist, he knocked the saboteur down and ran for the rock.

The locomotive, with its smoke and dazzling headlight, rushed upon him. With extraordinary courage and calmness he quickly rolled the big rock from the rails. The train roared past, throwing Nien Ssu-wang to the ground. . . .

The train stopped. Nien Ssu-wang was immediately rushed to hospital and experienced surgeons were brought by plane to attend him.

When Nien regained consciousness four days later, his memory was seriously affected. He could not even recognise fellow fighters who came to see him. A nurse pointed to a portrait of Chairman Mao on the wall and said to him: 'Look, there's Chairman Mao.'

Nien Ssu-wang opened his eyes, fixed his gaze on the portrait and with a great effort, said in a low voice: 'Chair—Man—Mao.'

Then he lost consciousness again. Several days later when he was again conscious the nurse was so happy that she suggested to him that they sing together 'The East Is Red', a song in praise of Chairman Mao.

> *The east is red, the sun rises,*
> *China has brought forth a Mao Tse-tung. . . .*

Though his voice faltered and he often stumbled for the words, he finished the song. Every word, every line the hero sang expressed his profound love for our great leader Chairman Mao.

Though he had several relapses, Nien Ssu-wang's condition steadily improved and he was soon able to speak and eat. One morning a doctor brought him a pencil and paper. 'Write something, your name if you like,' he said to Nien Ssu-wang.

Nien Ssu-wang thought for a while and then wrote with great care, 'Chairman Mao.'

But he was still not fully recovered and his memory was poor. He did not recognise his closest comrades from his own squad. Trying to test his memory, his company leader said: 'Ssu-wang, try, try your best and tell me about your family.'

After thinking for a while, the soldier said: 'I have Chairman Mao.' Asked where his home was, he replied, 'Peking.'

When Nien Ssu-wang left for Peking to receive further treatment, his comrades-in-arms came to see him off. The company political instructor said: 'Comrade Ssu-wang, I hope you will be patient in the hospital and "Be resolute. . . ."' Nien Ssu-wang finished for him this quotation from Chairman Mao: '. . . fear no sacrifice and surmount every difficulty to win victory.'

The young hero's love for and loyalty to Chairman Mao our great leader is boundless. At that crucial moment when people's lives and state property were in danger, he acted according to Chairman Mao's teaching and, by his heroic action, performed a glorious deed of service to the people. Although he was badly injured and his memory impaired, he still remembered Chairman Mao. In his heart is a never-setting red sun – our most respected and beloved great leader Chairman Mao!

Peking Review, 17 November 1967

Questions and further work

The Foolish Old Man was one of the few traditional stories still taught in Chinese schools under Mao. What is there about it which you think would make it regarded as a suitable story to be told to young people in Communist China?

2 Compare Documents 2 and 3. In what ways do they show a different attitude towards the family, and the duties of children towards their parents?

3 Nien Ssu-wang (Document 4) was one of the many young heroes whose example children were encouraged to follow.

(a) What do you think children were intended to learn from this story?

(b) How convincing do you find the story?

17 Conflicts and crises

In 1968 a British journalist was interviewing a Vietnamese farmer. Nguyen Ho was in his fifties. He had fled from North Vietnam to a camp in the south. There had been, he told the journalist through an interpreter, 'too much trouble, too long'. It was an answer which might have been repeated many times by people in various parts of the world. Neither the efforts of the United Nations nor the possibility of a nuclear catastrophe, proved sufficient to ensure permanent peace.

Wars in Asia

Korea

In Europe grave difficulties had arisen as the victorious Allies sought to decide the fate of previously German-occupied countries. Similarly in Asia, after the departure of the Japanese, Communist and non-Communist powers jockeyed for influence in the post-war world. In some cases there were added complications. Amongst the territories seized by Japan were a number of European colonies. For people living in these parts of Asia, freedom often meant not just freedom from the Japanese, but also from their former European rulers. This was true of the Indonesians, who fought for, and won, their independence from the Dutch in 1949. It was true also in Vietnam.

But the first international conflict to arise in Asia after the war, was in Korea, which the Japanese had ruled for most of this century. In 1945, the north surrendered to the Russians; the south to the Americans. Like Germany, Korea was divided into occupation zones, with a line of latitude (in this case, the 38th parallel), as the boundary.

It was not intended that this division should be permanent. But attempts to form a national government for the whole of the country failed. When the occupying troops withdrew in 1949, they left behind a Russian-supported Communist government in North Korea, and an American-backed government in South Korea. There were numerous incidents as the two sides faced each other uneasily either side of the 38th parallel. Then, on 25 June 1950, a large force of North Koreans, equipped with Russian arms, crossed the border, and moved rapidly south. It looked as if the days of South Korea were numbered.

In New York the Security Council of the United Nations held an emergency session to discuss the crisis. One member was missing. At the beginning of the year, the Russians had withdrawn because of the United Nations' refusal to recognise the new Communist government in China. They did not return until August. With no Russian veto (see chapter 14), the Security Council was able to call upon the members to give aid to South Korea. Many, particularly the United States, did so.

By September, these United Nations forces were trapped in a small pocket around Pusan. Their American commander, General MacArthur, saved the situation by a successful seaborne landing at Inchon. It was the biggest operation of its kind since the landings in Normandy six years earlier.

Within a month, the North Korean forces in the south had been

American marines land at Inchon: 25 000 men were put ashore

Tired and muddy American troops march along a road in Korea. The fighting lasted for two and a half years

defeated. The tables were now turned, and United Nations troops headed north across the 38th parallel. Their declared intention was to reunite the whole of Korea. But the Chinese saw this move as a threat to their position in Manchuria, and in the middle of October the first of 350 000 Chinese soldiers came to the aid of their fellow Communists. For the next two and a half years the war became a grim slogging match around the 38th parallel. When General MacArthur proposed extending the war into Manchuria and against China itself, he was dismissed by President Truman.

Eventually the two sides reached an agreement of sorts. On 27 July 1953 an armistice was signed, fixing the cease-fire line almost on the 38th parallel. A war in which there were four million casualties finally ended in the same stalemate from which it had started. Although the tension has been reduced with the passing of time, a permanent settlement has yet to be arrived at.

Vietnam

During the Korean War, General Marshall was asked to describe America's policy. It was he said, 'to contain Communist aggression in different fashions in different areas without resorting to total war'. To carry out such a policy, he added, 'has not always been easy or popular'. Ten years later it was to become less and less easy and far more unpopular. The United States became involved in a war in another part of Asia – in Vietnam.

The horrors of war were all too familiar to the peoples of Vietnam. Formerly part of the French colony of Indo-China, they had fought against the Japanese occupation forces, and then against the returning French. In 1954, after three months of carnage, the pride of the French Army was defeated at Dien Bien Phu, and France was forced out of Indo-China. 'Anybody who gets himself involved in a ground war in Indo-China', commented General MacArthur, 'needs his head examined.' Future American politicians were to wish they had heeded his warning.

Like Korea, Vietnam was now divided into north and south. A Communist government led by Ho Chi Minh ruled in the north, and an unpopular, American-backed, leader governed in the south. The

American soldiers rush to leave Khe Sanh in Vietnam

The horrors of war were all too familiar to the people of Vietnam: the road to Saigon (capital of South Vietnam) shortly before it was captured by the Communists in 1975. They re-named it Ho Chi Minh City

United States sent military advisers and equipment but the guerrillas from the north came to control more and more of the country. A succession of governments came to power and were overthrown in South Vietnam.

In 1964, the character of the war changed, as American and North Vietnamese warships clashed in the Gulf of Tonkin. It was, the American government claimed, an 'unprovoked attack'. Within a year, the number of American troops in Vietnam had risen from 23 000 to 184 000 (a number that was eventually to treble). Raids by American bombers began; eventually the tonnage of bombs used against the North Vietnamese exceeded the tonnage dropped by American planes in the Second World War.

But it was a war in which, despite their immense firepower and sophisticated weapons, the Americans could make little progress. It was hard to distinguish friend from foe. The man planting rice in the fields might be an innocent farmer or a Communist soldier. Villages captured during the day would be reoccupied by the enemy during the night. As the slaughter continued and American casualties mounted towards their final total of nearly 350 000, protests against the war became louder in the United States.

Negotiations for peace began in Paris in 1968, but for almost five years there seemed to be as little progress at the conference table as there was on the battlefield. Not until January 1973 was President Nixon able to announce on television that 'we have today concluded an agreement to end the war and bring peace with honor in Vietnam and in South East Asia'. This was not how the North Vietnamese representatives saw it. The agreement was, said Le Duc Tho, 'the crowning of thirteen years of valiant struggle which the Vietnamese people have conducted against American imperialism and a group of traitors in the country'. Whichever view was the correct one, the war was over for America, if not for Vietnam. American troops went home. Without them, South Vietnamese resistance gradually crumbled. Vietnam was reunited under a Communist government in 1975.

The Middle East

In 1970 a British VC10 (see the photo below) was hijacked and the pilot forced to land in the desert. There, after several days of negotiations, the passengers were allowed off, and the aeroplane was blown up. In 1972, masked gunmen shot a number of athletes taking part in the Olympic Games. By these, and other similar attacks, the terrorists responsible were forcing the world at large to take notice of their demands. Who were they, and what did they want?

The hijackers and the gunmen were Arabs. What they wanted, and

Jubilant Palestinians on the wreckage of the VC10

The Jews ruled Palestine in Biblical times. When they were conquered by the Romans, the Jews had become scattered all over the Roman Empire. In 1897 the Zionist movement began agitating for the setting-up of a Jewish homeland in Palestine. They believed that Britain had promised to support their claim in 1917.

The Arabs Followers of the Prophet Mohammed, they had conquered and settled in Palestine in the seventh century. Thirteen hundred years later, they formed over ninety per cent of the population. They believed that Britain had promised to support their independence in return for the help they had given in fighting the Turks during the First World War.

Palestine became part of the Turkish Empire at the beginning of the sixteenth century. The Turks in Palestine had been defeated by a British army during the First World War.

The British governed Palestine after the First World War under a League of Nations mandate. They allowed Jews into Palestine, but found it difficult to control the numbers as persecution of the Jews by Hitler increased. In 1947 Britain informed the United Nations that she was withdrawing from Palestine.

still want, was that part of the Middle East which used to be called the Holy Land, then Palestine, and is now largely Israel. Behind their demands lie nearly two thousand years of history.

On 14 May 1948 the last British troops and officials left Palestine. David Ben-Gurion, the leader of the Jewish population, proclaimed the new state of Israel, which was immediately attacked by the surrounding Arab countries.

The Palestine problem

Against all the odds Israel survived. In 1949, although the Arab countries still refused to recognise Israel's existence, fighting between the regular armies ceased. For the time being, the war was carried on by small irregular forces on both sides. The hijackers of the VC10 were following in their footsteps.

Three times in the next twenty-five years, full-scale war between Israel and the Arab countries broke out again, and the Middle East remains a troubled and embittered part of the world.

1956: The Suez Canal, in which Britain was a major shareholder, was nationalised by the new ruler of Egypt, Colonel Nasser. Whilst Israeli forces advanced across the Sinai Desert, British and French troops attacked the Canal Zone. Condemned by the United Nations, all three were forced to withdraw.

1967: In the Six Days War Israel overran parts of Egypt, Jordan and Syria.

1973: Egypt and Syria launched a joint attack on Israel in the hope of recovering their lost territories. After early successes, they were driven back by the Israelis. Together, the United States and Russia managed to bring about a ceasefire.

Cuba

On the morning of Tuesday, 16 October 1962, intelligence photographs were shown to John Kennedy, the president of the United States. The photographs had been taken two days earlier from an aeroplane specially designed to fly at high altitude, the U2 spy plane. They showed rocket-launching sites being built on the island of Cuba, 140 kilometres off the coast of Florida. When completed, it would be possible to fire missiles from Cuba at targets over 3200 kilometres away.

Since 1959, Cuba had been led by Fidel Castro. He was a Communist. So nervous was the United States government at having Castro for a neighbour, they had supported an attempt to invade Cuba and overthrow him. Although it resulted in humiliating defeat, Castro feared that there might be a next time. And next time, it might be more successful. When Russia offered to supply him with weapons for defence, he gratefully accepted.

But the photographs which Kennedy saw that Tuesday morning showed preparations for weapons which were clearly intended for more than defensive purposes. The rockets launched from these sites would be capable of landing a nuclear warhead on most of the major cities of the United States.

For six days President Kennedy went into secret session with his closest advisers. A handful of men discussed moves which could bring about a nuclear war. Their advice differed; and whatever decision was reached, there were risks involved.

(1) Do nothing

For: America had rocket sites in Turkey, closer to Russia than Cuba was to America.

Fidel Castro

President Kennedy was shown photographs of Russian rocket sites on Cuba.

Against: To have rocket sites in Cuba would greatly strengthen Russia's position.

(2) Bomb Cuba

For: Would show that America was prepared to take strong measures when her security was threatened.

Against: Russians would be killed. No certainty of destroying all the sites. America would appear to be bullying a much smaller country.

(3) Stop all Russian ships carrying weapons to Cuba (a blockade)

For: Need not involve any fighting or loss of life. Could still use other methods if it failed.

Against: Would not remove the rockets already in Cuba.

What would your advice to President Kennedy have been? You may be able to think of possibilities other than those listed here.

On 22 October, President Kennedy announced his decision on television to viewers who didn't even know a world crisis existed.

All ships of any kind bound for Cuba from whatever nation or port will, if found to contain cargoes of offensive weapons, be turned back. . . .

It shall be the policy of this nation to regard any nuclear missile launched from Cuba against any nation in the Western hemisphere as an attack by the Soviet Union on the United States, requiring a full retaliatory response upon the Soviet Union. . . . Our resolution (to the Security Council) will call for the prompt dismantling and withdrawal of all offensive weapons in Cuba, under the supervision of UN observers. . . .

Russian ship approaching Cuba, photographed from an American aircraft

As Kennedy was speaking, Russian ships were heading towards Cuba. Two days later, all but one changed course. American warships closed in. At this moment, the two most powerful countries in the world stood, in the words of the American Secretary of State, 'eyeball to eyeball'.

The ship was stopped. Its cargo was not found to include weapons, and it was allowed to go on its way. In a letter sent to the American president on 26 October, Khrushchev agreed to withdraw the missiles from Cuba. The crisis was over.

1948	State of Israel proclaimed
1950	Beginning of Korean War
1954	Defeat of French at Dien Bien Phu
1956	Nationalisation of the Suez Canal by Egypt
1959	Fidel Castro came to power in Cuba
1962	Cuban missile crisis
1964	Increased American involvement in Vietnam
1967	Six Days War in the Middle East
1973	American withdrawal from Vietnam
	War of Yom Kippur between Israel and Arab countries

Using the evidence: the Suez crisis

The crisis in 1956 over the Suez Canal was a grave threat to world peace.

Block-ships sunk in the entrance to the Suez Canal at Port Said, 1956

It was debated in many sessions both of the Security Council and the General Assembly of the United Nations. On 2 November, the General Assembly passed a resolution:

Resolution 997 (ES–I)

The General Assembly

Noting the disregard on many occasions by parties to the Israel-Arab armistice agreements of 1949 of the terms of such agreements, and that the armed forces of Israel have penetrated deeply into Egyptian territory in violation of the General Armistice Agreement between Egypt and Israel of 24 February 1949,

Noting that armed forces of France and the United Kingdom of Great Britain and Northern Ireland are conducting military operations against Egyptian territory,

Noting that traffic through the Suez Canal is now interrupted to the serious prejudice of many nations,

Expressing its grave concern over these developments,

1 Urges as a matter of priority that all parties now involved in hostilities in the area agree to an immediate ceasefire and, as part thereof, halt the movement of military forces and arms into the area; ...
6 Decides to remain in emergency session pending compliance with the present resolution.

562nd plenary meeting
2 November 1956

In this exercise, you should look at the crisis as it was seen by some of the countries and personalities involved.

Dag Hammarskjold – Secretary General of the United Nations.
Abba Eban – Representative of Israel at the UN.
Cabot Lodge – Representative of the USA at the UN.
Omar Loutfi – Representative of Egypt at the UN.
Pierson Dixon – Representative of Great Britain at the UN.

1 The Secretary General's task is to:
   (a) Prepare a report of events in the Middle East since 26 July, for consideration by members of the General Assembly at their meeting on 2 November;
   (b) produce a map of the area, showing,
   (i) the boundaries of Israel and Egypt at the start of the crisis; the position of the Suez Canal; the Sinai Desert;
   (ii) the positions of Israeli, British and French troops on 2 November; the withdrawal lines proposed by Britain and France.

Carry out these requirements as if you were Secretary General.

2 Each representative has a policy brief of his government's position with regard to the crisis. After reading the policy brief (see pages 222–3), decide whether or not you, as your country's representative, support each of these points raised during the debate. Copy out the table overleaf and indicate approval with a tick, disapproval with a cross.

	Abba Eban	Cabot Lodge	Omar Loutfi	Pierson Dixon
Israel is waging an aggressive war.				
Israel's actions are a move to stop Egyptian attacks which have been taking place over a long period.				
Israel and Egypt should accept the Franco-British proposal that they withdraw their forces ten miles (sixteen kilometres) either side of the Canal.				
Israeli troops should withdraw behind Israel's existing frontier.				
Britain and France are using their armed forces in an attempt to bring peace to the Middle East.				
Britain and France are right to use force.				
The Suez Canal is an international waterway which should be open to ships of all nations.				
The fighting in the Middle East is a threat to world peace.				

3 Which representative's position do you find it most difficult to decide upon? Why?

To: Israeli Ambassador to the United Nations
Subject: UN Resolution 997
The Ministry of Foreign Affairs issued the following statement on 29 October 1956:
Israel has taken the necessary measures to destroy Egyptian *fedayeen* (commando) bases in the Sinai Peninsula.

These units, organised some two years ago by the Egyptian government and forming part of the Egyptian regular army, were intended to spread terror in Israel by acts of indiscriminate murder, mining, and sabotage. . . .

Within the last week twenty-four Israeli casualties in dead and wounded were caused by mines planted by the *fedayeen* in the Negev territory. . . .

It is not Israel which has sent murder gangs into Egypt. It is Egypt which week after week and month after month sent such gangs into Israel.

It is not Israel which has sought to strangle Egypt's economy and life by illegal blockade at the Suez Canal. It is Egypt which in its pursuit of a one-sided state of war has done these things. . . .

. . . Colonel Nasser has ignored his international obligations under the Charter of the United Nations . . . to permit free passage through the Suez Canal for the vessels of all nations at all times.

To: United States Ambassador to the United Nations
Subject: UN Resolution 997
(a) Statement in the UN Security Council by Secretary of State Dulles, 9 October 1956:
The Suez Canal, to be sure, goes through what is now Egypt, and in this sense the Canal is Egyptian. But the Canal is not, and never has been, a purely

internal affair of Egypt with which Egypt could do what it wanted. The Canal has always been, from the very day of its opening, an international waterway dedicated to the free passage of the vessels of all nations ... Egypt cannot rightfully stop any vessel or cargo from going through the Canal.
(b) The President stated the United States position, in a television broadcast on 31 October 1956:
... the direct relations of Egypt with both Israel and France kept worsening to a point at which first Israel – then France – and Great Britain also – determined that, in their judgement, there could be no protection of their vital interests without resort to force. ...

We believe these actions to have been taken in error. For we do not accept the use of force as a wise or proper instrument for the settlement of international disputes.

French soldiers move cautiously into Port Said

To: Egyptian Ambassador to the United Nations
Subject: UN Resolution 997
The Foreign Minister sent the following letter to the President of the United Nations Security Council on 30 October 1956:
... The governments of the United Kingdom and of France are taking as a pretext for their actions the present fighting within Egyptian territory between the attacking armed forces from Israel and the defending forces of Egypt.

Neither this nor any other pretext can possibly justify actions taken by the British and French governments.

This threat of force (is) ... in flagrant violation of the rights of Egypt and of the Charter of the United Nations. ...

In the meantime and until the Security Council has taken the necessary measures, Egypt has no choice but to defend itself and safeguard its rights against such aggression.

Sincerely yours,
Mahmoud Fawzi

To: United Kingdom Ambassador to the United Nations
Subject: UN Resolution 997
The Prime Minister has made the following statements in the House of Commons:
(a) *30 October 1956*
... we have called upon both sides to stop all warlike action by land, sea and air forthwith and to withdraw their military forces to a distance of ten miles (sixteen kilometres) from the Canal. Further, in order to separate the belligerents and to guarantee freedom of transit through the Canal by the ships of all nations we have asked the Egyptian government to agree that Anglo-French forces should move temporarily – I repeat temporarily – into key positions at Port Said, Ismailia and Suez.
(b) *31 October 1956*
Throughout recent months and, in particular, since the seizure of the Canal, the Egyptian government have kept up a violent campaign against Israel, against this country and against the West. The Egyptian government have made clear over and over again, with increased emphasis since the seizure of the Canal, their intention to destroy Israel, just as they have made plain that they would drive the Western Powers out of the Middle East. ...

In these circumstances, is there any Member of this House who can consider Egypt as an innocent country ...?

As to our own request, to both sides, to cease fire and to withdraw, Israel accepted that request last night and declared her willingness to take practical steps to carry it out. The Egyptian government rejected it.

18 America at home

'My God, they've killed Jack'

On 22 November 1963 the president of the United States was shot. It was shortly after mid-day, in the city of Dallas in Texas. The presidential car was heading a motorcade through the city. With President Kennedy in the car was the governor of Texas, their two wives, a secret service agent, and the driver, also a secret service agent. As the shots rang out, both the president and the governor were hit. One bullet blew off the top of the president's head. Clutching her dying husband to her, Mrs Kennedy cried out, 'My God, what are they doing? My God, they've killed Jack, they've killed my husband. Jack, Jack!' At 1 p.m. the hospital doctors announced that the president was dead.

The assassination of President Kennedy was a horrifying and, in some ways, a mysterious event. The shooting took place in front of numerous witnesses. There was even a film of it, taken by one of the spectators. The suspected killer was arrested within hours, only to be shot himself two days later (watched by millions on television) as he was

Americans read about the assassination of their president

being moved from police headquarters. A Commission of Inquiry studied all the evidence and published its report in twenty-six volumes, yet still some doubts remain.

One point at issue has been the number of shots actually fired at the president. Was it two or three? According to the commission and to some historians who have considered the evidence, there were two. The first bullet entered the back of the president's neck and came out through his throat.

Continuing its flight the bullet had passed through Governor Connally's back, chest, right wrist, and left thigh, although the governor, suffering a delayed reaction, was not yet aware of it.

Seconds later, a second bullet hit the president in the head.

Not so, claims Governor Connally. According to him, it was not the same bullet which struck both the president and himself, but another one.

When I heard that first shot and was starting to turn to my right to see what had happened, Nellie [his wife] saw the president's hands reaching for his throat. I started to look around over my left shoulder, and somewhere in that revolution I was hit. My recollection of that time gap, the distinct separation between the shot that hit the president and the impact of the one that hit me, is as clear today as it was then.

Lee Harvey Oswald: arrested for shooting the president, but was he alone?

This is more than a disagreement over a matter of detail. If, as Connally claims, there were three shots, there must have been more than one assassin. The time-lag between the first shot and the one Connally says hit him was too short for both shots to have been fired by one man. At least two men must have been involved. But if there was a second man, he has never been found.

Un-American activities

Elected when he was forty-three, Kennedy was the youngest president the United States had had. Why he was assassinated remains as uncertain as some other aspects of that Friday in Dallas. Certainly, some of his policies had been extremely unpopular with a section of the American population. They felt that he had not taken a tough enough line with, for instance, Negroes and Communists. On the day of his visit, the local newspaper, the *Dallas News*, contained an advertisement edged in black like a funeral announcement. Signed by an organisation calling itself 'The American Fact-Finding Committee', it claimed that the president was selling food to the same Communists who were killing Americans in Vietnam. He had, it suggested, made a secret agreement with the American Communist Party.

Jack Ruby: he shot Oswald, watched by millions of television viewers

Fear of Communism had been especially strong in America during the years after 1945. It was the height of the Cold War. A handful of spies had been found guilty of passing atomic secrets to Russia. Mao Tse-tung had come to power in China. American troops were fighting in Korea. Under these circumstances, it was easy for people to be per-

*Threats, lies and rumours:
McCarthy listens to one of his aides*

suaded that there was a Communist conspiracy to undermine the United States. One man was more than ready to convince them. Waving a piece of paper in his hand, the Junior Senator for Wisconsin, Joseph McCarthy, made a speech at Wheeling, West Virginia. 'I have here,' he announced, 'a list of names that were made known to the Secretary of State as being members of the Communist Party and who nevertheless are still working and shaping policy in the State Department.' Like much else he claimed, McCarthy's list turned out to be a fraud. But, between 1950 and 1954, he became the most feared and powerful man in American politics.

By spinning a web of threats, lies and rumours, McCarthy told Americans that what they most feared was indeed happening. There was a plot to destroy the American way of life and bring Communism to their country. People in all walks of life – civil servants, politicians, teachers, film-makers, writers – were ruined simply because McCarthy, without a shred of evidence, said that they were Communists. He was even able to bring down the highly respected George Marshall (see page 181), such was his influence.

McCarthy's own downfall came when he challenged the US Army. He wildly accused the army of being riddled with Communism. The army fought back, in a battle that was seen by twenty million television viewers. For the first time the audience was able to see McCarthy's tactics; the way in which he bullied and screamed at innocent people. By the time it ended in a victory for the army, McCarthy's career was over. He was condemned by the Senate, and fell from power as rapidly as he had risen. Within three years he was dead.

'Liberty and justice for all'

McCarthyism was a short-lived, but brutal stain on American life. The continuing problem of the relationship between the two races, black and white, has a much longer history. In 1862, a proclamation published by President Abraham Lincoln, declared.'That on the 1st day of January, AD 1863, all persons held as slaves within any State . . . shall be then, thenceforward, and forever free.' Although it required the Civil War to enforce it, slavery in the United States was abolished.

Negro Americans now form more than a tenth of the population of the US. Many live in the big cities of the north, to which their families moved in search of a more prosperous life than they could find in the south. But, although they have been free for over a century, black Americans have, on average, a shorter life expectancy, a higher infant mortality rate, a shorter education, higher unemployment and lower wages than white Americans/ In the 1960s, the tension caused by living on the edges of prosperity in the world's richest country, exploded into violence. There had been previous outbreaks of violence, but between 1965 and 1968, in particular, each summer saw rioting, looting, burning and killing in cities like Chicago, Detroit, Newark and Washington.

Under the headline 'What Next?' the American magazine *Time* described the situation in cities throughout the country in August 1967.

Detroit was a burned-out volcano, and although Milwaukee trembled, its authorities hammered down an iron lid that saved the city from massive hurt. Still, there was little peace in the nation's cities. From Providence, RI, to Portland, Ore., communities large and small heard the sniper's staccato song, smelled the fire bomber's success, watched menacing crowds on the brink of becoming mindless mobs.

Living in the world's richest country: looting in Philadelphia

The Negro civil rights leader Dr Martin Luther King was killed in 1968, and more riots followed. The aim of the civil rights movement was to help American Negroes do those things which the laws of the country said they had a right to do. The law gave Negroes the right to vote, the right to be educated in integrated (mixed black and white) schools, the right to travel on the same bus or eat in the same restaurant as white Americans. But some states and some people tried to stop Negroes from doing any of these. In the southern states in particular, civil rights workers met violent opposition and, occasionally, death. Slavery had ended but, in some areas at least, the Ku Klux Klan and its attitudes lived on.

We aren't for integration in any form. All my life I paid the premium for purity. You see sugar advertised 100 per cent pure; everything like that you pay a premium for. What we can't understand is why take the pure blood of the white race and mingle it with the Negro race. There's a certain class of white people will never integrate with the nigger.

Views like these expressed by Louisiana Grand Dragon, and the shoot-

The body of Dr Martin Luther King carried on a mule wagon through the streets of Atlanta

Victims of rioting in New York

ing of Dr King, encouraged some Negroes to look for less peaceful means of protest. Support for violent movements like the Black Panthers grew.

Various presidents had tried to make the two races in America equal. In 1948, President Truman had ended the practice of separating, or segregating, black and white Americans in the armed forces. Under President Eisenhower, racial segregation in state schools had been declared illegal, and in 1957 he sent troops to see that this was stopped at Little Rock High School in Arkansas. President Kennedy had done the same at the University of Mississippi, and was on the point of passing a civil rights law when he was assassinated. The law was eventually passed under his successor, President Johnson, in 1964. But the riots and civil rights movement of the 1960s showed that the passing of laws did not itself bring about equality. What was needed was to make them work and to improve the conditions under which too many Negro Americans lived.

Although real equality was not reached, and racial violence did not disappear, the situation did seem to improve in the 1970s. Greater help for the poor, the unemployed and the sick, more Negro politicians, more Negro mayors of big cities – all these have helped to ease the tension. But President Eisenhower's hope at the time of Little Rock, that there might be 'liberty and justice for all' in America, is still unrealised.

The road to Watergate

The way in which Americans choose the man who is to be their president is possibly the most democratic in the world. It is certainly the most complicated. Elections are held every four years. The would-be president has first to be chosen by his party, Republican or Democratic, as their candidate. This is done at the party convention in August, although there are primary elections to be gone through in various parts of the country during the months before. Once over this hurdle, the presidential candidate and his partner from the party, the vice-presidential candidate, campaign for the national election. This takes place in November. Strictly speaking, the voters in each state vote not directly for their choice of president, but for the people who will represent them in the Electoral College. The number of representatives varies according to the size of the population in each state. The Electoral College meets in December, where the representatives vote for the Republican or Democratic candidate, according to the way the people of their state voted. Thus, although the winner is known in November, he is not officially elected until the beginning of the new year. Finally, the new president takes office, or is inaugurated, in a ceremony in January.

The route to the White House, the official home of the American President, is long and exhausting. Most presidents will usually have spent some years in one, or both, of the Houses which form the

Congress (Parliament) – the House of Representatives and the Senate. Once in office, the president is both head of state and prime minister. But unlike the British prime minister, for example, the party to which he belongs may not have a majority of the seats in Congress. This can mean that the president finds it difficult to get the laws he wants passed through Congress. Should the president die in office, the vice-president automatically takes his place until the next election. This has happened twice in recent times: in 1945, Harry Truman took over from Roosevelt, and in 1963, Johnson succeeded Kennedy after the tragedy in Dallas.

In 1972, Richard Nixon, who had been Eisenhower's vice-president, lost to Kennedy in 1960, and had finally been elected in 1968, stood for re-election. He won by an overwhelming majority. But his triumph was

Investigating Watergate: the Senate Committee examines one of the conspirators

Right Members of Congress listen to the tapes which damned the president

short-lived. Before the election took place, five men were caught red-handed after breaking into the Democratic Party's headquarters in Washington – a luxury block of flats known as the Watergate. They were no ordinary burglars. Police found on them a variety of electronic gadgets for eavesdropping. Even more startling than the 'bugs' they were carrying, was the list of their accomplices. They were working for leading members of President Nixon's staff. Gradually, through many trials and investigations, the trail led closer and closer to the president himself. How far was he involved in the goings-on inside the Watergate? Nixon denied all knowledge of it, but was he telling the truth? His refusal to allow tape recordings of conversations in his office to be heard in public created even more suspicion. The demands for his trial or resignation grew. Finally the tapes were heard. They damned the president. Cornered, Nixon confessed that he had lied, and resigned. For the third time in thirty years, a vice-president replaced a fallen president. President Ford pardoned the former president, thus ending the biggest political scandal and crisis in a hundred years. But memories of the Watergate affair still remained when Ford was defeated by the Democrat, Jimmy Carter, in the 1976 election.

Two presidents: Nixon, and Ford, who pardoned him

1950	Beginning of McCarthyism
1957	Desegregation at Little Rock High School
1963	Assassination of President Kennedy
1964	Civil Rights Act passed by President Johnson
1968	Assassination of Martin Luther King
	Richard Nixon elected president for the first time
1974	Nixon resigned after Watergate scandal

Using the evidence: whitewashing Watergate

These extracts are taken from *All The President's Men*, written by Carl Bernstein and Bob Woodward, two reporters who were closely involved in uncovering the scandal. The newspaper they worked for was the *Washington Post*.

(1) [A press briefing held at the White House, 16 October 1972. The break-in at the Watergate took place on 17 June. Ziegler was President Nixon's Press Secretary.]

Ziegler: The President is concerned about the technique being applied by the opposition in the stories themselves. I would say his concern goes to the fact that stories are being run that are based on hearsay, innuendo, guilt by association.

Question: Who is the opposition?

Ziegler: Well, I think the opposition is clear. You know, since the Watergate case broke, people have been trying to link the case with the White House . . . and no link has been established . . . because no link exists. Since that time the opposition has been making charges which are not substantiated, stories have been written which are not substantiated, stories have been written that are based upon hearsay and on sources that will not reveal themselves, and all of this is being intermingled into an allegation that this administration, as the opposition points out, is corrupt. . . . That is what I am referring to and I am not going to comment on that type of story.

Question: Why don't you deny the charges?

Ziegler: I am not going to dignify these types of stories with a comment . . . it goes without saying that this administration does not condone sabotage or espionage or surveillance of individuals, but it also does not condone innuendo or source stories that make broad sweeping charges about the character of individuals.

(2) [Later that day, the Director of the Campaign to Re-elect the President held a press conference:]

The goal of all presidential candidates: John Adams, the second President of the United States, was the first American leader to live in the White House

. . . George McGovern and his confederates are now engaging in the 'politics of desperation'. We are witnessing some of the dirtiest tactics and hearing some of the most offensive language ever to appear in an American presidential campaign.

Lashing out wildly, George McGovern has compared the President of the United States to Adolf Hitler, the Republican Party to the Ku Klux Klan, and the United States Government to the Third Reich of Nazi Germany. . . .
[He asked why the *Washington Post* hadn't investigated:]
The Molotov cocktail discovered on October 8 at the door of the Newhall, California, Nixon headquarters?

The extensive fire damage suffered on 17 September by the Nixon headquarters in Hollywood, California?

The arson of 25 September which caused more than $100,000 in damage to the Nixon headquarters in Phoenix, Arizona?

(3) [Two days later, Ziegler held another press briefing at the White House]:
I will repeat again today that no one presently employed at the White House had any involvement, awareness or association with the Watergate case. . . .

In the briefing yesterday and the day before yesterday, I made it clear that no one in the White House at any time directed activities of sabotage, spying, espionage, or activities that related to following people around and compiling dossiers on them or anything such as that.
(4) [On 30 April 1973 President Nixon addressed the nation on television. On his desk were a picture of his family, and a bust of Abraham Lincoln.]
I want to talk to you tonight from my heart. . . . There had been an effort to conceal the facts both from the public, from you, and from me. . . . I wanted to be fair. . . . Today, in one of the most difficult decisions of my presidency, I accepted the resignations of two of my closest associates. . . . Bob Haldeman and John Ehrlichman – two of the finest public servants it has been my privilege to know. . . . The easiest course would be for me to blame those to whom I delegated the responsibility to run the campaign. But that would be a cowardly thing to do. . . . In any organisation, the man at the top must bear the responsibility. That responsibility, therefore, belongs here in this office. I accept it. . . . It was the system that has brought the facts to light . . . a system that in this case has included a determined grand jury, honest prosecutors, a courageous judge, John Sirica, and a vigorous free press. . . . I must now turn my full attention once again to the larger duties of this office. I owe it to this great office that I hold, and I owe it to you – to our country.

. . . There can be no whitewash at the White House. . . . Two wrongs do not make a right. . . . I love America. . . . God bless America and God bless each and every one of you.

Uncovering the full story of Watergate proved to be long and complicated. The Nixon Administration fought hard to cover up the truth.

Questions and further work

1 In Documents 1 and 2, what efforts are made to:
  (a) deny that the White House was involved;
  (b) discredit the reports in the *Washington Post*;
  (c) claim that the rival candidate for the presidency was making wild accusations;
  (d) show that the *Washington Post* was biased in its reporting?

2 At the press briefing on 18 October (Document 3), Ziegler was questioned about his use of the word 'directed'. Why did some reporters there feel that this word was deliberately misleading?
3 In Document 3, does Ziegler deny that White House employees were involved in the events at the Watergate?
4 Look carefully at the description and wording of President Nixon's television address. In what ways did Nixon attempt to inspire Americans with confidence in him as their president?

19 Britain and Europe

All join hands

All join hands

Like all 50p pieces issued in 1973, this one differs from those of other years. The difference lies in the design on the 'tails' side. You have

'I look forward to a United States of Europe': Winston Churchill and cheering Londoners. The war in Europe was over

probably seen many like it, perhaps without realising what the design represents. 1973 was the year in which Britain joined the European Economic Community – better known as the Common Market. The nine hands, firmly joined together, stand for the nine member countries of the Community.

A European idea

As far back as the 1920s, European politicians spoke of a 'European idea'. 'Let each one of us,' said the German Foreign Minister in 1925, 'first be a citizen of Europe.' But, during the years which followed,

Signing the Treaty of Rome, 1957

becoming 'a citizen of Europe' did not seem attractive to many people if it meant joining with Fascists and Nazis. In the Europe of Mussolini, Hitler and Stalin, lasting friendships between countries were not easily made. Yet, even in one of the blackest periods of the war for Britain, Winston Churchill could write: 'I look forward to a United States of Europe . . . I trust that the European family may act unitedly.' It was a message he repeated after the war, when he was no longer prime minister, and Europe was a scene of desolation and chaos.

With help from the United States under the Marshall Plan, Europe began the task of rebuilding. And, with American dollars, came a move towards greater unity in Europe. The Organisation for European Economic Co-operation (OEEC) was formed to oversee the distribution of Marshall Aid. Two years later, the Council of Europe, a kind of European Parliament, came into being. Unlike other parliaments, it had very little power. It could not pass laws, but it could be a meeting-place where countries might discuss their joint problems.

A more positive step was taken in 1951. Six countries – France, Italy, West Germany, Belgium, Luxembourg and the Netherlands – came together in the European Coal and Steel Community (ECSC). They agreed to share and develop these two important industries together. It was a great success. The amount of steel produced by the six countries grew rapidly.

Encouraged by this success, they looked for ways to enlarge it. If it could work with coal and steel, why not with other industries? If it was successful in industry, why not in agriculture? Out of their discussions came the Common Market. Under the terms of the treaty they signed in Rome in 1957, the six countries agreed that they would buy and sell to each other on equal terms. It would be, for trading purposes, as if they were all part of the same country. Goods coming into the Common

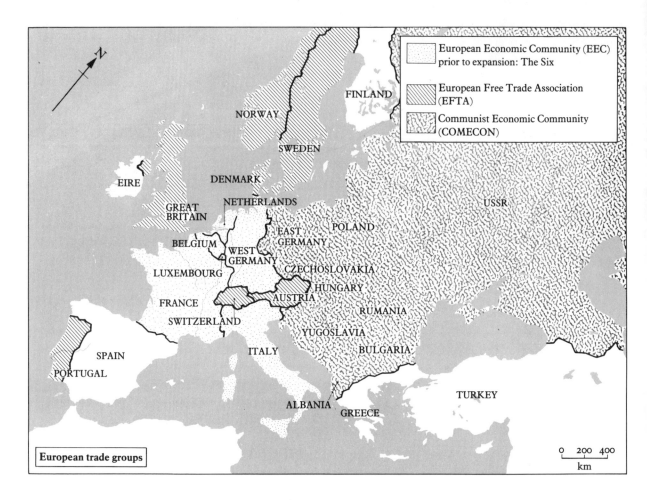

European trade groups

Legend:
- European Economic Community (EEC) prior to expansion: The Six
- European Free Trade Association (EFTA)
- Communist Economic Community (COMECON)

0 200 400 km

Market area from outside would be taxed, so that they would be more expensive and sell less well. Workers in one member country would be quite free to look for jobs in another. Eventually, it was hoped, the Six would join together politically as well as economically, then they really would be well on the way to forming a 'United States of Europe'.

Britain – in or out?

Like the ECSC before it, the Common Market appeared to live up to expectations. Trade flourished, wages rose, people prospered. West German development was so rapid that it was spoken of as an economic miracle. Meanwhile, British industry and the standard of living of the British people, seemed to be lagging behind.

Britain had been part of the OEEC, and British representatives had sat in the Council of Europe. But, on the question of membership of the Coal and Steel Community, the British government gave a firm refusal. They looked for support not from union with Europe, but across the Atlantic, from the United States. Thus, when the Coal and Steel Community became the Common Market, Britain remained outside.

Instead, faced by the success of the EEC, Britain played a leading part in creating a rival organisation, the European Free Trade Association. Formed two years after the Treaty of Rome, EFTA was a much looser body than the Common Market. Although its intention was to develop free trade between the seven member countries, there were no joint measures to impose taxes on goods from non-members. Nor did it aim at future political unity. The Seven did not prove strong enough to take on the might of the Six. Increasingly, there were those in Britain who felt that their country's future lay in joining the Common Market.

One of these was the Conservative prime minister, Harold Macmillan. In 1961 he announced that Britain would apply for membership. Most of the members welcomed Britain's application. President de Gaulle of France did not. Britain, he claimed, was not yet ready to become a wholehearted member of the European club.

She has in all her doings very marked and very original habits and traditions. In short, the nature, the structure, the very situation that are England's differ profoundly from those of the continentals.

There were many in Britain who agreed with de Gaulle. After eighteen months of negotiations, Britain's request was refused.

Four years later, with a new prime minister, and a new party in power, Britain tried again. For a time, it looked as if Harold Wilson might succeed where Macmillan had failed. But again de Gaulle said no. Not until the third time of asking, after de Gaulle's death, did Britain, along with Denmark and Eire, join the Six. In spite of continued opposition, it seemed that the European idea was growing – even in Britain. Had Britain finally gained not only a new role in the world, but

President de Gaulle welcomes Mr Macmillan: but that was in 1960

De Gaulle says no. What reason for de Gaulle's refusal is suggested by this cartoon?

Chancellor Adenauer of Germany agrees: Macmillan hopes; de Gaulle suspects

Britain enters Europe. The prime minister, Edward Heath, signs the Common Market Treaty

also the path to lasting prosperity which had proved so difficult to find since 1945?

Rebuilding the country

Even before the fight against Japan had been won, Britain's wartime coalition government had broken up. In a landslide victory the Labour Party had come to power. Churchill, at the very moment of his triumph in war, had been rejected. Remembering the disappointments which had followed the ending of the First World War, the electors chose the party which promised them jobs and houses for all.

The new government faced a hard task. Although better off than most countries in Europe, Britain was exhausted and heavily in debt. Thousands of derelict bomb sites were all that remained of some

Electioneering, 1945-style

people's homes. There were shortages of food, fuel and clothes. Rationing remained part of everyday life, and in some cases was actually tighter than it had been during the war. It now included bread which had escaped wartime rationing. Although rationing on most items was gradually removed, food rationing had not disappeared six years later, when the Labour government ended.

But, whatever shortages and difficulties there were, the people had been promised a new and better Britain, and this was what they expected the government to create. The government's hopes of doing so relied mainly on two policies: (i) nationalisation, (ii) National Insurance and National Health.

The Labour Party comes to power: Clement Attlee succeeds Churchill as prime minister

Lord Beveridge, who launched the attack on the 'five giants'

Under plans for nationalisation, industries such as mining and the railways were taken over, and run by, the government. On the whole, it made little difference to most people that they were now, as it were, part-owners of large industries. There were still complaints, not helped by a fuel crisis during one of the worst winters in living memory, in 1947. People's lives were more obviously affected by the government's schemes for social and medical reforms. Largely based on the Beveridge Report (see chapter 13), these mounted a massive attack on his 'five giants'.

Social insurance fully developed may provide income security; it is an attack upon Want. But Want is only one of the five giants on the road of reconstruction, and in some ways the easiest to attack. The others are Disease, Ignorance, Squalor and Idleness.

Money raised from a weekly contribution by workers and employers, and from taxation, was to pay for a system of social security and medical treatment 'from the cradle to the grave'. On 5 July 1948, the welfare state arrived. The *Daily Mail*, which had suggested delaying the government's plans until the country could better afford them, summed it all up:

On Monday morning you will wake in a new Britain, in a state which takes over its citizens six months before they are born, providing free care and services for their early years, their schooling, sickness, workless days, widowhood and retirement. Finally it helps defray the cost of their departure. All this with free doctoring, dentistry and medicine – free bath chairs too if needed – for four and elevenpence [24½p] of your weekly pay packet.

Better times ahead

Throughout 1950, curious Londoners could watch a strange collection of buildings going up on the banks of the Thames, not far from Waterloo Bridge. Since the war this had been a neglected area of bombed-out offices and warehouses. Now it was being transformed. Out of this rubble rose the tall, thin, cigar shape of the 'Skylon',

The Festival of Britain: the Skylon

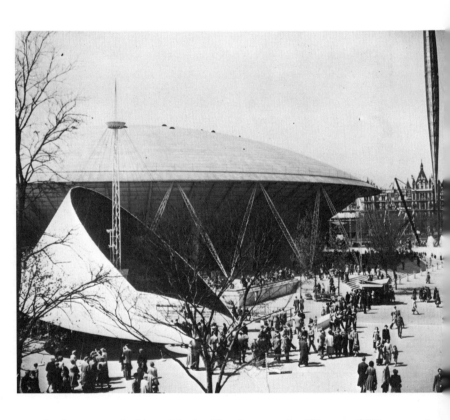

The Festival of Britain: the Dome of Discovery

seemingly suspended in mid-air. Nearby was the 'Dome of Discovery', like some vast recently-landed flying saucer. Dotted around were brightly painted pavilions and restaurants. This was the main site of the Festival of Britain, opened by the King and Queen on 1 May 1951. (The Festival Hall is still standing.)

At the festival were displayed the very latest in British products and inventions. The bright colours and modern designs were in marked contrast to the drabness of the past ten years. It was, as Herbert Morrison, the minister mainly responsible, put it, 'the people giving themselves a pat on the back'.

It was also the people bidding farewell to the Labour government. They were defeated in the General Election in October, and Churchill and the Conservatives were returned to power; power which they held for the next thirteen years.

The Festival of Britain marked more than the end of the Labour government. It also marked the end of a hard slog of rebuilding the

A better and brighter Britain: the Bull Ring Centre, Birmingham

damage caused by war. Now people were ready to enjoy the results of their labours. Although there were continuing economic problems, there was a growing rise in the standard of living. Factories produced more goods, people earned higher wages and worked shorter hours. They were able to buy cars, television sets, and numerous items which had once been luxuries for the few. With greater leisure, there was a boom in holidays abroad. Not everybody, of course, shared equally in this increased prosperity, but in general people were better-housed, better-fed and better-clothed than they had ever been. It was in the hope that these developments would continue, that Britain joined the Common Market in 1973. By then Britain had moved a long way, both socially and economically, from her position at the beginning of the century, when, for many workers, 50p was half a week's wages.

1948	Great expansion of welfare state
1951	European Coal and Steel Community formed
1957	Treaty of Rome
1961	First attempt by Britain to join the Common Market
1973	Britain joined the Common Market

Using the evidence: consumer society and welfare state

1 Conduct your own survey into the spending habits of a sample group of people whom you know. These are only some of the questions that you might ask.
(a) How many families possessed a car, a refrigerator, a washing machine in 1945, 1955, 1965 and 1975?

Members of the consumer society

(b) What proportions of the family income are spent on major items of expenditure (e.g. housing, food, fuel, clothing)? If possible, compare this with a family's expenditure ten or twenty years ago. Present your findings in tabular form.

2 On a map of your local area, show (a) manufacturing industries; (b) service industries (e.g. garages); (c) shops.
How many people are employed in each of these?

3 What methods are now used to try to persuade people to buy goods or to use services? How have these methods changed during the last thirty years?

4 Discover the size of the population of your area (a) in 1945, and (b) at the present. Then answer the following:
(i) How many doctors and hospitals were there in the same area in 1945?
(ii) How many are there today?

5 What other welfare services provided by the state are available in your area?

20 Poverty, population and development

In a book published in 1968 a Methodist missionary described how:

The other day a Zambian dropped dead not a hundred yards from my front door. The pathologist said the man had died of hunger. In his shrunken stomach were a few leaves and what appeared to be a ball of grass. And nothing else . . . (his) total possessions, according to the police, were a pair of shorts, a ragged shirt and an empty Biro pen.

Later in the book, he quoted from a report on world poverty:

Within this narrow world . . . the small white Christian and Western minority are rich and grow richer. They make up not more than twenty per cent of the world's people. They consume some seventy-five per cent of the world's income. Moreover, they grow richer by not less than three per cent per year. In 1965, they *added* to their existing national incomes some seventy thousand million dollars – a figure which is considerably larger than the entire national income of all Latin America and twice as large as that of India or Africa.

The contrast between rich and poor can be found in all parts of the world. In South America, in Asia, in Zambia, there are those who lead comfortable and prosperous lives. In the richest countries there are people who do not share in the general prosperity. But for the greater part of the population of North America, or Europe or Australasia, there is little threat of grinding poverty and hunger, much less of starvation. This was not always so – even in the twentieth century.

Measuring poverty in York and Calcutta

In 1899 Seebohm Rowntree began an investigation into poverty in his home city of York. Britain was then at the height of her prosperity. Yet Rowntree found that out of every seven people living in York, two had not enough food, fuel and clothing to lead healthy lives. One person in every ten lived in 'primary' poverty. That is, their wages were so low that even if they spent their money on nothing else, they could still not afford the bare necessities of life.

York was not unusual. During the Boer War large numbers of volunteers had been rejected by the army because they did not come up to the required physical standard. Between 1893 and 1902 more than one-third failed the medical examination. This did not include the very many who hadn't even been considered worth examining!

In 1936, and again in 1950, Rowntree carried out further surveys in York. The number of people living in 'primary' poverty had declined dramatically – to one in twenty-five in 1936, and to less than one in sixty by 1950. Most people were noticeably better off.

Rowntree was concerned with individual poverty – with people whose incomes were too low to buy the bare necessities. In 1899 he put the poverty line – the amount needed to keep a family with three children for a week – at £1.08. By 1950 this had risen to a little over £5.00. He had to take account of changes in the value of money – what it would buy. Another difficulty in calculating the poverty line is in deciding what the 'bare necessities' are. In 1950 Rowntree decided that they should include items like the cost of a wireless licence, travel, and

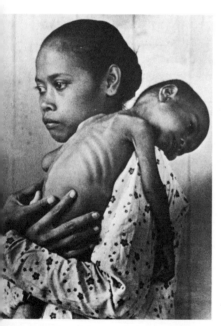

Starvation and disease threaten young and old alike: an Indonesian child suffering from malnutrition

various other personal expenses. Such items, whilst necessities to people in mid-twentieth century Britain, would be considered luxuries by many elsewhere. This makes comparison between countries difficult. As a missionary working in India has said: 'The poorest man in Britain is a millionaire compared with the ordinary person in Calcutta'.

I was taken by two members of the staff of the Calcutta Metropolitan planning organisation to look at a bustee (shanty slum). . . . Farthest from the road were the newest residents. . . . They had built shelters mostly out of discarded bamboo baskets salvaged from the rubbish of the city markets.

'World's Worst City' was the title given to this description of a visit to Calcutta by a British journalist. Here 100 000 people spend the night sleeping on the pavements. In 1968 Calcutta had a population of over 7½ million. By 1986 this will have increased to between 12 and 13 million. 'The squatters already nest with the rats on almost every square foot of land not built on. If we imagine their number doubled we are moving towards the unspeakable.'

Elderly Indian villagers in a relief camp in Madhya Pradesh, 1966

The widening gap

The simplest method of making general comparisons in wealth between one country and another is to compare the average yearly income per person. This figure is arrived at by dividing the total value of what is produced in the country by the number of people living in it. To make comparisons easier, the different currencies are converted into American dollars.

In the early 1950s, this calculation showed that whilst in the USA the average income was $1870, in Burma and Uganda it was only $50. Switzerland and Sweden were the richest of the European countries, with incomes of $1010 and $950. Britain and Belgium were next with about $800 each.

Twenty years later, as you can see from the table below, although the poor countries were not growing poorer, the gap between rich and poor was widening.

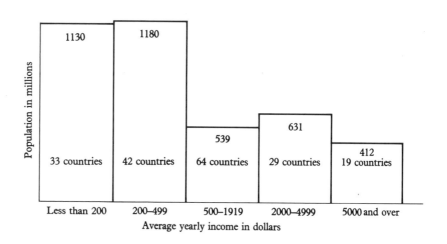

Rich and poor 1974
(Adapted from the World Bank Atlas, 11th edition, 1976)

It is not just in Europe and North America that incomes are highest. Numbered amongst the nineteen wealthiest countries in 1974, those with an average income of $5000 or more, were Brunei, Kuwait, Qatar and the United Arab Emirates. Their wealth is based on oil which has greatly increased in price during the 1970s. At the opposite extreme, there are thirty-three countries where the average income was less than $200. In 1974 some sixty per cent of the world's population were surviving on an income of less than $500 a year.

Population explosion

Standing in the way of economic development in Africa and Asia – of increasing average income – is a staggering increase in population. If the present rate of growth continues, the world's population (about 3892 million in 1974) will have almost doubled by the year 2000. This is the 'population explosion'.

Increases or decreases in the size of population are the result of changes in the birth rate and death rate. These figures are the number of children born in a year to every thousand adults; and the number of deaths in a year out of every thousand people. These diagrams illustrate how changes in these rates affect the growth of population.

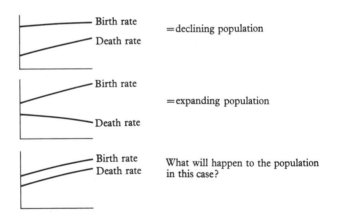

During the last two centuries enormous advances have been made in the treatment and control of disease. In Europe and the USA these advances came slowly. Their effect on the population was gradual. At the height of Britain's population boom in the nineteenth century, for example, the growth rate was never more than one and a half per cent per year. In 1974 the population in many countries was expanding at the rate of three or four per cent. This explosion of population in Asia and Africa is very largely the result of the rapid introduction of medical advances, particularly since the ending of the Second World War.

The attempt to control infectious diseases on an international scale first began in the middle of the nineteenth century. In 1902 the Pan-American Sanitary Bureau was set up in Washington. After the First World War, the League of Nations created a health organisation. But a

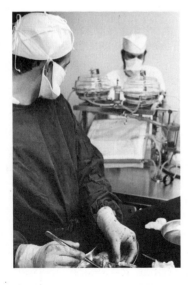

Medical advance: an organ transplant operation in progress

larger-scale international organisation was needed. In 1948 the World Health Organisation, an offshoot of the United Nations, was formed. It provides a number of services, but its main aim is to conquer the major

The fight against disease: insecticides on sale in Senegal

diseases of the world. Helped by medical discoveries, WHO has had some dramatic successes.

In Sri Lanka an insecticide, DDT, which first appeared in 1944, virtually wiped out the malaria-carrying mosquito in a matter of years. This, and other measures, halved the death rate in five years. In Britain a fall in the death rate of this size took seventy years.

But in Sri Lanka, as in similar parts of the world, the decline in the birth rate has been nothing like as steep. Hence, the population explosion is the result of (1) a dramatic fall in the death rate and (2) a continuing high birth rate.

Feeding the multitude

It is not only medical science which has helped more people to stay alive longer. The world has produced more food. Over the last century whole new areas of land have been used for farming. With fertilisers, better irrigation, and the use of machinery, the land has been farmed more effectively. As the population has increased, so has the amount of food produced. But for how long can it keep pace?

Despite the work of bodies like the Food and Agriculture Organisation set up by the United Nations in 1945, many people still go hungry. A survey carried out by the United Nations in 1963 found that throughout the world, 'ten per cent to fifteen per cent of the people are undernourished and up to half suffer from hunger or malnutrition or both'.

Can the threat of starvation be removed? In some recent years there have been encouraging signs. For five years after 1967 improved agricultural methods resulted in better harvests. Then widespread drought wiped out many of the gains that had been made. The Food and Agriculture Organisation remains confident.

Fortunately as the problem grows so do the means of meeting it. Modern technology has already put into man's hands the tools to solve the problem if only he is able, or is enabled, to use them. Technology has developed new varieties of plants and livestock which produce a much greater yield than the varieties they replace ... it has devised new fish-finding and fish-catching techniques, and new ways of getting the catch to the consumer in the freshest condition. The problem, then, is not what to do but how to get it done.

Perhaps the time is approaching when people need no longer die because all they have to eat are leaves and grass.

Trade and aid

By the beginning of the twentieth century most of the countries which are now the world's richest had changed from mainly agricultural to mainly industrial societies. This was how they became wealthy. But the developing countries – those with low incomes and growing populations – are not industrialised in this way. Nor can they afford it. More people need not only more food, but more houses, more schools, more roads, more health services, more of everything. There is little money left to buy machinery, build steelworks or erect oil refineries. They have little to sell. Therefore, they are forced to look to the richer countries for help.

Desert locusts: huge swarms of these insects can devour hundreds of square kilometres of crops. Only action on an international scale by the Food and Agriculture Organisation can control them

Aid to the developing countries is given for various reasons. It is given to gain allies, to support American or Russian interests. It is given to increase trade. If people are better off they will be able to buy more of the goods made in Europe or the USA. It is given because people believe that no one should be forced to live like the squatters of Calcutta.

For whatever reasons aid for the development of the countries of Africa and Asia is given in a number of ways. Some is channelled through organisations like the International Bank for Reconstruction and Development, better known as the World Bank, which was established in 1946. In 1964 the United Nations Conference on Trade and Development was set up to assist developing countries. Aid is given directly by one government to another. Large private companies build industrial plants.

But for much of the world the progress towards economic development remains slow, the problems difficult to solve. It seems that only when there is a fall in the birth rate as dramatic as that which has taken place in the death rate during the third quarter of the twentieth century, will the gap between rich and poor narrow. Until then, as one writer has put it, 'a developing country is like a bottomless pit. Its people can never reach a reasonable standard however much money is poured in.'

Indonesia: the rice harve

Index

Acknowledgements

The author and publishers wish to acknowledge the following photograph sources:—

Associated Newspaper Group Ltd p. 98; Associated Press pp. 132 left, 216, 238 top; Aufnahme des Heeresgeschichtlichen Museums pp. 31, 32; Barnabys Picture Library p. 165 left; Bettmann Archive Inc p. 84; Bilderdienst Suddeutscher Verlag pp. 27, 28, 43, 128, 129, 180, 182, 188; Black Star p. 217; Trustees of British Library pp. 141, 155 bottom, 156, 171 left; British Museum Newspaper Library pp. 47, 104, 105, 110 top, 138, 153, 160 bottom; Brown Brothers pp. 88 bottom, 92, 94, 96/97; Bundersarchiv, Koblenz p. 117; Camera Press Ltd pp. 195 bottom, 196, 198/199, 202 bottom, 208 top, 209, 230; Central Press Photos pp. 12 right, 53, 65 bottom, 103 bottom, 119, 124, 133, 137, 144/145, 148, 169 top and bottom, 192, 214; F.A.O. pp. Title page, 245, 248, 249; Courtesy of the Ford Archives/Henry Ford Museum, Dearborn, Michigan p. 89; John Hillelson Agency Ltd pp. 187, 199, 208 bottom, 219 top, 224, 226; I.B.A. pp. 142 right, 155 top left and right, 157 top right; Illustrated London News pp. 186, 204; Imperial War Museum pp. Cover/title page, 15 left, 26 left, 36, 38, 39, 40, 41, 42, 44, 45, 48, 54/55 top, 55 bottom, 59, 62, 70, 140, 142 left, 143, 145, 146, 159 top right, centre, bottom left, 160 top left and right, centre, 172 bottom, 173, 177; Institute of Contemporary History & Weiner Library p. 123; Institute of Social History, Amsterdam p. 114; Keystone Press Agency Ltd pp. 121 bottom, 131, 181, 185, 190, 191, 195 top, 206, 213 bottom, 220, 223, 229, 235; John Laing & Son Ltd p. 241; Library of Congress p. 90; London Express News & Feature Service p. 197; Marks & Spencer Ltd p. 242; Mary Evans Picture Library p. 15 right; N.A.S.A. Title page; National Portrait Gallery, London p. 49 bottom; Novosti Press Agency pp. 24, 76, 77, 78, 79, 80, 82/83 top, 179 top; Paul Popper pp. 112, 149, 159 bottom right, 162 bottom, 164, 165 right, 166 bottom left and right, 169 centre, 171 right, 172 top, 174, 178, 179 bottom, 198, 215, 225, 227, 228, 237 top; Press Association p. 234 top; Punch pp. 54/55 bottom; R.T.H.P.L. pp. Title page, 10, 12 left, 13, 20, 23, 24, 26 right, 34, 49 top, 52, 55 left, 64, 65 top left and right, 68, 69, 70/71, 88 top, 90/91, 99, 100, 101, 102, 106, 109, 110 bottom, 127, 130, 132 right, 136, 166 top, 167, 193, 213 top, 234 bottom, 238 bottom, 239, 240; Franklin D. Roosevelt Library Collection pp. 93, 95; Snark International pp. 113, 136/137, 237 bottom right; Society for Cultural Relations with USSR pp. 115 bottom, 184; Société Royale des Amis du Musée Royal de l'Armée p. 56; Sovfoto pp. 82, 83, 218; Syndication International p. 61; Tass from Sovfoto p. 115 top; The Times p. 103 top; Ullstein Bilderdienst pp. Title page, 24, 29, 33, 57, 71, 74, 86, 116, 118, 120, 121 top, 152; United Nations p. 176; Official U.S. Air Force Photo p. 219 bottom; U.S. Army Photograph pp. 147; U.S. Navy Photographs pp. 154, 157 top left, 158, 162 top; left, 158, 162 top; U.S. Travel Service p. 231; H. Roger Viollet pp. 202 top, centre, 205, 206, 207; Wilfred Weston p. 11; W.H.O. pp. 244, 246, 247.

The author and publishers wish to thank the following who have kindly given permission for the use of copyright material:

The Africa Publications Trust for an extract from The Africa Digest, October 1971; W. H. Allen & Company Limited for quotations from The Habsburgs by Dorothy G. McGuigan; Associated Book Publishers Ltd for an extract from The House That Hitler Built by Professor Stephen H. Roberts, published by Methuen & Company Ltd; Associated Newspapers Group Limited for an extract from the Daily Mail, 5 July 1948; Columbia University Press for an extract from the Report of the League of Nations Commission of Inquiry on Manchuria from The Manchurian Crisis 1931–33 by S. R. Smith; The Conde Nast Publications Inc. for an extract from the Franklin D. Roosevelt Library Collection, © 1933, 1961; Curtis Brown Limited on behalf of Viscount Templewood for extracts from Nine Troubled Years; Mel Calman for an extract from The Evacuees, editor B. S. Johnson, published by Victor Gollancz Limited; Jonathan Cape Ltd for an extract from The Morning Deluge (1972) by Han Suyin; Cassell Ltd for an extract from The Second World War by Sir Winston Churchill; Marshall Cavendish Partworks Limited for extracts from The War Papers, Part 60; The Controller of Her Majesty's Stationery Office for extracts from Parliamentary Papers, 1919, Volume LIII CMD 153; Documents on British Foreign Policy 1919–1939, 3rd Series, Volume 7; Parliamentary Debates, House of Commons Official Report, 5th Series, Volume 559, 6.11.56 and an extract and diagram from Booklet published by Ministry of Home Security, 1942; Peter Davis Limited for an extract from Hunt for the Czar (1971) by G. Richards; J. M. Dent & Sons Limited for an extract from The Hundred Days to Hitler by R. Manvell and H. Fraenkel; Victor Gollancz Limited for an extract from The Burning of the Reichstag by D. Reed; Granada Publishing Limited for extracts from The Road to Sarajevo by Vladimir Dedijer, published by MacGibbon & Kee Limited; Hamish Hamilton Limited for an extract from Only Yesterday by F. L. Allen; George G. Harrap & Company Limited for extracts from The USA in World Affairs by A. E. Campbell and China by A. Cotterell and D. Morgan; A. M. Heath & Company Limited on behalf of Robert Sherwood for an extract from The White House Papers of Harry L. Hopkins, Volume 1; Heinemann Educational Books Limited for an extract from No Easy Walk to

Freedom by N. Mandela; David Higham Associates Limited on behalf of Erich Maria Remarque for an extract from *All Quiet on the Western Front* by Maria Remarque; Hodder & Stoughton Limited for extracts from *Memoirs*, Volume 2 and *Year of Decisions*, 1945 by H. S. Truman; Houghton Mifflin Company for an extract from *The Lean Years: A History of the American Worker* by Irving Bernstein, © Irving Bernstein; Hutchinson Publishing Group Limited for extracts from *Ten Years After: A Reminder* by Philip Gibbs, *Mein Kampf* by Adolf Hitler and *Twenty Letters to a Friend* by Svetlana Alliluyea; Michael Joseph Limited for an extract from *The Death of a President* by William Manchester; Macmillan Publishing Company, Inc, for an extract from *Readings in European History* by Leon Barnard and Theodore B. Hodges; The Observer Limited for an extract from an article 'Hungary Ten Years After' by Patrick O'Donovan featured in *The Observer*, 1966; Penguin Books Limited for an extract and part of a figure adapted from *Lusitania* by Colin Simpson (Penguin Books 1974), copyright © Colin Simpson, 1972 (first published Longman 1972); A. D. Peters & Company Limited on behalf of J. B. Priestley for an extract from a record *BBC Scrapbook 1914* by J. B. Priestley; Phoebus Publishing Company for extracts from *Twentieth Century Scrapbook* – History of the Twentieth Century; *History of the Twentieth Century*; 'The Nuremberg Trial' by R. Manvell and H. Fraenkel from *History of the Second World War*, Volume 8, Nos 7 and 12, 1969 and *History of the Second World War*, Volume 6, No. 17; Martin Secker & Warburg Limited for extracts from *The Rise and Fall of the Third Reich* by William Shirer, *The Reichstag Fire* by Fritz Tobias and *All the President's Men* by Carl Bernstein and Bob Woodward; Souvenir Press Limited for an extract from *The Sokolov Investigation*, 1972 by J. E. O'Conor; Times Newspapers Limited for extracts from *The Times*, 28 April 1937, and *The Times*, 19 October 1975; A. P. Watt Limited on behalf of Robert Graves for extracts from *Goodbye to All That* and *The Long Week-end* by Robert Graves and Alan Hodges; A. P. Watt Limited on behalf of the Estate of the late Field-Marshal Montgomery of Alamein for an extract from *The Memoirs of Field-Marshal Montgomery*.

Every effort has been made to trace all the copyright holders but if any have been inadvertently overlooked the publishers will be pleased to make the necessary arrangement at the first opportunity.